The life record of H. W. Graber

H. W. Graber

Alpha Editions

This edition published in 2022

ISBN : 9789356898929

Design and Setting By
Alpha Editions
www.alphaedis.com
Email - info@alphaedis.com

Contents

Preface

The purpose of this narrative is to hand down to my children, and to present to my friends, an intimate, personal account of a life which has not been without interesting episodes, and which has been lived during the most eventful period that this Nation will, in all probability, ever know.

Though a large portion of my story will deal with incidents which occurred during the great sectional strife of the sixties, it is not intended as a history of that great calamity, but is meant, simply, to be an account of incidents with which the writer was personally associated.

The Great Strife which so nearly disrupted our country is over. For many years we of the South have been dwelling amicably with those of the North—this is as it should be. We are, united, the greatest country on the face of God's footstool. And to both the North and the South belongs the credit.

The mistakes of certain Northern fanatics, which were not, I believe, dictated by general Northern sentiment, have long been rectified. The Government at Washington today is, I know, truly representative of the entire country. The tragic blunders which were evident in the South during what has been called the "Reconstruction Period" would not be possible today. The country has become a unit.

In perfect love and friendship for all the good people of the United States, irrespective of location, and with no sectional feeling other than an abiding love for my South, I write this story. I hope it may be found to be not without interest.

H. W. GRABER.

CHAPTER I

My Earliest Recollections

I was born in the city of Bremen, Germany, on the 18th day of May, 1841. My father was a native of Prussia, and my mother of the Kingdom of Hanover. They were married in the city of Bremen in 1839. There were five children born unto them; a daughter, the oldest of the family, died in Bremen; the others moved with the family to Texas. I was educated at a private school, starting at six years old, up to the time of our removal to Texas in 1853.

In connection with the ordinary literary course, the French and English languages were taught in the higher grades in which I had just entered, but when father decided to move to Texas, he had me drop the French and employed an additional private teacher to come to our home and give me English lessons, which enabled me to speak the English language on our arrival in Texas.

Our father was a manufacturer of fine mahogany furniture and established a profitable trade on this with New York, exporting more of his furniture than was sold at home, though he had quite an extensive local trade, as his styles and work were very popular, all of his furniture being hand carved.

The great Revolution of 1848, which caused great stringency in financial affairs of the country, forced him to mortgage his home, and from this he never recovered. It was this condition that induced his removal to Texas.

Father and I came to Texas a year in advance of the balance of the family, for the purpose of getting acquainted with the country and its conditions. Then, the year following the rest of the family came over. We settled in Houston, Texas. We came over on a large sailing ship, as steamships were very few, and we came by way of New Orleans, where we found a great yellow fever epidemic, though we escaped it this year.

I forgot to mention that, when a child about four years old, I was playing on the river front, sliding up and down on a plank with one end in the water, the other end on the steps leading down to the water, when I lost my hold, slid into the river and under the bottom of a schooner, coming out on the opposite side, where one of the sailors caught me by the hair just as I started under the third time. I was carried home unconscious. This proved my first narrow escape from death, of which I had many during life.

Soon after our arrival in Houston, father worked in an undertaking establishment for a man by the name of Pannel, but during the first summer, both father and mother were taken sick with typhoid fever and died within one week, leaving me, the oldest of the family, then thirteen years old, to take care of the rest of the children.

We had an uncle, father's brother, living on Spring Creek, in the upper part of Harris County, who took charge of our sister and a younger brother until I could make provisions for them to come back to Houston, there to get the benefit of the schools.

During the yellow fever of that fall my brother, next to me, died with yellow fever.

I forgot to mention that soon after arrival in Houston I secured a position in the large retail grocery establishment of F. Bauman, and, subsequently, in the wholesale grocery establishment of C. E. Gregory, where I soon became shipping clerk and an expert marker of freight, with the marking brush; so much so that when a lot of freight was turned out on the sidewalk (to be shipped by ox-wagon, which was the only means of transportation out of Houston before the day of railroads) and when marking this freight, passersby would stop and watch me, as I was the youngest shipping clerk in Houston, which of course made me feel very proud.

After a year or more in the service of this wholesale establishment I was offered a position in a retail dry goods establishment of G. Gerson, where I became familiar with the dry goods business. After about a year, Gerson decided to open a general merchandise establishment at Waxahachie and place his cousin, Robert Angleman, in charge of the same, and, for this purpose, loaded about a half dozen ox-wagons with part of his Houston stock and employed me to go to Waxahachie and clerk for Angleman.

In place of going up to Waxahachie on the stage, our only means of travel then, I begged them to allow me to go with the wagons, as I was anxious to camp out and hunt on the way, but I took a great fancy to driving one of the wagons, the driver of which permitted me to learn, and I became somewhat expert in handling six yoke of oxen, each one of which had a name, such as "Red" or "Ball," or "Jerry." The oxen seemed to know their names when called on to move up, followed by the crack of the big whip, and it is hardly necessary to say when this outfit entered Waxahachie, preceded by this team, this little boy was driving, popping his whip as loud as any of the men. I felt I was the biggest man among them.

Angleman's business proved a great success—selling goods for cash and also taking pecans in trade for goods at fifty cents a bushel. These pecans were shipped by wagon to Houston and from thence to New York, where they netted from sixteen to eighteen cents per pound. Angleman's business was the first Jewish establishment in Waxahachie, and ultimately grew to be the largest business in that section of the country.

My sojourn at Waxahachie of about two years proved the most pleasant of my life, as everybody seemed to be my friend, and took a special interest in me because I was the only orphan child in the place and was without a home. While there I boarded at both hotels; first at the Rogers House and next at the Ellis House.

CHAPTER II

I ABANDON THE PRINTER'S TRADE AND TAKE UP SURVEYING.

After two years in Waxahachie, I decided to move back to Houston, where I concluded to learn the printer's trade, and for this purpose secured a position in the office of the Houston Telegraph, which, at that time, perhaps, had the largest circulation and was the leading paper in the State. It was published by Allen & Brockett. Soon after entering this office and acting as printer's devil for a while, they promoted me to the job office, where I became expert in doing fancy work, such as marriage notices, ball invitations, etc., but I was unable to collect any salary; these people were always hard up for money, and I never got anything out of it but my board and sufficient money for clothing. I finally became disgusted and went to Galveston, where I had an offer from a man by the name of Spratt, who published a little paper called the Ignis Fatuous or Jack o' the Lantern. As the name indicates it was a humorous paper, containing criticisms in a humorous vein, of leading politicians of the city and the State. It was one of the most popular periodicals then published, selling at ten cents a copy, by newsboys, without having any left over each week. Here, too, I failed to get my pay, though I set up the whole paper and made up the forms, which were sent up to the Gazette's office on Friday, where it was struck off ready for the sale of the paper on Saturday. I did my work at Spratt's home, where he had set apart a room containing cases. I had board at the same place.

Spratt was a billiard fiend and, as soon as he got the money for his papers on Saturday, he would stay in town, play billiards until his money was exhausted, come home about Tuesday, and then prepare to furnish matter for the next issue. I worked with him for about sixty days. Failing to get my pay, I became disgusted and concluded that the printer's trade was a good thing for me to drop. I then went back to Waxahachie and again went to work with the Angleman house and formed the acquaintance of an old land surveyor by the name of James E. Patton, who employed me to go with him on surveying expeditions, just for company, paying me a good salary. I furnished my own horse and arms, the latter of which he never carried. He was firm in the belief that Indians would never trouble him, although it was said that he was taken prisoner by the Indians, having been caught surveying lands down on Chambers' Creek in Ellis County. They turned him loose, which was considered one of the most remarkable cases of Indian generosity ever known on the frontier, as they always killed surveyors whom they caught locating land.

It was also related of this old man, that, in the early days, when he surveyed lands in Ellis County, he substituted chain carrying by hobbling his ankles just the length of a vara, and stepped off the land, in place of measuring it with a chain. Colonel Patton was one of the most popular surveyors and land locaters in Texas. His compensation for locating headright certificates was one-half of the land, which made him one of the richest men in lands, at the time of his death, in that section of the State.

My first trip with Colonel Patton was to Fort Belknap, Texas, where he had formed the acquaintance of a man by the name of Gibbons, who moved there from Arkansas and owned about a dozen negroes, with whom he cultivated a considerable plantation just across the river from Fort Belknap. Gibbons had an Indian wife, a Delaware, who was dark complected like other Indians, but she had a younger sister, who married General Tarrant, an old Texas pioneer and Indian fighter, after whom Tarrant County is named. General Tarrant made his home in Ellis County and he and Colonel Patton were great friends. General Tarrant happened to be on a visit at Gibbons' when we arrived there on our first expedition, and we were made to feel at home before starting out surveying.

It was the custom there for surveyors to make up a party of a half dozen or more to go on these expeditions, for protection against Indians who were then roaming over that whole section of the country. There was an Indian agency about twelve or fifteen miles below Belknap, in charge of Captain Shapley Ross, the father of General L. S. Ross, then a boy like myself. This agency was composed of remnant tribes of Indians, probably a half dozen or more, whom the Comanche Indians had run in off the range. These Indians had the protection of the United States Government and, of course, pretended to be friendly. The most uncivilized Indian in this agency was the Tonkawa, who, it was claimed, were cannibals. I remember as we passed through Keechie Valley, on our way to Weatherford, we stopped at a store for about an hour, resting and talking, when the storekeeper told us of a trouble he came very near having the day before. It seems a Tonkawa Indian had offered to trade him a pony for a young Kentuckian, who had just come out from his State and was clerking in the store. He asked the Indian what he wanted to do with the Kentuckian if he accepted his offer. The Indian told him that he wanted to eat him. The young man got a gun and was about to shoot the Indian, when the storekeeper stopped him and made the Indian leave.

There was another Indian agency at Camp Cooper, about forty miles west of Belknap, presided over by a man by the name of Neighbors. This agency had a tribe of the Southern Comanches, who were also run in by the Northern Comanches, or Apaches. These Southern Comanches claimed to be friendly with the whites in order to have the protection of the United

States Government, but they, and occasionally the Ross Agency Indians, were believed to be responsible for many of the raids on our exposed frontier; especially the Indians at the upper agency at Camp Cooper. These raids became frequent; one of them culminating in the murder of two families in Jack County, and the carrying off of a little boy and girl as prisoners. Being hotly pursued by Rangers and citizens, they were forced to abandon the boy, whom they threw into the brush to be found by the pursuers. He made the statement that he was taken upon a horse, behind a red-headed white man, who seemed to be the leader of the band. This red-headed white man was seen in the Indian camp, located up on the Canadian River, at different times, by scouts.

Major Neighbors, while on a visit to Fort Belknap, became involved in a dispute with one of the citizens, who charged that his Indians were responsible for many of the raids on our frontier. The dispute resulted in a fight and Major Neighbors was killed by the citizen. His death created quite an excitement on the frontier, as he was a United States officer and the Government asked an investigation of the affair, but there was never anything done about it.

While on my first trip with Colonel Patton, while we were making our headquarters at Gibbons', we found General Tarrant and his wife, the sister of Mrs. Gibbons. This lady, by the way, was as fair as most of the white women on the frontier. Their adopted son, Jesse, was about my age. Gibbons had two sons, one about my age, the other a year younger. We boys became great friends, and sometimes engaged in hunting and fishing.

One day we four decided to go fishing at the mouth of a creek, where it emptied into the Brazos, about three-quarters of a mile below the house. We cut fishing poles at a thicket near the creek. After fishing a while without any result, we got tired and commenced shooting with our pistols, of which each had one. All boys of our age always then went armed with six-shooters, the custom of the frontier. After shooting at a log in the creek, thereby emptying our pistols, we did not reload, not deeming it necessary just then, and decided to go in bathing in the river. The river being very low, was only running on the Fort Belknap side, and we had to walk a considerable distance on a sand bar to the water. Having just stripped ourselves of our clothing, ready to go in, we heard voices calling on the south bank of the river and discovered a group of men beckoning to us to come over to them. These proved to be General Tarrant, Colonel Patton, Gibbons, his overseer and a blacksmith, who, with his wife, occupied a log cabin on Gibbons' place, he being at work for the troops at the Fort.

When we reached this party of men we were asked where we had been. When we told them that we had cut our fishing poles at a thicket, they commenced laughing and guying this blacksmith, telling him that his wife had mistaken us for Indians and concluded that this was a sufficient explanation of the alarm about Indians that she had created. This blacksmith insisted on going down to this thicket, saying that he was satisfied that his wife was not frightened and made no mistake; that she must have seen Indians there, but they would not hear to it, and in going up to the house, stopped at the cabin and told this woman that it was us boys that she saw, in place of Indians. She, too, insisted that they were mistaken, that there were surely Indians in that thicket, but they paid no further attention to the matter and went home.

It was the custom there to tie all horses in the yard, around the house, which was done that night. When we woke next morning we found all of our horses gone. When they then investigated the thicket where we boys cut our fishing poles, they found plenty of Indian signs, such as small pieces of buffalo meat and moccasin tracks. The matter, of course, was reported to the commandant of the fort, who got his troops ready to start in pursuit the next evening. This was about the character of protection afforded by the United States troops. If rangers had been stationed there, they would have been in the saddle in less than an hour and continued the pursuit until the Indians were caught up with.

CHAPTER III

INDIAN TROUBLES—MY FIRST VENTURE IN BUSINESS.

This bold raid of these Indians stirred up General Tarrant and he determined to raise about five hundred volunteers in the frontier counties, to break up a big Indian camp, under a celebrated chief, Buffalo Hump, that was known to exist on the North Canadian, and for this purpose he canvassed the frontier counties and had no trouble in having volunteers sign to go out on the expedition. He fixed the time of departure from Fort Belknap on the fourth day of July, which was most unfortunate, as the time of his canvass was in the early part of May, when during the long interim the Indians had been quiet, and had made no raids into the settlements. The volunteers who subscribed had lost interest in the matter and would not go.

I was one of twenty who subscribed to go from Ellis County, and believe I was the only one that ever started. About this time Colonel Patton had arranged to start on another surveying expedition, in conjunction with a party of surveyors, in charge of Gid Rucker, who had a contract for running the center line of a twenty-mile reserve, granted by the State to the Memphis & El Paso Railroad Company. This center line was run on the thirty-second parallel. Colonel Patton went along to locate land certificates, of which he had a great many, and was anxious to see the country up on Hubbard's Creek in Young County. Hubbard's Creek is a tributary of the Clear Fork of the Brazos.

When we reached Weatherford we found General Tarrant very sick, not expected to live, and he died a few days afterwards, which, of course, broke up the expedition for which I had enlisted. Colonel Patton then induced the railroad company's surveyors to make me a proposition and pay me two dollars per day to simply go along as company, they being anxious to have a sufficient crowd to overawe any attack Indians might contemplate.

After reaching the eightieth milepost, Colonel Patton had them run down ten miles to the southern boundary of the reserve, which was done, and a most magnificent country developed. It seems Colonel Patton had requested Mr. Rucker to get a sketch of that section of the country from the General Land Office at Austin, and gave him money to pay for such sketch, and when he asked for this sketch Rucker told him that they told him at the Land Office that the whole country was vacant; that there had been no surveys recorded in that section. Colonel Patton then struck out alone, riding around and, after a few hours' investigation, became disgusted, having found quite a number of rock piles and blazed trees, indicating that the country was not vacant and had been well surveyed over by others.

Colonel Patton then told me that he was going back home, his whole trip was a failure, that he wouldn't stay with a crowd that had deceived him so grossly. He planned to go back by himself, but I told him he should not do so—if he was going back I would go with him. The whole party started back to the center line, where we quit work. It was now late at night, the moon shining brightly, and we were about ten miles away from water, which we needed for our horses, before we could go into camp. After riding over the high, rolling prairie on this beautiful night, some seven or eight miles, coming over a ridge we discovered a few camp fires in the bottom of Hubbard's Creek, which, of course, were thought to be Indian fires by our party. After consultation, we decided to make a charge on them and scatter them. For this purpose we drew up in line, having altogether about twenty men, and moved on them cautiously. When within a few hundred yards of the bottoms, we were halted by a vidette picket, who from his brogue, proved to be an Irishman. This indicated to our party that the camp was of United States troops, and not Indians.

On arriving in camp we found Major Van Dorn with a troop of cavalry, on his way from Fort Phantom Hill to Camp Cooper. The major, of course, was glad to have us camp with him. During the night, Mr. Rucker learned that Colonel Patton intended going straight for the settlements, without company except myself. Major Van Dorn sent for Colonel Patton and begged him to go to Camp Cooper with him, where he would no doubt find company from there to Fort Belknap, and then again from Fort Belknap to Weatherford, all of which were dangerous routes for one or two men to travel alone, on account of Indians, but Colonel Patton wouldn't listen to such advice, claiming the Indians would never bother him and he would have no trouble in getting back to the settlements with me.

The next morning we struck out in a straight line for the settlements, all alone, without taking any provisions, as the old man was mad with Rucker and would not ask for them, nor accept any when they were offered.

This ride to the settlements proved one of the most trying the old gentleman had ever been subjected to. It was, likewise, for me. We were without water for a day and a half, when we struck running water in the North Fork of Palo Pinto, and the second evening, late, we found a small cornfield, about three or four acres, with a board shed and a pile of ashes, indicating that this corn was made by some parties who had camped there and finally abandoned on account of Indian depredations. We then found a well-beaten path from this, leading in the direction we were traveling. About six or eight miles from there we found a house, the home of a frontier settler, with a wife and two children. All were much rejoiced at seeing us and insisted on our staying a week, which, of course, we had to decline and left the next morning, on our way home to Waxahachie, which was reached in due time. This ended my frontier visitation, determined never to go outside of the settlements again, which I never did.

Soon after reaching Waxahachie, I was induced to accept a position with a Mr. Leander Cannon at Hempstead, Austin County, who was then conducting the largest mercantile business in that section of the State. After serving about a year in the dry goods and clothing department, I was induced by Mr. Cannon to take charge of his books, which I did for about six or eight months, when he decided to sell out and offered me his business, giving me all the time I needed to pay for it, if I would enter into copartnership with one J. W. Fosgard, his former bookkeeper, who was an educated, college man, from Sweden. Fosgard was very egotistic and overbearing and I knew we could never get along, therefore, I declined Mr. Cannon's generous offer. He sold out to Fosgard alone.

A short time after, I had an invitation to join R. P. Faddis in the purchase of the business of Young & Bush, who, at the time, had a better stock of goods than Cannon and made us a very attractive offer, giving us all the time we wanted to pay them. This offer we accepted, constituting the firm of Faddis & Graber. Faddis was the bookkeeper of Young & Bush, and was a very popular man with the trade, which was largely composed of the leading and richest planters in that section of the Brazos country, and we soon built up a profitable business, though unfortunately, for us, our country soon became involved in sectional troubles, which prevented our restocking our reduced stock of goods and finally culminated in secession and war.

War Record

CHAPTER IV

MY FIRST MILITARY EXPERIENCES.

R. P. Faddis was a native of Minnesota, raised and educated there, and was about nine years my senior. He was more familiar with the true conditions in the North than I was.

When war was threatened, before Sumter was fired on, minute companies were organized in many of the important towns of Texas; forts and arsenals on our frontiers were taken possession of by the State, and the garrisons shipped North. A Captain Stoneman collected about five hundred picked troops at Fort Brown and refused to surrender. Colonel Ford, an old commander of Texas Rangers, collected about three hundred men and demanded the surrender of the fort, which was refused.

An old New Orleans boat, called the General Rusk, was dispatched to Galveston for reinforcements. On its arrival there, telegrams were sent to Houston, Hempstead and Navasota, which places had organized companies, for the companies to report by twelve o'clock that night for passage on the General Rusk, for Brazos, Santiago. Twelve o'clock that night found four companies aboard of this boat, coasting down the Gulf in a storm, without ballast, rolling and making us all seasick; nearly five hundred men lying on the lower deck. We finally arrived at Brazos Santiago, where we found some other citizen soldiers in the old army barracks, including the Davis Guards, under command of Captain Odium and Dick Dowling.

After two weeks' camping on Brazos Santiago Island, Captain Stoneman surrendered Fort Brown, and, after disarmament, was sent North with his troops. We then returned home and resumed our civic avocations.

We next organized a cavalry company, commanded by a Captain Alston; Hannibal Boone, First Lieutenant, and W. R. Webb, Second Lieutenant. I was offered the second lieutenancy, but declined, saying I would only serve in a private capacity. I was not a military man, and never expected to be. In about thirty days we were called to hasten to Indianola on horseback, where they had collected more troops, which had refused to surrender. We immediately started there and, when near Victoria, we got information that these troops had also surrendered, making it unnecessary to go any further, and we again returned home to resume our several pursuits. The company then disbanded and largely merged into a new company, organized for frontier protection against Indians. I remained at home, attending to my business with Faddis.

A couple of young Englishmen had come to Hempstead about a year before and started a foundry and machine shop, the second one in the State. They were both experts in their business and good men, receiving the financial support of the community, and soon owed our firm a large amount of money for advances to their hands and monies loaned.

In July, 1861, the same year, Colonel Frank Terry, a large sugar planter in Fort Bend County, and Thomas Lubbock of Houston, returned from the battle of Manassas, where they had served as volunteer aides on the staff of General Beauregard and through their intrepid daring and valuable services, were commissioned to raise a regiment of Texas Rangers.

Immediately upon their return, they issued a call for volunteers, to serve during the war, in Virginia; the men to furnish their own equipment. The response was prompt; in less than thirty days ten companies of over one thousand men were on their way to Houston to be mustered into the service of the Confederate States Army for the war. The personnel was of the highest order, some of the best families in South Texas were represented, many were college graduates, professional men, merchants, stockmen and planters; all anxious to serve in the ranks as privates; all young, in their teens and early twenties; rank was not considered and when tendered, refused; the main desire was to get into this regiment.

I told Faddis our firm must be represented, on which we agreed, and that I wanted to join, but he insisted that it was his time to go, that I had been out twice, and I finally had to yield him the right. He then subscribed to join. The day he was ordered to Houston to be mustered in, he declined to go and frankly told me that he only signed to keep me from going, and he did his best to persuade me not to go. He said that the South was deceived in the spirit and strength of the North; that the North had every advantage of us—they had the army and navy, the arsenals, the treasury and large manufactories, as well as five men to our one; the whole world open to them, while we had nothing, our ports would be blockaded and we would be forced to depend upon our own limited resources, and, as to relying upon the justice of our cause, in the language of Abraham Lincoln, "might was right and would surely conquer." I told him I could not agree with him and was satisfied the war would not last three months. As soon as we could drive these people back into their own territory, they would be willing to let us alone. "I am going to take your place, Faddis." I had about an hour to arrange for board for my young brother and sister and Faddis agreed to look after them and pay their board out of my interest in the business, which he pledged himself to continue for our mutual benefit.

When we parted I expected to return inside of three months; he expected he would never see me again, as I might be killed and, if I should return, that I would be a crippled, subjugated man.

Faddis continued the business as far as he was able and finally, to protect us, had to take over the foundry and machine shop, arranging with our Englishmen to run it for him. He then, to keep out of the army, turned his attention to repairing old guns, making swords and other arms, and finally, on the persuasion of his English friends, cast a nine-inch Armstrong gun, the only one ever successfully made in the Confederacy.

This drew the attention of the Confederate Government, who impressed our property, paid him eighty thousand dollars for it and gave him a permit to stay in Brownsville and run cotton into Mexico, returning with goods.

On my return from the army, after four years, I heard of him through a party who knew him in Brownsville. This party reported that Faddis had more gold than he knew what to do with, and I concluded that I was fixed, too, but I was unable to communicate with him, as we had no mails, and did not hear from him until after two years, when he returned to Hempstead broke. He had lost all in grain speculations in Chicago.

I next proceeded to Houston, where I was mustered in with the balance of the regiment, to serve in Virginia, during the war. While in camp at Houston, we organized our company, electing John A. Wharton of Brazoria County captain of the company; who, on his election, made up a speech, in which he said that he had no ambition to gratify more than to command Company B, that he expected to return captain of Company B and did not want any promotion. He was offered by the balance of the regiment in connection with our company, the office of major. The balance of the commissioned officers of the company were Clarence McNeil, first lieutenant and Theodore Bennett, second lieutenant; and the noncommissioned officers were distributed among the different sections from which the company was made up; nobody caring for an office of any kind, as a private was generally the equal of any officer in command. All went to do their patriotic duty and contribute their mite for the success of the cause.

We now started on horseback. After reaching Beaumont we returned our horses to Texas, having to take boat to Lake Charles, Louisiana, from whence we were forced to walk to New Iberia, carrying our saddles and other equipment on wagons, across the country. At New Iberia we again took boat for New Orleans; this was the only route open, as our ports had been blockaded for some time, both at Galveston and at the mouth of the Mississippi River.

During our stay in New Orleans for three or four days, we had a good rest and waited for the balance of the companies to catch up. Colonel Terry received a telegram from General Albert Sidney Johnston at Bowling Green, Kentucky, stating that he had been ordered to take command in Kentucky, and requested Colonel Terry to urge the men to come and serve under him and, by way of inducement, authorized him to say that we should be mounted on the best horses that Kentucky afforded and that we should always remain a separate and distinct command, never to be brigaded with any other troops as long as he lived. General Johnston was well acquainted with the character of Texans, regarding them as fearless and enthusiastic people, proud of their Texas history; and, knowing the young men composing this regiment would endeavor to emulate the example of the heroes of the Alamo, Goliad and San Jacinto, on which point, he was not mistaken. General Johnston had been connected with the army, under General Houston, and had also engaged in sugar planting near the Kyle and Terry plantation in Fort Bend and Brazoria Counties, where a great friendship sprang up between him and Colonel Terry. Colonel Terry's influence with the men of the regiment was unlimited and he had no trouble in persuading the men to accept General Johnston's offer and serve with him in Kentucky.

While in New Orleans Colonel Terry made an official visit to General Twiggs, an officer of the old army, who had resigned, and tendered his services to the Confederacy, and who was then in command at New Orleans and the Southwestern territory. Colonel Terry, while there, asked information on the matter of obtaining cooking utensils and tents. When General Twiggs, who had served many years on the frontier of Texas, laughed him out of countenance, saying, "Who ever heard of a Texas Ranger carrying cooking utensils and sleeping in a tent?" It is needless to say that this matter was not mentioned again by Colonel Terry.

Our company arrived at Nashville, Tennessee, ahead of the balance of the regiment, where we were quartered in the Fair Grounds, there to await the arrival of the rest of the companies. I forgot to mention we started out with the name of the "Texas Rangers," with a reputation we had never earned, but were called on to sustain; how well we did it, we leave history to record our services during the four years we served the Army of the West. While I would not make any invidious distinction as between our regiment and others who served under Forrest, Wheeler and Wharton, I am proud to be able to say that opportunities were afforded us, largely by accident, that demonstrated our ability to meet every expectation of department commanders, as evidenced by the following expressions during the war:

"With a little more drill you are the equals of the old guard of Napoleon."—General Albert Sidney Johnston. "I always feel safe when the

Rangers are in front."—General Wm. J. Hardee. "There is no danger of a surprise when the Rangers are between us and the enemy."—General Braxton Bragg. "The Terry Rangers have done all that could be expected or required of soldiers."—Jefferson Davis.

While camped in the Fair Grounds, the citizens of Nashville, largely ladies, came rolling in, in carriages and buggies; all anxious to see the Texas Rangers, about whom history had written so much about their fearlessness and being great riders. Colonel Terry called on not a few of our men to ride horses that were taken out of buggies and carriages, for the purpose of showing their horsemanship—the most popular feature being a deposit of gold coins on the ground, the rider to run at full speed, stooping down and picking them up. This extraordinary feat, in connection with their general appearance; being armed with shotguns, six-shooters and Bowie knives, seemed to sustain their idea of the Texas Rangers that fought at the Alamo, Goliad and San Jacinto and served under Jack Hayes, Ben McCollough and other Indian and Mexican fighters. The regular army equipment for cavalry was the saber, the carbine and six-shooter. This difference in equipment alone indicated that the Texas Ranger expected and would fight only in close quarters. After a pleasant stay at Nashville of nearly two weeks, we were ordered to go by rail to Bowling Green, Kentucky, where we found an army of infantry and artillery and three regiments of cavalry. Here we drew our horses by lot and it was my good fortune to draw first choice out of about a thousand horses tied to a picket rope. When all were ready to make their selection I was directed to where these horses were tied and ordered to make my selection, which I was not permitted to do with any degree of deliberation. Having about a thousand men waiting on me, all anxious to make their selection, a comrade, seeing I was confused and embarrassed, offered to exchange his thirty-second choice for my choice, paying me a liberal bonus. I was glad to accept it, mainly to get time to look around among the rest of the horses, believing I would stand a better chance to get a good mount. I had got short of money by that time, as we paid our own expenses, except transportation, and this comrade was glad to pay me for my first choice. We had no time to take out a horse and try his gaits, and it proved largely guesswork in the selection of the horses. The best gait for cavalry service is a long swinging walk and fox trot; unfortunately my thirty-second choice proved a pacer.

After drawing our horses and preparing everything ready for active service, the regiment under Colonel Terry was ordered on a scout to Glasgow, Kentucky, where we were kindly received by its citizens and took up our quarters at the Fair Grounds. Here the regiment spent several days pleasantly, feasting on the good things brought in by the ladies of the town.

The second day Colonel Terry ordered Captain Ferrell, with his company and Company B, of which I was a member, to the little town of Edmonton, Kentucky, where it was reported a part of a regiment of Federal cavalry were quartered.

We started at night, which proved to be one of the coldest we had ever been out in, riding all night. When nearly daylight, we reached the suburbs of the town. I was riding a very spirited and nervous horse, which refused to be quieted, while riding in line. In order to keep him quiet, I had loosened the strap on his curb, which proved to be a mistake. Nearing the town, the order came down the line "Silence in ranks," and soon my horse got to prancing. I jerked him by the reins, throwing him on his haunches, when the hammer of my shotgun struck the horn of the saddle and fired off my gun, which raised the alarm in town. Immediately the order was given "Form fours; Charge!" which excited my horse to such an extent that he broke ranks and flew up the line to the front. Carrying my shotgun in my right hand, I was unable to check him without the curb and he ran away with me, carrying me up into the town on the square, about three hundred yards in advance of my command, where I succeeded in checking him. For this I was reprimanded by Captain Ferrell, who would not receive my explanation that the horse ran away with me and claimed that I was too anxious to get there first.

Had the garrison not received information that we were moving on them for an attack and left during the night for Mumfordsville, instead of occupying the town as we expected, I no doubt would have been killed in this, our first charge.

Captain Ferrell had orders from General Johnston to try to capture a spy by the name of Burrell, who was making this town his headquarters and who always stopped at the hotel. As soon as we entered the square we were ordered to surround the hotel, which was done promptly. Captain Ferrell then called the proprietor to the door, told him to tell the ladies in the house to rise and dress, as he would have to search the house for Burrell. The hotel man said that Burrell was there the evening before, but left for Mumfordsville and was certainly not in the house. Captain Ferrell told him that it made no difference, but to hurry up, he was going to search the house.

The house was partly a two-story building, which had been added to the gable end of the one-story building and the stair landing, built against the gable of a one-story house, with a solid wood shutter covering, and opening into the attic of the one-story building. The ladies took their own time about getting ready for our search, perhaps nearly an hour; some of them in the meantime coming to the door and repeating the proprietor's statement—that Burrell had left the evening before. When they announced ready, I being near the door, dashed in ahead of all the rest and up the stairs, when I discovered the wooden shutter, which I jerked open, peering into the dark attic. Daylight had now fairly lit up the surroundings and I discovered, through the light of the cracked shingles, what I took to be a bundle of clothing at the far end, under the corner of the roof. I cocked both barrels of my gun and called out, "Come out; I see you; I'll shoot if you don't." He answered, "Don't shoot." If he had not answered I, no doubt, would have concluded, and perhaps others that followed me, too, that it was an old bundle of plunder. Proceeding down stairs with the prisoner, Burrell, who proved to be quite an intelligent and good-looking gentleman, I carried him into the parlor, where the ladies had congregated. They were all in tears, with some of our boys laughing at them and telling them they were story tellers.

Captain Ferrell, immediately on entering the square, detailed two men for each road leading into the town, to picket these roads about one-half mile from town. We built log fires on the square to keep us warm during the day until about three o'clock in the evening. A citizen then came in and, in an excited manner, told Captain Ferrell that a large cavalry force was moving in between us and Glasgow, with a view of cutting us off from our main command. The pickets arrested everybody coming into town and by three o'clock we had about fifteen or twenty prisoners, including some four or five Federal soldiers, who rode in on them, thinking the town was still occupied by Federal troops. On receiving information about this large cavalry force moving on a road between us and Glasgow, Captain Ferrell gave the order to mount and form fours, selecting what prisoners (about seven or eight, including Burrell) and the soldiers, to take with us, and turning the balance of them loose. He then placed me in charge of the prisoners, with four others to help guard them. We then commenced our retreat to Glasgow. When about three miles from town, another citizen dashed up to Captain Ferrell, who rode in advance of the column, and reported the same large cavalry force occupying our road some few miles ahead of us. Captain Ferrell, who, by the way, was an old frontiersman, Indian and Mexican fighter, dropped back and ordered me to tie Burrell's ankles together, under the horse's body and if we got into a fight and he attempted to escape, to not fail to kill him the first one. I don't think I ever did anything during the war that I hated as bad as I did to tie this man's ankles under the horse, but it was my orders from a man I knew would not permit any plea for its modification, and I had to obey.

After riding about eight or ten miles, in this way, feeling sorry for Burrell in his pitiful plight, I couldn't stand it any longer and told him if he would promise me he would not make a break when the guns opened, that

I would unloose the ropes and free his legs, for which he thanked me. Then I told him to be careful and carry out his promise, for if he did attempt a break, I would surely shoot him.

It seems that the report of these citizens proved only a ruse to induce us to liberate our prisoners, as we were never fired on or again heard of any Federal Cavalry in our front and safely reached Glasgow, where we still found the balance of the regiment in camp.

Colonel Terry sent our prisoners to Bowling Green, highly pleased with the capture of Burrell, for whom he had a special order by General Johnston. I am satisfied Burrell was sent to Richmond, Virginia, and was ultimately exchanged, as I saw the name of a Colonel Burrell, commanding Kentucky troops mentioned in a war history, published in the North some years after the War and on which point I trust I was not mistaken, and that he is still in the land of the living.

CHAPTER V

Our First Engagement

We now took up our line of march for Ritters, a point on the Louisville & Nashville Pike, between Cave City and Woodsonville, with Hindman's Brigade of infantry and a battery of four pieces, camped at Cave City, a few miles in our rear, and established our permanent camp, for the purpose of scouting and picketing. This camp at Ritters in winter proved to be a very trying one to us, raised in Texas in a mild and genial climate. We had a great deal of snow and rain and the exposure on scouts and picket duty soon developed pneumonia, measles and other troubles, necessitating our patients to abandon camp life. They were sent to the hospital at Nashville, where the ladies of Nashville were daily awaiting trains. They would not permit patients to be carried to the hospital but would take them to their private homes for personal care and treatment. They showed a partiality for the Texas Rangers, no doubt largely through sympathy, as we had left our distant, comfortable homes, burning all bridges behind us, to fight for them and their country. Our regiment soon dwindled down from a membership of one thousand to not more than about four hundred for duty; many of the sick were permanently rendered unable to return, while a great many died.

After serving nearly a month in the capacity of picket and scouts, General Hindman, anxious to bring on an engagement with the enemy, who were camped on Green River at Woodsonville and Mumfordsville, conceived the idea of moving his camp. Instead of avoiding a collision, as he had orders to do, he moved right toward the enemy's lines, ordering Colonel Terry, with our regiment, to move about a mile in his advance.

I was on picket duty, with part of a company, at Horse Cave, about three miles south of the main pike from Bowling Green to Louisville, when Captain Ferrell of the regiment, with part of his company, came by and took us along, moving towards Woodsonville on a dirt road running parallel with the pike on which were Hindman's Brigade of infantry; with the Louisville & Nashville Railroad running between the two. Just as we came in sight of Rowlett Station, a point on a high ridge this side of Woodsonville, we discovered the regiment, with Colonel Terry and General Hindman about fifty feet in advance, moving in the direction of Rowlett Station. Colonel Terry and General Hindman then discovered a Federal line of infantry lying down behind a rail fence in front of them. Hindman's infantry were at least a mile behind, coming on, when they discovered the enemy. General Hindman ordered Colonel Terry to withdraw the regiment and let him bring up the artillery and infantry, and dislodge them from their position. In the meantime, Captain Ferrell, in command of the party I was with, had discovered the enemy in our front, which was just across a railroad cut, spanned by the pike bridge. Colonel Terry, in place of obeying the order of General Hindman to withdraw, answered, "General Hindman, this is no place for you; go back to your infantry," and called on Captain Walker, who was in the rear with the balance of the regiment, to come on, form into line and charge. Simultaneously with his charge on the west side of the railroad, we, under Ferrell, charged the enemy in front of us, behind the rail fence. As soon as we moved forward, other Federals, behind trees and rocks, on small hills on both sides, opened fire on us. Their troops behind the fence held their fire until we got within fifty yards of them, then turned loose. In less time than it takes to tell it, we charged them, delivering our fire of double-barreled shotguns, breaking down the fence and getting among them with our six-shooters. In a few minutes we had run over them, although they numbered two to one, and to save themselves many of them "possumed" on us, and feigned being dead, and by that means saved their lives, though the main portion of them fled towards Woodsonville, where, down in the edge of the timber, they were met by heavy reinforcements. In this charge we lost a number of our best men, killed and wounded. Among the killed was Colonel Terry, which proved an irreparable loss, as no doubt, considering his fearlessness and dash, as also his ability as a commander, he would have proven another Forrest, a Napoleon of cavalry. General Hindman brought up his infantry and artillery, a battery of four pieces, with which he opened on their fort at Mumfordsville, and also on their line of infantry in the woods about a half mile below us. The fort responded, but largely overshot us and our battery. This proved our first baptism by fire. General Hindman was notified by a scout that the enemy was crossing Green River in very heavy force, near the Mammoth Cave, moving in our rear, which necessitated falling back to Cave City. We brought off the bodies of our dead and wounded, the remains of Colonel Terry being sent to Texas in charge of Captain Walker, who was wounded, and the balance of the wounded were sent to hospitals at Nashville.

The enemy we fought at this point proved to be the Thirty-second Indiana Regiment, under Colonel Wilich, a German regiment, said to be the best drilled regiment in Rousseau's Army.

We next established our camp at Bell Station, a few miles in advance of Cave City, where we continued scouting and picketing for the army. Both armies now remained quiet for several months, collecting reinforcements for a final clash; the rigors of the winter affecting our army perhaps more than it did the Federal army, as they were used to a colder climate. Our regiment was especially affected.

While encamped at Bell Station, I had a messmate by the name of McDonald, who was taken sick with pneumonia and was unwilling to be sent to the hospital at Nashville. He insisted on being taken to some good private family in the neighborhood. I succeeded in finding the family of Isaac Smith, an old gentleman who had six sons in Breckenridge's Brigade of infantry, and living about three miles from our picket stand with his wife and two daughters. These good people were willing to take McDonald and nurse him, our own surgeon attending him and myself assisting in nursing him, frequently spending the night there. The oldest daughter was also very sick, attended by a citizen doctor in the neighborhood, who also took a deep interest in McDonald.

One day I received orders to report to the command; that Bowling Green was being evacuated. We were ordered to join the army as quickly as possible, Hindman's Brigade having already arrived at Bowling Green. This information proved to be bad news for McDonald, who was already convalescent, but still very weak. He begged and pleaded to be taken to Bowling Green and Nashville, saying he did not want to be captured. Old Mr. Smith, then perhaps fifty-five years old, decided to hitch up his wagon, as he had no buggy or hack, and haul McDonald to Bowling Green in a wagon, as he wanted to refugee and stay with his boys in the army; he feared to stay at home, surrounded by ugly Union neighbors.

We now put a mattress in the wagon, with plenty of bedclothing. We put McDonald in the wagon, well protected from the cold, and, after a sad parting with the family, proceeded to the Bowling Green pike, the old man driving the wagon and I following on my horse. We reached Bowling Green near night, just in time to witness the last cannon shot striking one of the main pillars of the railroad bridge, which was an iron extension, and saw it drop into the river. We crossed on a covered wooden pike bridge.

On our arrival in town, we inquired for a good place to leave McDonald for the night, which we were unable to find, but were recommended to go out about two miles to a Mr. Roe's, who had a large flouring mill. This we did, and found excellent quarters for McDonald and myself for the night; old Mr. Smith driving back to town and taking the Nashville pike to try to find Breckenridge's Brigade of Infantry, with which his sons were connected.

During the night we had a very heavy snow. Mr. Roe had his buggy hitched up and drove McDonald to the railroad station in town, myself following. Roe was unable to remain with us, as we were expecting the enemy to cross the river any moment and enter the town, hence left us by the side of the track and returned home.

After a while, Colonel Wharton, with about fifteen or twenty men out of our regiment, was ordered to destroy the depot and proceeded to fire it. A train with a few passenger coaches and an engine to pull it, was standing on the track on the outside, waiting for orders to move. A good many convalescent soldiers from the hospital, including my friend McDonald, squatted down by the roadside, waiting for the coaches to be opened. As soon as the fire started in the station, the enemy opened a battery on the place, using shells, which exploded all around us. The engineer got scared, uncoupled his engine and pulled out, leaving our train at the mercy of the artillery fire. Looking around for some kind of a vehicle to take McDonald out of there, as he was too feeble to attempt to ride my horse, I rode up town and found a two-horse wagon, loaded with hams, flush to the top of the bed, which the driver had taken from our commissary building and was hauling home. I stopped and told him that I had a sick friend down at the station; that I wanted him to go down there and haul my friend away. He said he wouldn't go down there for anything in the world. I pulled out my gun and told him to go; and he went.

Arriving at the place, we cut open some infantry baggage that had blankets tied to the knapsacks and put about a half dozen blankets on top of the hams, lifting McDonald and laying him on top, covering him with more blankets. In the meantime, the station was about consumed and the artillery had ceased firing. After getting up on the square and finding our troops had all left, I told this man that he would have to drive on the Nashville Pike until we could catch up with our command, which he did most reluctantly and only under the persuasion of my gun.

About a mile and a half below town we found our regiment drawn up in line of battle. I sent for our surgeon, who examined McDonald and said to the driver, "You will have to drive on down the road until we catch up with my ambulances." The driver said that he wouldn't go any further; said I, "If you don't, we will have to hold on to this team until we unload; I am going to save these hams for our regiment." They were meat that belonged to our commissary. He said that he wouldn't go any further, that we could take his team and wagon and go to —— with it. The fellow was evidently afraid that we would force him into the army; he thereby lost his team and wagon, which we had no idea of taking, and he could have saved them by continuing with us.

Our army now took up its long line of retreat for Nashville; our regiment covering the rear without any engagements, or the firing of a single gun. On reaching Nashville, crossing the Cumberland River on the suspension bridge about midnight, we got information that Port Donaldson had surrendered, which made it necessary for our troops to leave Nashville in great haste, which they did; protected in the rear by our regiment. The army continued to Shelbyville, while we were ordered to Fort Donaldson, to cover the escape of many men of the Fort Donaldson army, whom we met scattered all along the road. The weather was most severe.

The winding up of this winter I had a sad experience. About midnight, the second night out, we pulled into a cedar grove by the side of the road, the ground of which was soft and muddy. We tied our horses to the trees around us, and arranged as best we could, to get a little rest and sleep, putting down our oilcloths next to the mud, then our saddle blankets and each having a good blanket and overcoat for cover. My messmate, John Cochran, laid by me, and we soon dropped into a sound sleep, being tired and worn out, and without having had a bite of anything to eat that day and no forage for our horses.

Waking up some time during the night, I felt a curious feeling about my head. Putting my hand to my head I found my hair clotted with blood. I woke up Cochran, my companion, and told him that some one had struck me over the head with a gun, which proved a mistake. Our horses being tied in the cold, without any feed, had pulled the length of the rope and commenced pawing, when one of them pawed me on the head with a sharp shoe, which caused a deep cut of my scalp. We then decided we would move through the woods until we could strike some house, and soon struck a country road. After traveling perhaps a mile, we discovered a little log house by the side of the road and through the cracks of the batten door, we saw a bright fire burning on the inside. We knocked on the door, which was answered by a very old gentleman, whom we told that we wanted to come in and dress my wounds. He asked who we were. We told him we were Confederate soldiers, camped near there and the cause of my hurt. He received us very kindly, invited us into his main room, which contained a double bed where his old wife was sleeping. As soon as she saw my bloody condition, she jumped up, dressed, heated some water and with nice clean towels, commenced bathing my head and dressing my wounds. She then went to work, put some clean sheets and pillowcases on the bed and insisted on our lying down and taking a good nap, while she prepared breakfast for us.

While we told them that it was dangerous for us to sleep in a bed, as we were not used to it and it would give us a cold, we were compelled to take the bed on their refusal to listen to anything else.

When we awoke next morning after daylight, the old lady had a splendid breakfast of fried chicken prepared for us, fine biscuit and good

Confederate coffee—made of rye and parched sweet potatoes; everything on the table was neat and spotlessly clean and I do not think we ever enjoyed a meal during the whole war better than we did this.

When we prepared to leave, we asked the old gentleman for our bill; he seemed to feel hurt, and said, "The idea of charging a Confederate soldier for anything he had!" This was out of the question with him; all he asked, if we ever happened in that neighborhood, in twenty miles of him, to be sure to make him another visit, for he hoped to meet us again. Thanking them for their exceeding kindness, we then walked back to camp, where we found many of our comrades still in deep sleep, with no forage for the horses.

In the course of a few hours the bugle called to saddle up, and we resumed our march to Shelbyville, and caught up with a good many of our retreating infantry. Here we spent two days and had our first taste of an attempt at discipline by Major Harrison, who was then in command; Colonel Wharton being sick somewhere on the line of our retreat.

It seems that Major Harrison met a couple of our men in town without permission and ordered them to return to camp immediately, which they refused to do. When he returned to camp he ordered these men arrested by the camp guards and placed on the pike, marking time. A Mr. Sam Ash of Company B (now still living in Houston) went to these men and led them back to camp, telling them that no such disgraceful punishment should be inaugurated in the regiment. The infantry were passing frequently and we considered it a disgrace to the Texas Ranger to submit to such punishment. Major Harrison finally yielded and passed the incident, but to a great extent, lost the respect of the command.

The army now continued its retreat through Shelbyville, Huntsville, Decatur to Corinth, Mississippi, without incidents of note, except the burning of bridges behind us. We also destroyed the magnificent bridge across the Tennessee River at Decatur.

It may be not out of place, before going further, and to give the reader a better idea of the character of the Texas Rangers, to mention an expression of Hardee's. While passing through Huntsville, Alabama, some ladies, in company with General Hardee, were standing on the sidewalk, watching us pass, cheering and waving their handkerchiefs at us, when one of them remarked to General Hardee, saying "General, the Rangers are the best soldiers you have; are they not?" He told them no, he was not stuck on them, saying that they would not submit to any discipline or drill; but he was willing to say that in a battle, or when called on to meet a forlorn hope, the Rangers always responded. General Hardee was one of the strictest disciplinarians in our army and wrote the military tactics that were used by both sides.

We soon arrived at Corinth, where we were assigned a camp ground about two miles from the place, near a spring and we here witnessed new additions to the main army. Occasionally scouting parties from the regiment were sent out in different directions towards the Tennessee River, which duties were always performed to the satisfaction of the commanding officers.

CHAPTER VI

AN ACCIDENTAL INJURY—SHILOH—THE "MARK-TIME" MAJOR.

Our regiment, one night, was ordered out to report at daylight to some point up the Tennessee River, the night being very dark—one of the darkest nights we ever traveled in—and branches and small streams very boggy. Colonel Wharton, at the head of the regiment, was riding a very fast walking horse. We struck many places in these branches where it was only possible for one horse to cross at a time, and Wharton, as soon as across, would strike out in his fast walk, leaving the rest of his command to come on as best they could. This threw the rear end of the regiment considerably behind and we had to lope at full speed to catch up with our file leaders after crossing these bad places. In one of these races to catch up, my horse stumbled and fell, pitching me over his head, with my left arm extended, and I sustained a dislocation of my left arm. Considerably stunned by the fall, and suffering great pain from this dislocation, a comrade was sent back with me to Corinth, where I had a surgeon to replace my arm, with instructions to carry it in a sling until it got well. Our regiment returned the next night without having discovered any of the enemy and was then ordered to prepare three days' rations, as was also the rest of the army.

In the meantime, the enemy had landed a large force, under General Grant, at Pittsburg Landing. Our regiment was ordered out with no one knowing where they were going, until they moved in the direction of Pittsburg Landing. They were immediately followed by the whole army, and on the fifth of April, they engaged the enemy and fought the battle of Shiloh; our regiment was moved about on the field from right to left. As the dense woods did not afford an opportunity for mounted cavalry, they were unable to do much fighting, except, about ten o'clock the first day, they were dismounted and ordered to charge through a thicket at Owl Creek, which they had to do single file, and were shot down by a large infantry force as fast as the men made their appearance in the open. Soon realizing that it was impossible to dislodge the enemy from their position with this handful of men, they were immediately ordered to fall back. This proved the extent of their active engagement, but they served as a corps of observation on both flanks until Tuesday evening.

After the second day's engagement, Grant's army having been reinforced on Sunday night by the whole of Buell's army (as large as our army originally), our army was compelled to retreat, which was done in a heavy rain, rendering the road to Corinth almost impassable for artillery and ambulances. Realizing that our army was in great danger of being annihilated, General Beauregard sent for General Breckenridge, who was on the field with his Kentucky Brigade, ordering him to cover the retreat and try to save the army. General Breckenridge responded that he would protect the army if it cost the last man he had. This occurred on Tuesday after the battle. Our regiment, what was left of it, and Colonel Forrest, with about fifty men, were ordered to support General Breckenridge. Breckenridge's Brigade was drawn up near the old battlefield. In their front, about a quarter of a mile away, two lines of battle of the enemy were seen to form with a brigade of cavalry, mounted, in their front, covering their movement. Breckenridge's Brigade was then moved to the rear a short distance, to a position where they were hid by lying down. Our regiment, in command of Major Harrison, and Colonel Forrest with his fifty men, soon formed in front of Breckenridge, preparing to charge the enemy.

As heretofore stated, Colonel Harrison, up to this time, on our retreat, did not have the confidence or respect of the men on account of a blunder he committed at the small town of Jimtown in Kentucky, which caused him to be dubbed the "Jimtown Major;" then again, on account of his ordering some boys to mark time on the Shelbyville Pike, was dubbed the "Mark-time Major."

A large number of the regiment had been congregated on the pike, at the point from which Ash had led the prisoners, and when Major Harrison reached the spot, after hearing what had been done, he was met by angry glances on every hand for presuming to treat two gentlemen so inconsiderately. Disregarding their menacing looks Major Harrison called out, "Is there an officer of my regiment present who will execute my orders?" when Pat Christian (then a lieutenant in Company K) stepped to the front, with a salute, and said, "Major, I will." Then Major Harris ordered him to get a file of men and bring the two prisoners back to complete their sentence, and to inform him instantly if interfered with.

It was here that Christian, afterwards captain of his company, and then major and later lieutenant colonel, first attracted the attention of the regiment, afterwards so devoted to him, for his gallantry and his good traits of character, and here that the regiment had its first lesson in military discipline, under an officer temporarily unpopular, who afterwards won their high respect.

For the first time since our retreat, he was in command of the regiment, Colonel Wharton having been wounded, and very soon the enemy commenced a scattering fire, while the regiment was forming, occasionally striking a man or a horse. The men became restive and wanted to charge, but Major Harrison rode down the line saying to them, "Be quiet, boys, 'till your 'Jimtown Mark-time Major' gets ready for you," in a very cool and deliberate manner, and finally in ordering the charge said, "Now, follow your Jimtown Major." He led them on to the cavalry, which, in an impetuous charge, they drove right in among their infantry, and, on account of their being confused in the mix-up, the enemy fell back a short distance, and the regiment brought out a number of prisoners. While this charge proved a success, we lost a number of valuable men in killed and wounded. This was the last fighting on the battlefield of Shiloh.

I have not entered into any details of the battle, as history gives such a complete account, written by both sides, that its details are well known, and as the purpose of this writing is to recount my own personal history and because I was not actively engaged with the regiment during the battle, I find it unnecessary to give the details.

As heretofore stated, I was suffering with a dislocated arm, the effects of my fall, and did not move out with the regiment when they started on this trip; but on Sunday morning, hearing the guns of Shiloh in our camp at Corinth, I mounted my horse and struck out for the field. Unable to learn where our regiment was posted, I remained with an infantry command, offering my services to the extent of what I was able to do, but I was not called on during the several days' battle, except to carry a few orders from place to place.

I reached Corinth, Mississippi, where our camp was located, on Thursday, aiding and assisting about a half dozen wounded men of the Second Texas, allowing them to ride my horse when they were able. These men were completely exhausted, as they did nothing else but stand in line all day Sunday 'till four o'clock in the evening, firing their guns, and again on Monday, opposed to Buell's fresh army, which proved the hardest fighting during the battle. "All honor to the Second Texas."

Recalling General Albert Sidney Johnston's promise in a telegram to Colonel Terry at New Orleans, that we should never be brigaded as long as he lived; his death at four o'clock on Sunday evening cancelled this promise. General Beauregard then took command of the army.

A few days after the battle of Shiloh, having recuperated our horses, as well as the men, Colonel Wharton was ordered to report to a General Adams, who had a Kentucky regiment, and General Adams, with this regiment and the Eighth Texas, was ordered on a raid into Middle Tennessee, with instructions to capture and destroy everything of the enemy he could meet up with and was able to handle.

We crossed the Tennessee River at Lamb's Ferry, the ferry boat being propelled by a paddle wheel, driven by a horse-tread power. Here we left our wagons and all our extra luggage, as well as cooking utensils, awaiting our return, but the Federal cavalry a few days after, crossed the river, captured our entire storage and we never saw cooking utensils or tents afterwards, and were thereby reduced to the condition of the real Texas Ranger as on the frontiers of Texas.

Immediately after crossing the Tennessee River we struck a considerable infantry force, with artillery. General Adams, in place of attacking them, moved us around them in great haste, thereby avoiding a collision and getting away, leaving them shelling the woods for several hours, while we were making distance. We next struck the Pulaski Pike, finding about two hundred wagons, loaded with two bales of cotton on each and a guard of two men with each wagon. General Adams drew us out of sight and hearing and would not allow Colonel Wharton to capture this train, which could have been done without the loss of a man. But no doubt as General Adams suggested, in doing this we would stir up a hornet's nest and get the whole Yankee army in pursuit of us. Wharton was powerless to do anything, held back by General Adams.

When near the town of Fayetteville, Lincoln County, Tennessee, a citizen sent out by the garrison of the town, numbering about five hundred cavalry, told us to come in; they wanted to surrender; they were tired of the war and wanted to go home. General Adams conceived this to be a trick of theirs and declined their invitation, moving us around the town in the night by a path in the woods, guided by a citizen, thereby losing a splendid opportunity of capturing this garrison.

The second night after this, we camped at the town of Salem, about ten miles south of Winchester, and at Winchester the next night, where information reached us that about two thousand infantry, moving in wagons, and a battery of artillery, had been in pursuit of us and had been camped at Salem the next night after we were there, and was expected to follow us to Winchester. The road from Salem to Winchester was a straight lane with high rail fences on each side. At a point about equal distance between Salem and Winchester, was a large woods lot, running up to the lane, as noticed by Colonel Wharton. He suggested to General Adams that we go back, remain concealed in this woods, close to the road and when the enemy came along, riding in wagons, that we charge them and force them to surrender. This seemed good to General Adams and an opportunity he was willing to risk.

We moved around to this woods lot, remaining there until about daylight, when information reached us that the Yankees had already passed and were then occupying Winchester. We immediately returned to Winchester and found them drawn up behind a railroad cut, with a commanding position for their battery. They opened this battery on us, using shells, as soon as we came in sight. Then Colonel Wharton, riding 'round hunting a place to charge them, decided this could not be done without the loss of a great many men and a charge might result in failure; we, therefore, moved around Winchester, passing through Decherd's depot and pitched camp in Hawkins Cove, perhaps twenty miles distant from Winchester.

The second day in camp in Hawkins Cove, a citizen came and reported to General Adams that the Yankees were at his house with a couple of wagons, loading his meat, and begging him to send a small force to drive them away. A company of the Kentucky regiment and Company B of the Rangers, which was the company to which I belonged, were detailed for this service. When we reached this man's house they had already left with his meat and were driving fast, back into town. We struck a lope, endeavoring to catch up with them, but failed. The Kentucky captain, being the ranking officer, was in command; riding at the head of the column and running over the pickets on a bridge near town, he carried us right into the town, up to the courthouse square. This charge proved a complete surprise. We found the enemy scattered all over town and a large party of them in the courthouse, being the only parties we felt free to fire on, as there were no women and children about. We heard the artillery bugle and concluded to get out of there, which we did very promptly and in such good time the artillery never had a chance to fire a shot at us.

Some years after the war, a Winchester paper was sent me, giving an account of fifty Texas Rangers attacking two thousand infantry and artillery in their town, with a loss of only one man, who had his arm broken by an explosive ball.

We returned to our camp in Hawkins Cove. On that night General Adams came down to Colonel Wharton's camp fire and announced that he would start across the mountain, for Chattanooga, the next morning, and secure artillery, that he could not undertake to remain in Middle Tennessee without it. Colonel Wharton had become exasperated at General Adams' conduct the entire trip and told him to take his Kentucky regiment and go to Halifax with it, if he wanted to—that he intended remaining in Middle Tennessee and doing what he could to carry out the original order of General Beauregard.

After a few days' rest in Hawkins Cove, where the enemy did not attempt to molest us, a messenger reached us, with orders from General Kirby Smith at Knoxville, to report to Colonel Forrest at McMinnville, which Wharton did, as soon as we reached there. After a day's rest Colonel Forrest (who had the First and Second Georgia and a Tennessee battalion, all cavalry) in conjunction with our regiment, started, late evening, for Murfreesboro, which was then the headquarters for Tennessee, of the Federal Army, with Major General Crittenden in command. Murfreesboro's garrison consisted of the Ninth Michigan Infantry, a part of a regiment of cavalry located in their camp to the right of town, the Third Minnesota and a battery of artillery on the northwest of town. They had about one hundred prisoners in the courthouse, upstairs, with a strong guard downstairs.

Greatly outnumbering us, our success depended on a surprise. When near their advance picket on the pike, Colonel Forrest asked for some Rangers to capture this picket without the fire of a gun, which was done in very short order. He then had a consultation with the commanders of the different regiments, and it was decided that Colonel Wharton, with our regiment in advance and the Second Georgia next in column, attack the Ninth Michigan and the cavalry camp on the right. To reach them he had to turn into a side street about two or three blocks from the courthouse, where Colonel Forrest halted, awaiting for his part of the command to come up to take them through town to the Third Minnesota and battery camp, ignoring the courthouse as much as possible.

After our regiment had passed into the side street, following Wharton, Forrest discovered that the Georgians and Tennesseans had failed to come up and immediately decided to take what was left of our regiment and lead them to the attack on the Third Minnesota and the battery north of the town. This gave him a force of only about fifty or sixty men. By this action he cut our company about half in two, which threw me into the first set of fours at the head of the column, with Forrest riding by my side, on my right. Nearing the courthouse, a couple of Federals up in the second story door, dropped down on their knees and raised their guns to fire, but Forrest and I fired ahead of them. When Forrest fired his pistol, his horse dodged almost in front of me, just as I fired, very nearly shooting Forrest through the head. I have often thought what a misfortune this would have been, as I came very near killing a man who turned out to be the Napoleon of cavalry.

In the upper story of the courthouse were confined about one hundred prisoners, some of Morgan's men, but mostly civilians, and the courthouse was guarded by about one hundred men, who fired on us through doors and windows. We moved around the courthouse, some to the left and some to the right, as the courthouse was standing in the middle of the square immediately fronting the center of the street we came up on. About the time we reached the courthouse, Wharton, with the balance of the regiment, had charged the Michigan camp, many of whom were asleep in their tents, and the noise of the battle reached us about the time we fired into the courthouse. As stated, Forrest with about fifty men in columns of fours, except a few that were left on the courthouse square, shot down by courthouse guards, moved on to the north of town, where he lost his bearings and was compelled to get a citizen out of his house, to pilot us to the Minnesota camp and battery. When we reached there we found the men up and dressed and the battery opened on us, throwing a few shells among us, which scattered us and caused the disappearance of Forrest. We were in an old field, and on leaving, I was called by a Kentuckian, who had volunteered to go with us into the fight and had his arm shattered by a piece of shell, begging me to not go off and leave him. He was hardly able to sit on his horse. I rode up, taking his horse by the bridle, leading him up to a fence in the edge of the timber, with a scattering fire directed on us. I dismounted and let down the fence, leading his horse over it. While doing this, noticing I was trying to get off a wounded comrade, they gallantly ceased firing on us. I now led my wounded friend through the woods, until we reached a house, about a mile from there, when the gentleman at the house hitched up his buggy, and, placing my friend in the buggy, he drove around the town, with myself following, leading the wounded man's horse, until we reached a point about a mile below town, where we found the Rangers collecting what was left of them, out of the Michigan camp fight and also the few men who were with Forrest in the old sedge field when fired on by the Third Minnesota and battery.

The regiment formed and gathered at this point about a mile below town, awaiting further orders, with Wharton, wounded again, directing the formation, when a messenger came from Forrest, who was then up town with his Georgia and Tennessee battalions, ordering us back up into town. After joining the Georgians and having displayed about three times as many men as he really had, by moving them around a block, in sight of the enemy (who had gathered and formed, in a splendid position, supported by their battery) Forrest went in, under a flag of truce and demanded their immediate surrender, telling them that he had five men to their one and was determined to take them; that if he had to make another charge on them, on their own heads be the responsibility; that the little fight had, was only with his advance guard, that he had five hundred Texas Rangers he couldn't control in a fight, and the responsibility was with them. After deliberating on the matter for a few minutes, they raised the white flag and surrendered. The result of this surrender was a parole of eighteen hundred and sixteen privates at McMinnville, the further capture of forty-seven commissioned officers, including Major General Crittenden, with Colonel Duffield of the Ninth Michigan badly wounded in the Michigan camp; thirty-eight wagonloads of valuable stores; a magnificent battery of four pieces of artillery and several million dollars' worth of commissary and quartermaster's stores, destroyed by fire.

I would also mention the release of two citizen prisoners confined in the jail, who were condemned to be hung the next day, as spies. The wife of one of these men, with many other ladies, witnessed our passing through Woodbury. Learning that we were going to Murfreesboro, she wrung her hands and begged and plead with us to bring her husband back. Some of the men who heard her, answered that we would surely bring her husband back, which we did the next day.

A dastardly act I will recount here—of one of the Federal guards stationed at the jail. When he found we were about to capture the town, he set fire to the jail, which no doubt would have burned the poor prisoners, but the fire was promptly extinguished by several of our men, who succeeded in capturing the fellow who started the fire and in taking him before General Forrest. Forrest pulled out his pistol and killed him on the spot, a well-deserved punishment.

On marching our prisoners to McMinnville, the commissioned officers who had been captured, were given the privilege of the pike, they taking a parole not to attempt to make their escape. When this high privilege was offered Major General Crittenden, he refused the courtesy, telling Forrest that he could not accept, as his government didn't recognize him as a regular Confederate soldier and only knew him as a guerilla. Forrest told him that it made no difference with him and he furnished him with a guard of two Texas Rangers, dressed in buckskin, wearing Mexican sombreros. These men were somewhat wild in appearance, no doubt, to General Crittenden. After riding along with his guards for an hour or two, one man on each side of him, occasionally nodding at each other, the general concluded that perhaps they were planning to kill him, and had them take him up to Colonel Forrest, when he asked Forrest to parole him and give him the privilege of the pike, like the rest; saying he verily believed that these men would kill him.

After paroling the privates at McMinnville, permitting them all to retain their private property, which included a magnificent set of silver band instruments, Forrest told the officers that they would have to be taken to Knoxville to General Smith's headquarters and directed Colonel Wharton, who was wounded, with Company B, his old company, to take charge of them, the battery and thirty-eight wagonloads of valuable stores. He requested Colonel Wharton, when he got safely up on top of the mountain, by way of Sparta, to send back a messenger, reporting that fact, and I was sent back with this message to Colonel Forrest.

Reaching Sparta about daylight, I could not find any one who could tell me the whereabouts of Forrest's command, and struck out, back in the direction of McMinnville, when incidentally I met a citizen, who reported that they were camped at a certain place in the woods between Sparta and Lebanon, which I succeeded in finding about noon. Reporting to Colonel Forrest that Wharton had got up on top of the mountain safely with his prisoners, artillery and wagons, I told him that I didn't feel like going back to catch up with my company, going to Knoxville, lying around in camp and that I wanted to remain with the regiment and asked his permission to do so. He kindly consented and told me to report to the regiment and stay with them.

CHAPTER VII

I AM WOUNDED AND CAPTURED.

The Rangers now felt that they were commanded by somebody who meant business and that there was plenty of work in store for them. After remaining in this camp another day, we started for Lebanon, in the night, where it was understood a considerable cavalry force of the enemy were camped. Reaching the town about daylight, we formed fours and charged in, being greeted by ladies, through their windows, waving handkerchiefs and cheering, with no Federal cavalry in town, they having moved to Murfreesboro during the night, in great haste, learning we were on the way.

Here at Lebanon, we found, as in nearly every town we had been in in Middle Tennessee, a strong Southern people, who, while we were camped there for two days, gave us a great feast of everything that was good, which was heartily enjoyed by the whole command. Forrest, on being interviewed as to what was next on docket, said that he was going to take Nashville, though strongly fortified, and garrisoned by an infantry force of not less than ten thousand men under General Nelson.

On the early morning of the third day, we started out on the main Nashville pike, moving along at an ordinary gait, occasionally meeting citizens, out from Nashville, saying there was great excitement among the Yankees, and they were digging additional pits and preparing a strong defense. When we reached within twelve miles of Nashville, we struck a road leading through the cedars, to La Vergne, a station between Murfreesboro and Nashville. Before reaching La Vergne, General Forrest detailed about two hundred Rangers, under Captain Ferrell, to meet and capture a train from Murfreesboro, at La Vergne, which they succeeded in doing, capturing a large number of commissioned officers, who were on their way home on furlough, and capturing also the mails and express freight. Among these prisoners I will mention the kind-hearted and excellent business man among us today, a Mr. Fordyce, of the Pierce-Fordyce Oil Association, one of the largest oil concerns doing business in Texas.

Forrest, with the balance of the command, went to work tearing up the railroad between La Vergne and Nashville, burning trestles and bridges and tearing up the track. We then again retired to McMinnville. Before leaving in front of Nashville, Colonel Forrest asked for a detail of about fifteen or twenty men, who were selected from the Rangers and joined by four or five of Morgan's men, who happened to be along. I was one of this party, and we were all under the command of a Captain Gordon, who proved to be a reckless fellow, unfit to command such a party successfully. We crossed Cumberland River near Lebanon, in a bend called Little Dixie. Little Dixie was settled with some of the strongest Southern and most liberal people in the State, and regarded as a safe haven for the wounded Confederate soldiers, whom these good people would nourish and care for, to the extent of any character of risk. While crossing there, we promised the ladies if any of us were wounded, we would not fail to make our way back, so they could take care of us until able to join our command. Our orders from Colonel Forrest for the expedition were to collect information on the disposition of the Federal forces, preparatory to a general raid of our cavalry.

After crossing the river, we moved up towards the Louisville & Nashville Railroad, circulating through that section quite extensively, gathering information, and, on our return, we decided to capture a railroad train, with the mails from the army, which always proved very valuable, as the soldiers were always writing home on the movements of their army, which proved most valuable information for our headquarters.

In accordance with our plans, we struck the Louisville & Nashville Railroad between Woodburn and Franklin, at a point about equidistant between the two places; watering our horses at a branch within hearing of a Union man's house, who was awakened and decided that we had about three hundred men, supposing us to be of Morgan's command. Riding around in the branch, as we did, led him to the conclusion that we had about three hundred men. We struck the railroad about daylight, when we removed a few spikes, spreading the track, for the purpose of stopping the train and, being in a thick woods out of hearing, with no settlement near, we all laid down for a short nap. The mail train from the army was due at this point about eleven-thirty; another mail train from above was due about twelve o'clock, with numerous freight trains, carrying troops and war material, due throughout the day, also trains returning with wounded and discharged soldiers.

We heard the mail train whistle, from below, when it reached Franklin, and nothing of any other train, waiting until between three and four o'clock in the evening. I became satisfied that we were going to be caught in a trap and so told Gordon, insisting on leaving there, but Gordon refused to listen; he had just about sense enough to lose what he had. Finally, between three and four o'clock we heard the train, and immediately took position by the side of the track, having nineteen men for the fight, two of the men remaining with our horses, in the rear. All that could get trees for shelter, within twenty feet of the track took position behind trees, while eight of us, unable to find trees convenient, laid down flat on the ground. Very soon the train came up, turning a bend in the road about a half mile below us. The engineer, to fool us, put on more steam, making us think that they were entirely ignorant of our presence, and stopped right at the place we had shifted the rail. Soon they were right on us and began firing with about three hundred muskets, killing seven of our party, who were lying on the ground and jumped up, and badly wounding me, but the balance of our party, eleven strong, behind trees, with six-shooters, drove those fellows off the train on to the other side of the track. There the commanding officer, Lieutenant-Colonel (Blank), succeeded in forming about a hundred men in line in about twenty minutes, so he stated to me at the hospital at Bowling Green, where he made me a visit about a week after, furthermore stating that he believed if we had had about twenty-five more men we would have gotten his train. It seems that this was the first time these people were ever under fire and when under the impression that we had three hundred of Morgan's men, they were no doubt demoralized at the noise of their own guns.

The citizen at whose house we watered our horses at the branch had spied out our exact location on the railroad, a desolate place, where Morgan's cavalry had captured a train before. He went to Franklin, where he met the train from the army, reported three hundred of Morgan's men, when they ran the train back to Gallatin, Tennessee, unloaded the mails and express freight and took this regiment aboard, also notifying other trains that we were on the road, which caused their delay.

While the Federals were jumping off the train on the other side, we fell back to our horses, mounting, leaving the horses belonging to the men that were killed; not knowing at the time just who was left behind. I was able to run back and mount my own horse, with the assistance of a comrade. We hurried out of there, taking the road by which we had come, by this Union man's house, where I stopped to get me a drink of water. I had just been relieved of my pistol belt, and had grown very weak and faint from the loss of blood, which had collected in my boots, and was about to fall from the horse when I was caught by a comrade. Some one called out, "Here they come!" This aroused me. I made them hand me my pistols. We drew up in line in the lane and saw a party in the edge of the timber. Drawing our pistols we waved them at them and urged them to come on, which they didn't do. We soon discovered that they were only parties from the train who had found our dead men's horses and were afraid to come forward.

We now continued our march on this country road about eight or ten miles. I became too weak to travel and, satisfied that being encumbered with me would cause them all to get captured or killed, I insisted on their leaving me, believing that I was done for, anyway.

We soon reached a Mr. White's (an humble log house) who had two sons in Breckenridge's Brigade, and had with him his wife and daughter. He was an ardent Southern man and promised my comrades that I should have every attention, if left with them. Before leaving, I begged them to let me keep my pistols, which they failed to do, thinking it was best to leave me disarmed, as it proved to be.

My comrades then proceeded in haste to get out of that neighborhood and made for the Cumberland River, our main army then being near Chattanooga. In about an hour a citizen doctor came to see me and filled my wound full of cotton, in order to check the bleeding, saying that this was all that he could do for me; he had to hurry back home, lest he was caught giving me his attention, believing his neighbors would hang him and burn his family out of house and home, as this section of the country was inhabited by a desperate, vindictive Union people.

During the evening a young man called and claimed to be a good Rebel, saying that he had an uncle, who was also a good friend of the South, living up in the mountains, and if he could succeed in taking me there, that I would be perfectly safe. He arranged with me to come that night, with a hack, and take me to his uncle's, which he failed to do.

Mr. White's house was a double log house, a room at each end, with about a ten-foot hall in between, but no porch in front, a step at each room, leading out into the yard and heavy batten doors covering the door opening. Old Mr. White occupied a bed in the room with me, while his wife and daughter occupied a room at the other end. They had improvised a cot for me, in the middle of the room, so they could get around it. They used wick and tallow lamps for lights, which created a bad smell in the room and annoyed me a great deal, as I had considerable fever. Some time after midnight I begged the old man to extinguish his lamp, and very soon thereafter, I heard voices in the yard and immediately a pounding on the door with the butt end of a gun. The reader can imagine my feelings; I was satisfied they were Tories and my time had come. I would then have given a kingdom for my pistols and, no doubt, would have opened on them as they came in. They called and demanded of the old man to open the door quick. He told them to wait until he could strike a light, which he did. I was in position, from where I lay, to notice them coming in and to my great relief, saw a lieutenant and ten men in uniform, passing around me. Here was one time I was glad to see the Federal uniform. When they got up to my bunk, I feigned sleep and listened to what they had to say. The lieutenant asked the old man if I was badly hurt. He told him to turn down the sheet and he could judge for himself, when the lieutenant expressed his surprise and said, "I'm afraid we won't be able to move him." Now I concluded it was my time to say something. I opened my eyes and feigned bewilderment, looking up at them. The lieutenant asked, "Are you hurt much, sir?" I told them no, I did not think I was, and couldn't understand why I had been left there. The lieutenant asked if I thought that I could stand to be hauled to Woodburn, a station about five miles from there and the first station this side of Bowling Green. I told him I was satisfied I could stand it all right. He then ordered the old gentleman to direct him where he could find feed for his horses, also to have breakfast for his men by daylight and have his own team and wagon ready to haul me to their camp at a church about four miles from there, where the balance of his regiment, the Eleventh Kentucky Mounted Infantry, were camped.

About daylight they started for their camp, with me lying on a mattress in the wagon. We reached camp in due time. The lieutenant-colonel commanding the regiment, which had been started in pursuit of our party, then stood up on the wagon wheel and questioned me as to where the balance of our party had gone. I told him they had gone up on the railroad towards Louisville, where they expected to capture a train before they returned to the army, thus directing him off their trail, as they were making great haste to cross the Cumberland River and were avoiding pursuit.

When this officer called to see me at the hospital at Bowling Green, he referred to my throwing him off my comrades' trail, saying that he couldn't account for accepting my statement, as he did, but "you seemed so honest in your statement, that I believed you, and committed one of the greatest blunders I was ever guilty of."

After questioning me at this camp, he sent a sergeant and two men, with a wagon, to haul me to Woodburn, the first station, where I was lifted into a boxcar on a train for Bowling Green.

Arriving at Bowling Green I was taken up to General Judah's headquarters, laid down on the floor of his room, surrounded by some soldiers, and he questioned me on the number of our party, what command we belonged to; he also asked if we had ever been engaged in that kind of warfare before. I told him that it had been the business of our regiment to destroy their line of communication, capture trains and everything else we were able to do to annoy the enemy, when he said, "Young man, you will never fire into another train." I told him that I expected to fire into many an one, that this little scratch would soon get well and I would be ready for service again. He said, "Young man, we've got a rope for all such fellows as you." I told him there was a higher authority than he, that would have my disposition. He said, "Who?" I told him, "President Davis." He laughed and said, "Jeff Davis has no authority here." I told him that I hoped it wouldn't be long before he would have. Feeling very irritable, with a hot fever on me, I was able to resent his threat in the manner I did and felt able to talk to him, although an officer of a high rank, in resentment of his threat.

I was then taken to their regular hospital, located on Barren River, about a mile and a half from town, where I was very kindly received by the surgeon in charge, who turned out to be a very sympathetic, kind-hearted man. I was furnished a cot, the same as their other sick, in the principal ward, and had a guard detailed to stay with me all the time. This guard consisted of two men, who were on duty every alternate six hours.

Under the care of this doctor and good nurses, I soon began to recover my strength and began to hope that I would be permitted to stay there until able to travel on foot, having no doubt I could make my escape out of there, when ready.

Unfortunately the Rebel ladies of Bowling Green, learning there was a wounded Texas Ranger at the hospital, would get permission from the provost marshal to visit the sick, he supposing that they meant the Federal sick. When admitted to the wards they would come directly to my cot and deposit flowers, fruit and cake, and encourage me in the belief that I would soon get well again.

My generous, kind-hearted surgeon would sometimes send and get fish or oysters for me, evidently in the belief that he was doing a last kind act for me, as he expected me to be court martialed and sentenced to death, having frankly told me so, trying to persuade me to take the oath, which I refused to do.

As soon as I was able to sit up and talk without effort and overtaxing my strength, we had several discussions about the conduct of the war and the merits of the two armies. On one occasion I said to him, "I'm going to make an assertion, Doctor, and before I make it, I want to qualify it by stating that you have many good, patriotic men in your army and you are one of them; but, taking your army as a whole, they are an army of hirelings, fighting for their bounties and their pay, and would not hold together thirty days if their pay was stopped." He spurned the idea, telling me that I was sadly mistaken, while there might be a few men that could be classed as hirelings, the bulk of their army were prompted only by patriotic motives and were not considering gain or pay. I said, "Doctor, I will prove my assertion right here in your presence," and called up some convalescents. Addressing one, I asked him, "What induced you to join the army and what are you fighting for?" He said, "I am fighting for the flag and the Union," but I said, "As a matter of fact, were you not paid a bounty?" He admitted that he had been paid six hundred dollars by his State. Then again, "What pay do you receive?" He said, "Twelve dollars per month." "What do you do with your money?" He said, "I send it home, for safety." "Why don't you spend it?" "I have nothing to spend it for." "Does your Government furnish you everything you need?" "Everything," he said. I interrogated a second one, whose answers were about the same. I then detailed the treatment our Government had been forced to accord our army, who were frequently without pay, often without rations or clothing, especially without shoes, sometimes forced them to go barefooted, leaving their bloody tracks on the road. "Now, boys, if your Government treated you in such manner, what would you do?" They replied, "We wouldn't fight for any such d—— Government; we would go home and stay there." I said to the doctor, "Withdraw your pay and rations from your army and you wouldn't hold them together for sixty days," on which point we could not agree and he said, "Graber, you are too good a man to be engaged in such a cause." I replied, "Doctor, that is just my opinion of you; you ought to wear the gray in place of the blue," all of which he took in the kindliest spirit. I frequently conversed with the ward master and some of the nurses, who seemed to have taken a great fancy for me on account of my bold, outspoken sentiments, and they sympathized with me in my helpless condition.

I had concluded to try to make my escape as soon as I got strong enough to undertake walking through the woods, over a rough country across the river. There were always a number of boats tied to the river bank. I would have had no difficulty in crossing Barren River. One night a guard on duty with me was sound asleep, snoring, with his head resting on the foot of my cot and I was wide awake. The nurse on duty went over to the ward master's bed, not far from my cot, and woke him up. He aroused himself, and the nurse in a low voice told him, "The guard is asleep; let us tell Texas to get away." The ward master said, "No, don't do that; you had better wake up the guard," which he did. A little pleading on my part then would, no doubt, have had their consent, but I was still too feeble to undertake the hazard.

After spending about a month at this hospital, the provost marshal had heard of the ladies abusing his confidence and calling at my berth only, and rarely ever having a kind word for the Federal sick, so he had me moved to the prison, where I found about twenty-five or thirty men confined, most of them Morgan's men and a few highway robbers, who sought the protection of the Confederate Government by claiming to belong to certain Confederate commands, which I was satisfied was not the case. Kentucky afforded a good territory for these highwaymen to operate, on account of this condition.

Arriving at this prison proved the commencement of my suffering and trouble, as the surgeon in charge was a brute. He came in and threw some soap and bandages at my feet and I never saw him any more.

The prison was a two-story stone building with a brick gable, with the side fronting the street; it had been a two-story residence, converted into a jail by attaching iron gratings in the large windows; it had only four rooms, two upstairs, occupied by the prisoners, and two downstairs, occupied by about twenty guards on active duty. There was also a room for the lieutenant commanding. There was a stairway, leading down into one of the rooms below, with a door at the foot of the steps. About two companies of infantry camped in the back yard, which was surrounded by a high board fence, and there was a sink in the back end of the yard. These troops were quartered in tents. The building was located diagonally across the street from a big hotel, which was occupied by the commanding officers, as headquarters.

Here I made the acquaintance of a Lieutenant Clark of Morgan's command, whose home was Bowling Green, where he was teaching before the war. Lieutenant Clark was a brother-in-law of Captain Tom Hines, one of Morgan's trusted lieutenants and the man that planned Morgan's escape out of the Ohio penitentiary. Lieutenant Clark and I were both held under the same charges for court martial, Morgan's command raiding Kentucky, destroying their line of communications and Forrest in charge of Middle Tennessee; it is hardly necessary to say that we became fast friends and plotted and planned escape, the only chance for which was frustrated.

Colonel Clarence Prentice, in conjunction with Major Kit Ousley, also of Morgan's command, was sent into Kentucky by our War Department to recruit a regiment for the Confederate Army.

Colonel Clarence Prentice was the son of the publisher of the Louisville Courier, which was largely responsible for retaining Kentucky in the Union. The family were divided in sentiment; the father was a great Union man and particular friend of Abraham Lincoln, while Mrs. Prentice and the two sons were strongly Southern in sentiment, the sons joining the Confederate Army.

Colonel Prentice, immediately on his arrival at his home, was captured and through the influence of his father, was sent around for exchange. Major Kit Ousley was captured near Bowling Green, in citizen's clothes, therefore treated as a spy and placed in prison with us, awaiting court martial. When Ousley was captured they found a letter on his person from Fountain Fox, whose home was in Elizabethtown, this letter stating that Fox had succeeded in raising a company of one hundred and four of the best young men of his neighborhood, ready to move at a moment's warning. They immediately sent up and arrested Fountain Fox and placed him in prison with us.

Fountain Fox's father also was an influential Union man, and the Fox family was divided like the Prentice family, Mrs. Fox and sons strong Southern sympathizers, and Mr. Fox a personal friend of Abraham Lincoln. When Lincoln commenced making his appointments abroad, he appointed Fountain Fox, Consul to Madrid, Spain. Consulting with his mother about the appointment, she advised him not to accept, telling him he would see the time very soon when he would blush to represent the American Government abroad. Taking his mother's advice, he declined the appointment.

After a short time, to appease his father's anger, he accepted a captaincy in the Home Guards, in which capacity he served about a year. On the reorganization of the regiment, he was appointed major, serving in this capacity about three or four months longer, when they were ordered to Franklin, Tennessee, to the front. He said, "Considering that all of his youth's companions and nearly all of his schoolmates were in the Southern army, he could not go down there and fight them" and made haste to resign.

Some sixty days after his resignation he met Major Ousley some distance from Elizabethtown, out in the country. Being well acquainted with him Ousley gave Fox a commission to raise a company for the Confederate Army, and he soon wrote Ousley the letter that was found on Ousley's person when he was captured, and which caused Fox's arrest.

His father immediately went to see the President and secured an order for his release, provided he would take the oath of allegiance to the United States and remain north of the Mason and Dixon's line during the war, also giving a bond of fifty thousand dollars, all of which he did, remaining in prison with us perhaps only two or three weeks. This prison was directly in charge of Major Erastus Motley, provost marshal, an old friend of Clark's before the war and a schoolmate of Captain Hines. He, like many Kentucky officers in such position, had made himself very obnoxious by his tyrannical treatment of the families of Confederate soldiers and seemed greatly prejudiced against Clark and myself.

CHAPTER VIII

THE ESCAPE OF MAJOR OUSLEY.

A court martial to try Major Kit Ousley was soon organized and his trial resulted easily in conviction, as he occupied the position of a spy, being captured in citizen's clothes. Very soon his sentence was returned from General Burnside, and approved by him, General Burnside being in command of Kentucky and Ohio, with his headquarters at Cincinnati.

Major Ousley, while recruiting up in the Blue Grass region near Lexington, married a very wealthy and beautiful young lady, who as soon as she heard of his capture and imprisonment at Bowling Green, came down to render what assistance she could, and succeeded in bribing a lieutenant, who had an office in town, paying him eight thousand dollars for his assistance. This officer kept her posted and gave her the information about the return that evening of the verdict of the court martial, approved by General Burnside, which was his conviction as a spy and his punishment death by hanging. He was to be placed over in the courthouse in irons under a special guard until the day of his execution, which was fixed for the 29th of May, while this information was imparted on the 14th of May.

Major Ousley asked permission that evening to go to a barber shop, which permission was granted by sending a special guard with him. At this barber shop he met his wife, who succeeded in obtaining a private interview with him, when she imparted the information about having bribed this lieutenant and the location of his office, which Ousley understood, as he was well acquainted in Bowling Green. She had also received from the lieutenant a pair of surgeon's shoulder straps and the password for that night, which was "Columbia," and which was imparted to Lieutenant Clark and myself by Ousley, after he returned to the prison.

Major Ousley had a visit that evening from several officers of the court martial, who seemed to be old acquaintances of his and had quite a long chat with them, with a good deal of levity, which of course was a matter of surprise to Clark and myself, as he seemed to be completely at ease. Considering his condition with his doom already sealed, we thought he displayed more nerve than any man we ever saw.

Major Ousley requested his officer friends, before they left him, to send him a bottle of brandy, which they did and which he distributed freely among the guards on duty in the lower room, hoping to load them up, and in doing this we were afraid he imbibed a little too much himself.

Now, it was imperative for him to make his escape that night, for, as stated, he was to be placed in irons the next day and kept in the courthouse under special guard. With Clark and myself, and other trusted friends in the prison, we planned that the only means of his escape would be to cut a hole through the plastering overhead large enough to admit a man into the attic; then take a sufficient number of brick out of the gable end which connected with the roof of a single-story house adjoining, all of which was done by the willing hands of our comrades; but a mistake was made in the location of the hole through the brick wall. This hole opened on top of a roof, on the side facing the street in full view of the headquarters on the other side. Major Ousley imparted the countersign to Clark and myself with an injunction and earnest request not to attempt to get out until after giving him four hours the start, as his case was the most desperate one and we had not been tried by the court martial. This promise we fully kept.

When Major Ousley passed through the hole in the brick wall on to the roof of the other house, it was drizzling rain and the night was very dark, so the hole could not be discovered on the other side of the street. He laid flat on the roof for a few minutes, then quietly crawled over the comb of the house, on the other side, out of sight of the street, then to the far end of the roof away from the prison and dropped down into the yard of a private residence when a large dog got after him, giving one bark and no more. Ousley told me afterwards that he hit this dog with his fist and said, "I reckon I killed him!" Some of the guards in our prison yard rushed to the fence and asked a lady who came to the door, what was the matter; she said, "Nothing that I know of, everything is all right over here," which seemed to quiet their suspicion, so they went back to their tents. Major Ousley soon was heard to come down the walk in front of our prison. He was halted by the guard, asking, "Who comes there?" "A friend with the countersign." "Advance, friend, and give the countersign." He gave the countersign and passed on down the street and found the lieutenant's room. The lieutenant told him it would not be safe for him to attempt to go out that night, but to go down into the river bottoms, stay there all next day, then return to his office, when he would have a horse and side arms for him and give him the new countersign for that night. Ousley went down to the river bottoms and spent the day until very near night. Then, being very hungry, he decided to go to a friend's house, who lived away out in the suburbs and get something to eat. Just before reaching his friend's house, he struck the big road and immediately heard the running of a horse behind him, which proved to be a man on horseback loping towards town. Though he did not suspect any such thing, the man evidently went to town and raised the alarm. On entering the house his friend's wife met him. She was well acquainted with Ousley, but her husband was not at home, and she, of course, was surprised and alarmed, as she knew that he was a prisoner. When he made known his wants, she rushed in and prepared a lunch, while he stood at the front door, watching. As soon as the lunch was ready, she invited him into the diningroom and took his place watching. Before he finished his lunch she rushed into the diningroom, saying, "My God, Major Ousley, you are lost, you are lost." He told her to keep perfectly quiet. "The safest place is among the enemy," he said, and grabbed a couple of biscuits, stuck them into his coat pocket, and started out of the front door when a couple of guards behind a rosebush, jumped up, threw their guns down on him and told him to halt. He cursed them and told them to get behind that bush. Major Ousley would see them, making them believe that he was one of their own officers.

I forgot to mention that he had the surgeon's shoulder straps sewed on to his coat at the shoulders, the same as was the custom in the Federal Army. As already stated, when captured, he had on a splendid double-breasted frock coat and black pants, all of which in the dark could easily be mistaken for a Federal uniform, hence on the spur of the moment, he made the two guards believe that he was one of their own officers. He walked to the gate and passing outside, walked very fast up the fence, and when about a hundred yards these men began to call, "Halt," when he broke into a run and left them firing after him, not receiving a scratch. While, of course, they ran after him I imagine they didn't try very hard to catch him, fearing perhaps that he had accomplices, prepared to defend him.

Major Ousley next circled around the town and again made his way to the lieutenant's room, who had a horse ready for him, gave him a couple of six-shooters and the countersign for that night. He boldly rode down the main street leading to Barren River bridge, where he gave the countersign to the guards, then up the pike towards Louisville.

After an all-night's ride he pulled up at a friend's house, where he decided to stay until Morgan's command came in there and go with them back to our main army, telling his friend his purpose. His friend said, "Major, you can't stay here; there is a brigade of Yankees camped at a spring about a mile from here and Colonel Gross, the commander, comes over occasionally and has a game of poker with me." Ousley told him that would not make any difference, he was going to stay anyway and take a hand with him at poker. He then proceeded to disguise; cut off a heavy mustache, and also cut his hair short, which made him look like a different man; and he actually stayed at this friend's house for nearly three weeks, joining his friend and Colonel Gross in several games of poker. He finally heard of Morgan's command in the blue grass region, mounted his horse to try to find them and telling his friend good-bye and to give him a half hour's start, and then to tell Colonel Gross who he was and tell him the next time they met pistols would be trumps. His friend said that he wouldn't do such a thing for anything in the world; he said, "Colonel Gross never will find out through me or mine who you were."

Major Ousley succeeded in finding Morgan's command and went out of the State with them, reporting to the War Department at Richmond, and was given a job in the department and an order forbidding him to re-enter the army. I met him again at Richmond, where he detailed all of the features and incidents of his escape from the time he dropped into the adjoining yard and knocked over the dog.

CHAPTER IX

IN PRISON AT LOUISVILLE, WHERE I WAS HONORED WITH HANDCUFFS.

Referring to Bowling Green prison, where Major Ousley had left us: Four hours after Ousley's escape, our friends in the prison boosted Clark and me up into the attic, when we found out to our dismay that the weather had cleared and the moon had risen sufficiently high to light up the front of our building, disclosing the hole in the gable. The general's headquarters being diagonally across the street with a guard's beat immediately in front, I whispered to Clark, "We had better wait until the corporal comes with his relief guard in front of the headquarters and watch their actions." Waiting about thirty minutes, a corporal with a relief appeared on the beat and the three stood for some time talking and looking up at our prison wall, which satisfied us that they had made the discovery of the hole and were only waiting for some of us to crawl out on the roof, when they would have shot us. We, therefore, decided it would be folly to attempt our escape that night, which proved a wise decision.

The next morning at roll call the discovery was made that Major Ousley was missing, which caused the greatest excitement; and immediately scouting parties of eight or ten men dashed up to the headquarters across the street for orders, and started out in a lope. All that day these parties called for orders and came back and reported at headquarters. Major Motley came up and saw the manner of Ousley's escape, and asked the prisoners who made those holes and assisted Ousley. None of us vouchsafed any information. He then sent for the most desperate prisoners, some that were not Confederates, as heretofore stated, and told them that their cases were bad, but if they would tell who assisted Ousley in making his escape, and tried to make their escape with him, he would do all he could to let them off as easy as possible. This we learned through two most excellent citizens, who were in the prison with us, and who were also taken out and offered their liberty if they would disclose Ousley's accomplices. One of these was a Colonel Lewis, living near Franklin; the other a Doctor Vertriece, a neighbor of Colonel Lewis. These men were imprisoned because of our raid on the railroad, which the reader will remember occurred between Franklin and Woodburn. It was the custom of the Federal commander, whenever Morgan, or any other troops, made a raid on the railroad, to arrest the most prominent citizens in the neighborhood.

After several days of questioning these prisoners, Major Motley came up; my friend Clark was asleep on a mattress the lieutenant of the guard had favored me with, on account of my being wounded. He was lying with his face to the wall. I was sitting on the window sill, looking out into the street when Major Motley walked up to where Clark was asleep and gave him a kick in the back, thereby waking him. Clark raised up and asked, "What do you want, Ras'?" when Motley produced a pair of handcuffs he had held behind him and put them on him. Turning around to me, he said, "I will have a pair here for you in a few minutes," but as it turned out fortunately there was not another pair of handcuffs in Bowling Green, and he had to send to Louisville after them. After he left the prison Doctor Vertriece suggested to me that I write a letter to Colonel Hawkins, who was then in command of the post, telling him that I was a wounded Confederate soldier, and that Major Motley had threatened to put handcuffs on me. I stated in this letter that our command had captured thousands of their men and had always treated them humanely and kindly, notably the Ninth Michigan and Third Minnesota, who, after we had paroled them and when parting with us, said, "If any of you Texas Rangers are captured, call for the Ninth Michigan and Third Minnesota, and we will see that you are well treated." In winding up my letter to Colonel Hawkins, I called on him as a gentleman and a soldier not to permit such an outrage perpetrated as that of placing irons on a wounded prisoner. This letter Doctor Vertriece succeeded in smuggling around Major Motley, bribing a guard to take it directly to Colonel Hawkins without Motley's knowledge, and we soon had an answer returned in the same manner from Colonel Hawkins, expressing his regret at our condition, praising Major Motley as a very kind-hearted and good man, and stating that he was satisfied he would do all in his power to alleviate our condition and suffering, and trusting that we would be able to bear up with our condition.

When I read the letter I threw it on the floor, and told Doctor Vertriece he was mistaken in his man; that Colonel Hawkins was no better than the rest of them. He picked up the letter, read it and told me that I was doing a great injustice to Colonel Hawkins, that I was simply misconstruing his position, that he could not have said anything more to me, a prisoner belonging to the army of his enemy, and could certainly not censure Major Motley, an officer of his own army, for his treatment of us, and furthermore suggested that if I would just wait he was satisfied that the handcuffs would not be put on me.

The next day Major Motley again visited our prison, walked up to Lieutenant Clark and took off his handcuffs, hardly able to look into his face. Turning around, he walked up and down the cell a few times in study, and finally stopped in front of me, saying, "Graber, I want you and Clark to understand that I have no personal feeling in this matter; you are prisoners, have been placed in my charge and keeping; you have tried to make your escape with Major Ousley, and, I am going to keep you here, if I have to chain you to this floor."

I frequently told Major Motley that if they were holding me for court martial, to bring my charges and specifications, to which he replied that I needn't be in a hurry, I would receive them sooner than I wanted to, perhaps, and, when finally brought, the charge was being a Guerilla; specifications, my own statement admitting to General Judah that we had been engaged in raiding their lines of communications and destroying them ever since we had been in the army. I concluded they need not resort to any trial, as I was prepared to admit the specifications. In this charge they gave my name, company and regiment, C. S. A. (so-called), which was virtually an admission that I was not a Guerilla, but by an order, No. 38, of General Burnside, all recruiting officers captured within his department should be treated as spies, and all raiding parties, not under a general officer, as Guerillas. Finally one day Major Motley came in about ten o'clock in the morning and ordered me to prepare to leave on the eleven o'clock train for Louisville. I asked him, "What for? Are you sending me up there for safe keeping, or to be treated as a prisoner of war?" He said, "Never mind about that; you will learn soon enough." When I reached Louisville I was taken to the general prison and there treated as a prisoner of war.

I found the Louisville prison a most excellent one; two barracks running parallel, with bunks on each side and a brick-paved yard in the center, with a splendid waterworks. At one end were the offices occupied by clerks and an officer who kept the roll; at the other end was the kitchen, connected on one side with a barrack, and on the other side having a passageway of about three feet, leading into the backyard in the rear of the kitchen, where they had the sinks, and this backyard was kept in a very filthy condition. We had three rations a day, with coffee in the mornings, the rations consisting of a chunk of light bread and a piece of pickled pork, already cut in proper size for each man, in tubs, on each side of the door. On the inside of the kitchen stood a tub, presided over by negro wenches who would shove these rations to us as we passed through, single file, into the backyard.

A negro official, called "Captain Black" by the prisoners, frequently stood on the outside of the door as the prisoners passed in to draw their rations. When some poor, emaciated prisoner, reduced by confinement, barely able to drag his feet, came along, he would curse, tell him to "Hike out, you d—m Rebel," and sometimes push them along. This made me fear this negro to the extent that I always avoided him and always moved quickly in his presence, determined never to give him an opportunity to insult me.

One day I was lying on my bunk, the second from the floor, about five feet high, which was the end of the bunks next to the door. I was feeling bad and having considerable fever, and was still suffering from my wounds, so I decided not to go out and get my dinner rations. All that were able had gone out, a few sick remaining in the barracks at different places. A little negro boy came to the door and looking up at me, asked if I was sick and didn't I want a cup of coffee. I told him yes, to bring me a cup and I would pay him for it. He brought me a small tin cup full of fine coffee, for which I gave him a twenty-five-cent bill.

While lying sipping my coffee, resting on my right elbow, "Captain Black" stepped into the door, and, on discovering me said, "What are you doing here, sir?" I said I was sick and didn't want my rations. He raised up on his toes and said, "Sick?" "Yes, I am sick, too," and he started to order me out when I lost all control of myself and, from my bunk, fell right over on him, grabbing at his pistol. I got my hand on it, but he jerked away before I could clinch it, but he thought I had it, saying, "Foh Gawd, Massa; don't, Massa!" then broke for the gate. Some of the prisoners witnessed the trouble and told the others when they came in from drawing their rations, which created considerable excitement and considerable sympathy for me, for it was believed that I would be placed in irons and in a dungeon.

In about half an hour after the prisoners returned from drawing their rations, one of them rushed up to me and suggested that I hide. He said, "That negro, with a big sergeant, is in the yard hunting you." I told him that I would not hide, but would go and meet them, walking out into the yard. The negro pointed me out to the sergeant, when he walked up to me and told me to hold up my hands. I asked him, "What for?" He said, "To put these things on you," producing a pair of handcuffs, which he had held behind him. I asked who ordered it done? He stated, Colonel Orcutt. I asked, "Who is Colonel Orcutt?" He said, "Commander of this prison." I told him, "All right; put them on; they are Yankee bracelets, and I consider it an honor to wear them."

After wearing these irons two or three days and nights, an officer in fatigue uniform, whom I took to be Colonel Orcutt, stepped up to me and told me to hold up my hands. I asked him what for? He said, "To take those things off." I told him he needn't be in a hurry, I had got used to them and considered it an honor to wear them. By this time he had unlocked them and taken them off. When I turned my back on him and mingled with the crowd, some of the prisoners told me that he started to strike me with them, which I hardly believe.

"Captain Black" very soon came to me and apologized, saying that he was very sorry for what he had done, and that he would never mistreat a prisoner again, that "Dese soldiers had put him up to it." I told him I would give him five dollars if he would steal those handcuffs for me. He said that he would be glad to do that, and would not charge me anything, and he soon reported that they had not been replaced in the office, where they used to hang, and that he couldn't find out where they were kept.

CHAPTER X.

CAMP CHASE—FORT DELAWARE—I CHANGE MY NAME FOR THE FIRST TIME AND AM FINALLY EXCHANGED.

After remaining in this prison about a month, a roll was called and the prisoners whose names were called, were ordered to get ready for exchange. We started next morning for City Point, as we were told, but when we reached Columbus, Ohio, we were ordered to march to Camp Chase, where we were quartered in barracks, partitioned into mess rooms of twenty-four in a mess. While here I was very uneasy, expecting to be called for at any time, to be returned to Louisville, as several of the prisoners had been so returned, to meet charges against them, hence concluded perhaps my name appeared on the roll through mistake, but I was fortunate enough to escape this fate and got along fine until I was taken sick with flux. While confined in this prison I was furnished a New York paper, I think it was the Tribune, giving an account of the hanging of one of our comrades of the regiment by the name of Dodd, who was captured near Knoxville, Tennessee, having had his horse killed in an engagement near there, and was ordered to make his way out as best he could. He was raised in Sevier County, and decided to visit his home, while there, and when captured, was taken to Knoxville, there tried as a spy by a court martial, convicted and sentenced to be hung. His conviction was secured on a pocket diary, which he had kept, recording his every-day work.

A correspondent of the New York Tribune, who visited him in the jail just before his execution, claimed he found him a very intelligent, educated gentleman, in fact, believed him to be a grand character, and his execution, which he witnessed, proved such a horrible affair that it elicited the following expression from him: "In the name of humanity and all that is decent, if the terrible exigencies of war require the deliberate taking of human life, let the prisoner be shot or give us the merciful guillotine."

Satisfied if the members of the regiment heard of Dodd's execution they would certainly retaliate, and in return the Federal Army would also retaliate, and as I was the only member of the Eighth Texas, their prisoner, they would certainly call for me for such purpose.

After remaining in this prison for a month I agreed with one of Morgan's men to tunnel out under the fence, and prepared to go to work that night. The fence was only about twenty yards from our mess room, the identical place where one of Morgan's officers had dug out a few months before and effected his escape. During this day we were suddenly called on to move and were again promised that we should be sent to City Point for exchange. All the sick in the hospital were furnished conveyances to carry them to Columbus, where we took train. As stated heretofore, I had a severe case of flux, which weakened me a great deal, and I was rendered unable to walk soon after we started on our march to Columbus, a distance of about four miles. We were marched by fours with a heavy advance and rear guard and a single file guard on each side of our column. After having marched about a mile I gave out completely, and my comrades reported my case to a lieutenant, marching by the side of us, who instructed me to sit down by the roadside and wait until the rear guard came up; then to tell them to make a detail to stay with me until I reached Columbus. Very soon after the main body had passed, one of the rear guards called out: "Hike out, you d—— Rebel," which, of course, made me resentful and I refused to hike out, telling him that I had orders to stop and tell some of the rear guard to bring me up to Columbus. By this time he had got pretty close to me and I happening to look around found him charging on me with a bayonet, which made me jump, and proved the best medicine I could have taken for flux. It simply infused new strength and enabled me to hike to Columbus.

At Erie, Pennsylvania, we were put in coal cars with the bottoms pretty thickly covered with coal dust, in which we were carried to Philadelphia, being marched through Chestnut Street to a boat landing.

Their object in moving us in these coal cars we construed to be a policy to make us look as dirty as possible. Many of our men, of course, were somewhat ragged, and, altogether, we appeared a motley crowd, in striking contrast to the heroes that had been cherished by our Northern sympathizers, called "copper-heads" by the fanatics of the North. In our march to the boat landing we were greeted by many intelligent ladies, who were standing on the streets watching our passing, and quite a number of them had their hands full of postage money, which was bills of denominations of less than a dollar, which they threw and scattered among us. After we reached the boat, on which we were ordered up on the second deck, a dray-load of cheese and crackers was sent down to us by some of the ladies, but the guards on the lower deck appropriated it, and, after eating as much as they wanted, sold the balance of it to all that had money. Then, adding insult to injury, they sent word to the ladies to send more—to be treated in the same manner. The boat then moved out down the river where our journey to City Point for exchange terminated at Fort Delaware, where we were unloaded and were roughly treated.

Fort Delaware proved to be the worst prison we had been in; dirty, with no water fit to drink. Our drinking water had to be taken from the canal inside of the levee, which had a green scum floating on top, and, on the lower part of the island, was used for bathing. After about two or three weeks, an arrangement was made with a boat called the "Osceola" to bring us water from the Brandywine River, which proved to be palatable and a great treat.

On our arrival at Fort Delaware we found about twenty thousand prisoners, a large part of them captured at the battle of Gettysburg; among whom were four or five hundred of Hood's Brigade, and also some from Granbury's Brigade, who were captured at Vicksburg. This created a sad impression on me and made me wish I was back in the saddle again more than I ever did, but there was nothing to do but submit. While here we also heard of the battle of Chickamauga, the first report of which was most encouraging, as it stated their army was annihilated and Thomas had fled to the mountains. This started the Rebel yell in the prison, and made us feel that we would soon be exchanged, but the next day's report put a damper on our enthusiasm, and made us feel sad indeed, as the report in this New York paper was that their army had rallied and were holding on to Chattanooga, with our army retreating, and, while their loss was very heavy in killed and wounded, ours was double. It made us realize that fate was against us, and we would never be able to gain a decisive victory, which would unquestionably secure our recognition by foreign governments.

As already stated, Fort Delaware proved the worst prison we had been in; smallpox broke out among us and nearly every other disease known. A large number died. Every morning they called at the big gate, "Bring out your dead!" and the dead were buried on the Jersey shore by a detail of prisoners.

Among one of these details one morning was a gentleman by the name of Simpson, from Houston, Texas, who belonged to Hood's Brigade. This man was born and raised in New York State and had lived in Houston only a couple of years, engaging in business and had become thoroughly acquainted with the character of our people, and especially the institution of slavery. In this short time he became one of the South's strongest friends, ready to give his life for her cause, as demonstrated by his joining the first troops Texas sent to Virginia.

Slipping away from the guards, he made his way to his old home, told his people who had heard that he was in the Rebel Army that he had recanted and taken the oath of allegiance to the United States Government, thereby reinstating him with his family, who lavished money and all else on him until he was fully recuperated from the effects of his prison experience, when he again shipped on board a steamer for Nassau, where he took a Confederate blockade runner and came South, to fight it out to the end. After the war he entered into copartnership with a man by the name of

Wiggins, constituting the firm of Wiggins & Simpson, which built a large foundry and machine shop. This they conducted for many years, and, at the time of his death, Simpson was wealthy and one of the most honored and esteemed citizens of Houston, never having expressed a word of regret over his conduct during the war.

It might not be out of place here to say that nearly all Northern-raised men among us within my knowledge pursued the same course. They invariably proved gallant soldiers and did their duty for the South to the limit of their ability, returning South after the war and spending the balance of their lives as our most honored citizens. We had twenty-six generals of Northern birth in the Confederate Army, twelve of whom were graduates of West Point, and were offered high rank in the Federal Army. This, no doubt, proved a hard problem for the North to understand, and only emphasizes the justice of our cause, because these men were prompted only by a conscientious motive, and faced suffering, death and disgrace in the eyes of their Northern friends by such a course.

While on this subject I would mention the case of General Pemberton, the gallant soldier who commanded at Vicksburg, and directed its defense to the last ditch. He was the son of wealthy parents in Philadelphia, who threatened to disinherit him if he didn't resign his commission in the Southern Army and come North, but he ignored their threat and continued in the Southern Army to the end.

Our suffering at Fort Delaware was almost unbearable. We were crowded into these barracks as thick as we could lie, with all character of sickness and disease among us, receiving additional prisoners occasionally to keep the barracks filled, with only two meals a day of three small crackers and an inch of meat. Many prisoners got desperate and attempted to swim the Delaware River to effect their escape, only to have their dead bodies found washed ashore on the Delaware or Jersey side of the river the next day.

A number of our men were shot without cause by the guard, who, we understood, were promoted for such act; still a few of the men made their escape by swimming the river, among whom I might mention Jim Loggins, a boy about eighteen years old, who belonged to Hood's Brigade. He is now a practicing physician of Ennis, Texas, a father of a large family of children, all highly regarded and respected citizens of their home town.

Prisoners seeking their escape would take canteens, tightly corked, and use them as life preservers. Referring back to the case of Jim Loggins: When he got into the river with others, the tide was running in fast, and the tide took him about five or six miles up the river before he reached a landing on the Delaware side. He then, with one companion, made his way through the State of Delaware into Maryland, crossing the Potomac, then through Northern Virginia, occupied by the Federal Army, back to Richmond, where he rejoined Hood's Brigade, and was in every important battle until the end of the war, surrendering at Appomattox.

Among our prisoners at Fort Delaware were the First Maryland Cavalry, captured at South Mountain, before the battle of Gettysburg. These Maryland men were the sons of leading families, largely men of great wealth in the State of Maryland. Their friends and families at home petitioned Governor Swann, of Maryland, to intercede for them with the Federal War Department, and permit them to take a parole to go home, and stay at their homes, until regularly exchanged, and it was generally believed success would crown their efforts. These men received clothing and money in the greatest abundance from their families at home, and were about the most genteel looking men we had in prison. In connection with this, I would mention the escape of one of their parties, who, being well dressed and clean shaven, wearing a white shirt and fresh collar, was watching the "Osceola" at the landing about ready to depart, and boldly slipped up on the levee, walked down to the guard, passing him while the guard saluted, mistaking him for a citizen visitor from Delaware City, who came over quite often, then passed on to the boat, walked up on its cabin deck, took a seat in front, with his feet cocked up on the guards, smoking a cigar, when the boat pushed off with him and he was never heard of by us any more, no doubt making good his escape.

Many incidents of interest I might mention, showing the loyalty of the Southern soldier under this most terrible condition, facing death daily, seeing his comrades carried out by the dozen for burial daily, with no prospect for exchange. Certainly history does not record such remarkable devotion to a country and cause.

In line with this, I might mention the effort of General Schoepf, commander of the fort and prison. He one day conceived the idea of creating a stampede among us, for which purpose he ordered out about three hundred East Tennesseeans, formed them in line and made a strong speech to them, telling them of the North's vast resources for the conduct of the war, and our diminishing, limited means for holding on; showing them the impossibility for our ever succeeding, with no prospect of exchange. Then he told them of the great prosperity of the North, where labor was in demand and wages high, of which they could take the benefit by taking the oath of allegiance and thus save their lives, recover their health and strength, live in peace and happiness the balance of the war, and, finally, he called on them, saying, "Now, all of you that are ready and willing to take the oath of allegiance, step three paces to the front." Only one man responded.

General Schoepf evidently thought that East Tennessee, as a section of country in the South, was the most disloyal to our cause, its citizens being largely Union people, and that these East Tennesseeans would certainly accept his liberal offer, and, by that means, make a break in our ranks. It is hardly necessary to say that he gave it up as a bad job, and did not attempt another such experiment. In connection with this, however, I regret to have to say that a few weak brothers were found in our ranks, who took the oath of allegiance and were then separated from the rest of the prisoners, in a special camp about a half mile distant, where they were designated by us as "Galvanized Yankees."

After spending a part of the winter at Fort Delaware, one morning there appeared a notice at what we called a postoffice, inside of the big gate, calling upon all Marylanders, prisoners of war, to appear at the gate with their baggage; which, of course, was construed to mean that Governor Swann had succeeded in his effort to secure a parole for these Marylanders, and that they would be taken to Washington for the purpose of being paroled and permitted to go home to remain until properly exchanged. This, of course, created considerable excitement and rejoicing among the Marylanders, which was shared largely by the rest of the prisoners, although they could not hope to ever be favored in the same manner. It was a source of comfort and gratification to us to know that some of our friends, at least, would be saved the sufferings and almost certain death, even if we could not share it with them.

While they were forming in line, by fours, headed for the big gate, an acquaintance belonging to Hood's Brigade, whose name was Robert Brantley, of Navasota, called to me and said, "Good-bye, Henry." I said, "Where are you going, Bob?" He said, "I am going to try to get out with these men." I said, "How are you going to try to do that?" He said, "I have two names and am going to answer to one of them at roll call." I said, "Bob, you do not want two names; you can't answer to both. If you will give me one of them I will try to go out with you." He said, "All right, come on." I had time enough to go into the barracks and get an oilcloth satchel, which had been given me at Bowling Green; then I had a magnificent cape overcoat, left me by Major Ousley in Bowling Green prison; with this coat on and this citizen's new satchel, the coat extending over the top of my boots, hiding partly worn butternut pants. I passed for a Marylander pretty well, seemingly as well dressed as they were, while Bob looked ragged, like one of these Hood Brigade men that had not had any clothing furnished them in some time, and appeared rather suspicious among this well dressed crowd. In giving me the name he retained the name of Charles Erbert, who belonged to the First Maryland Cavalry, and who had died in prison. The name of Charles Stanley, which he gave me to use, was the name of a son of a preacher Charles Stanley was sick in the hospital, and his father, ostensibly to preach to the troops at the fort, was permitted the privilege of a visit, mainly for the purpose of being with his son in the hospital.

The keeper of the prison roll was a Lieutenant Wolff, a renegade Virginian, who was also a "Galvanized Yankee." Wolff was also acquainted with many of the Marylanders, and particularly with Charles Stanley, on account of his father visiting there. Wolff's acquaintance with the Marylanders was through their clothing and money sent them, which passed through his hands.

We were soon marched out to the wharf, where the "Osceola" was awaiting us to carry us to the flag of truce boat, "New York," anchored in midstream, as the water was too shallow for her to come up to the wharf. We were held on the wharf for nearly an hour before a roll call commenced, during which time I suggested to Bob to separate, for him to take the opposite edge of the party to the edge that I would take, then to post himself on the circumstances of his man's capture and the location of his home in Maryland, telling him that we might be questioned, and, if posted, we could have a ready answer, thereby keeping down suspicion. Bob said he did not think there was any danger in that; his greatest apprehension was that he would be personally recognized by some of the Yankees, as he had been at work in the cook house, where he made the acquaintance of quite a number, and he thought perhaps Lieutenant Wolff might recognize him, while I had no fear of anything of that kind.

Finally a major, with several other officers, appeared. Lieutenant Wolff was already there. The major began calling the roll alphabetically. When he called the name of Charles Erbert, Bob failed to answer. I decided if he called it the second time that I would answer to the dead man's name, believing that Bob had lost his nerve and would not answer at all. When he called the name the second time we both answered, but I kept down, while he jumped up quickly. This drew the major's attention to him, and he never knew who it was that answered over on my side of the crowd. I forgot to mention that we were all squatted down on the wharf. When Bob walked out boldly, attempting to pass the major, on his way to the boat, the major stopped him. "What is your name, sir?" "My name is Charles Erbert." The major, without any further questioning, told him to take a seat and called up a guard to take charge of him. This sudden decision of the major that there was fraud was no doubt prompted by both of us answering to the same name, yet it created a suspicion with me that perhaps we had been betrayed, as they kept a lot of spies in the prison all the time. As considerable time was consumed in calling the names, down to the letter S, I had ample time to prepare for the issue, and when the name of Charles Stanley was called I jumped up and boldly went forward, passing him, without looking. I was favored by Lieutenant Wolff being engaged in shaking hands with one of the Marylanders and eating an apple with his back turned to the major when he called the name of Charles Stanley, evidently not hearing it, and which I did not permit him to call the second time. I therefore passed through unmolested. As heretofore stated, my appearance tallied pretty well with the rest of the Marylanders and Bob Brantley's appearance was in striking contrast with theirs.

After getting on the boat and mixing with the Marylanders, I was congratulated by them on my success and promised a good time when they reached home. As soon as all were aboard, the "New York" weighed anchor, when, the next morning, running down the coast on the Atlantic, we were told that we would have to remain down in the hold on the second deck until they could wash decks. They closed down the hatch and only permitted us to come on the main deck when we discovered that we were at Point Lookout, Maryland, under the guns of a thirty-two-pound battery, and the Potomac flotilla, and were then told to march out, and were led into what we called a "bull pen," where we found about ten or twelve thousand prisoners quartered in little A tents on the sand of the seashore, with nothing else to protect them from the winter's blast. Had we suspected their motive, we could have easily overpowered the guard on the big steamer, beached and burned her and scattered out in Maryland, without taking a parole. At Point Lookout our camp was laid off in State divisions, a row of little A tents on each side of a wide street with a cook house for each division at the head of it. We were here furnished rations the same as we had at Fort Delaware, by marching in and taking our position at the long table in front of each ration. Sometimes we had a cup of what they called bean soup, but it was always my misfortune to get a cup of bean water, the cook failing to stir up the soup and thoroughly mixing the beans with the water. Besides this, we had three crackers and an inch of meat. This we had twice a day, as at Fort Delaware, and considerable suffering on account of hunger was thereby entailed.

As stated, we were quartered in tents by State Divisions. Coming there with the Marylanders, under a Marylander's name, I started with the Maryland Division, but in connection with this, soon joined the Texas Division, Tennessee Division and Louisiana Division and drew rations with every one of these divisions, thereby securing three extra rations which I divided among my messmates.

In order to improve my time, with nothing else to do, I decided to try to learn the French language and for this purpose, joined a Louisiana mess, the men belonging to the Seventh Louisiana, who were Creoles and spoke nothing but French in their mess. In a short time, I was enabled to understand some of their talk and they, as well as I, thought I was getting along fine, and I believe if I could have continued with them six months I would have spoken French fluently.

While at this point General Butler was appointed Exchange Agent, this in response to the clamor of the people in the North, demanding exchange, as their people were dying in our prisons, as well as our people in theirs; but, the policy of their War Department, sanctioned by Abraham Lincoln, was not to exchange a prisoner if they could avoid it. They did not want to reinforce our army from that source when our country was about exhausted for men. To carry their point on this they cared very little for their men in our prisons and even openly claimed that it was a protection to their army to enforce non-exchange even at the sacrifice of the men in our prisons.

General Butler being placed in charge of the exchange, the Federal Government knew that they could throw the odium of refusal to exchange on the Confederate Government, because General Butler had been outlawed by our Government through President Davis' proclamation ordering him executed whenever captured, on account of his dastardly conduct while in command of New Orleans, which earned for him the name of "Beast" Butler. They well knew that his appointment as Chief Exchange Agent would forever place a barrier against exchange.

At this time General Marsden was in command at Point Lookout, and a Captain Patterson, aided by Sergeant Finnegan, in charge of the prisoners.

After the arrival of the Marylanders at Point Lookout, the Federal Government decided to relieve the crowded condition of Fort Delaware by transferring more prisoners to Point Lookout, which was done to a considerable extent.

General Butler, for political reasons, as well as to show his interest in the prisoners, made us a visit, and when his arrival was announced, proceeded in company with General Marsden and their respective staffs, to ride over to our enclosure. We were then called on by Captain Patterson, announcing his approach, to cheer him as he came inside. As soon as the big gate was thrown open and he rode in, perhaps five thousand prisoners had collected at the gate, many of them calling out, "Boys, here is the 'Beast;' " to which he paid no attention or to the name of "Mumford," the man whom he hung in New Orleans for tearing down the United States flag placed on his house on their first occupancy of New Orleans. When he and General Marsden attempted to enter the First Division, which was the Louisiana Division, the men called out "New Orleans." By this time such a crowd had gathered in this division that it was difficult for them to ride through, when General Butler decided not to go any further and returned to General Marsden's headquarters.

About two weeks later General Butler returned and entered the prison enclosure with General Marsden and their respective staffs; all armed with pistols, and having also an escort of about fifty cavalry. They were determined to push through the Louisiana Division, when again the insults thrown at them on his first visit were repeated. In reaching a Sibley tent, where a part of a company of the Louisiana Guard Battery were quartered, one of the young men, seeing General Butler passing in front of the tent, rushed out, took Butler's horse by the bridle and stopped him, proposed three cheers for Jeff Davis, which were given with a will by our ten thousand throats, then proposed three groans for the "Beast."

General Butler turned pale, looked at the men, seemed undecided what to do, surrounded by an angry crowd of at least ten thousand men, who although unarmed, he well knew were more than a match for him and his guards and that they would not stand any show for their lives if a single shot was fired. He decided it was best to move on and pass the incident. When nearly at the end of the division some one called "Magruder," which made him smile, as it referred to the battle of Big Bethel, which he commanded and lost to the Confederates commanded by General Magruder.

He next turned into the North Carolina Division, a brigade of conscripts, who had surrendered without firing a gun. On his entering this division the men cheered him, when he stopped and talked with them, asking how they were getting along. They told him they did not get enough to eat and were starving, and he turned to Captain Patterson and told him to add an extra cracker to the rations, which brought another cheer. He then passed through the division, being cheered frequently by these conscripts and returned to General Marsden's headquarters.

In punishment for the insults offered him in the Louisiana Division, he sent a regiment, composed of illiterate negroes from the plantations in North Carolina, to guard us. The immediate guard of the prison were on beats on a platform outside of the prison walls, which exposed their heads and shoulders to the prisoners inside of the walls. There were also guard beats at the head of every division between the tents and the cook houses. These negroes were very poorly drilled and disciplined, but fit tools in the hands of a vindictive enemy. As the men in the prison had never seen any negro troops, they gathered along these different beats to watch their performance. They came into the prison for guard duty, carrying their knapsacks as they were afraid to leave them in their camp, fearing that some of the other troops not on duty would rob them. A guard at the head of the Texas Division, tired of carrying his knapsack, deposited it at the end of his beat; as soon as his back was turned, one of the men picked it up and ran away with it. The negro, returning on his beat, discovered his knapsack gone and created a general laugh among the spectators by his puzzled look. Finally he said, "Men, you better give me back my knapsack or I'll call Marse Lieutenant." The men again laughed, when finally he called to the guard up on the fence, "Central, Oh Central! Call Marse Lieutenant and tell him one of dese here white folks stole my knapsack," when in due time the officer of the day came in on horseback, dashed up to the guard and asked what was the matter. The guard said, "Marse Lieutenant, some of these white folks stole my knapsack," which created additional laughter and merriment. The lieutenant called on the men to return the knapsack, and said that if they didn't, he would order a search of the camp. This they could not afford to have done. In the meantime, the negro said if they would just give him back his "bacca" and guarretype, he wouldn't care anything about the balance. The men then returned the knapsack to keep the camp from being searched.

Our troubles with this negro guard commenced the first night, when they shot into the camp whenever they heard any noise. They were undoubtedly instigated by their officers and the white soldiers.

There were a number of attempts to escape, one novel plan being evolved by the Marylanders. The smallpox broke out inside of the prison, and a pesthouse was established on the main land in the piney woods, about three or four miles from the Point. I forgot to mention Point Lookout is a peninsula, connected with the mainland by a very narrow strip, where a strong fort was located, and where these negroes were quartered. We also had an ordinary hospital inside of the enclosure, immediately in charge of Confederate surgeons, but supervised by a Federal surgeon, who would receive their report every morning on the conditions of the sick, the number of the dead, etc. A couple of Marylanders would blister their faces and hands with hot wire, giving it the appearance of smallpox; the Confederate surgeon would point out these two cases having developed smallpox during the night, when they were ordered out to the pesthouse. They were then carried in a one-horse cart out to the pesthouse in the piney woods, where they only had one guard on duty with his beat in front of the door. The Confederate surgeon immediately in charge, at this pesthouse, would add a couple of boxes in connection with others, for the dead that had passed away during the night, and would report these two men among the other dead of the night. These boxes were then buried by Confederate convalescents, and that was the end of it. The two Marylanders, during the night, had slipped by the single guard with his beat in front of the door, then managed to cross the Potuxan River, either by swimming or floating on planks or logs, there being an only bridge which had a strong cavalry guard and could not be crossed without the countersign.

When I was made acquainted with the scheme by Judge Wilson of the Hood's Texas Brigade, who was a Mason and had a number of Masonic friends among the Marylanders, there were two men out then and after giving them a reasonable time to get away, he had made arrangements for he and I to go out next, but alas, the two men out then were captured and exposed the whole plan, which put an end to it.

Another plan of escape was attempted by others, that of wading out in the bay on dark nights, in water deep enough to barely expose their heads, but when they got opposite the fort those shrewd Yankees had cast an anchor about a quarter of a mile out, to which was attached a rope and the rope attached to a bell inside of the fort, so when the prisoner, wading along in the deep water, would strike this rope, he would ring the bell, which invariably resulted in his discovery.

Other attempts at escape by some of the Marylanders, through bribery of the guard at the gate leading out on the bay shore, invariably failed. The guards would take the bribe, then report the case when he permitted the prisoners to pass out of the gate. The escaping prisoners would then be charged on by a lot of cavalry in waiting around the corner of the fence and shot down by them.

General Butler next conceived the idea to go to Richmond with a batch of prisoners and attempt an exchange, not for the purpose of relieving the prisoners, but simply to test his own case with the Confederate Government. On his arrival at City Point, it seems some arrangement was made that enabled him to deliver these prisoners, presumably in a fair exchange for prisoners held by us. In this batch of prisoners were a number of Marylanders, who thoughtlessly published in a Richmond paper their sufferings and hardships, as well as ill treatment at the hands of the Federal authorities, and particularly denounced Captain Patterson, who had charge of the Point Lookout prison, in most bitter terms. By accident Captain Patterson got hold of a copy of a Richmond paper containing these charges and with it, went to the Maryland Division, read it to the men and told them if further exchanges were had he would see to it that the Marylanders should be the last to leave there.

After this, the Marylanders in the prison, having denounced the article as ill advised and improper, began again to court the favor of Captain Patterson and, after several months, concluded that they had about succeeded in regaining his confidence. One morning they were notified to get ready to go to City Point for exchange. Of course, there was considerable enthusiasm among the Marylanders and I decided to go out with them, in the name of Stanley. We were marched out and carried into another bull pen, kept there five or six hours, when we were permitted to return into our old quarters and found the Tennessee Division had been placed aboard the flag of truce boat and sailed for City Point. It is hardly necessary to say that I was the greatest disappointed man among them, because I also belonged to the Tennessee Division.

In about two weeks the Louisiana Division was called for, to which I also belonged and availed myself of the Louisianan's name, the owner of which was dead, and passed out with them.

At the mouth of the James River we passed a fleet of gunboats and ships, and in due time arrived at City Point, where we anchored in midstream. The exchange agent, Major Mulford, immediately went ashore and telegraphed to Richmond our arrival. We were anchored here several days, expecting hourly a Confederate boat to put in its appearance with the equivalent of Federal prisoners to be returned in exchange. After several days, having been told that our boat surely would arrive the second day, and as it had not put in its appearance, we decided that there was a hitch somewhere and that we were liable to be carried back. We expected, hourly, a couple of gunboats to come in sight to escort us back to Point Lookout.

The situation, to us, began to look gloomy, and created a feeling of desperation. We were determined never to be taken back to look inside of another prison. In accordance therewith we soon made up a party of about a hundred, agreeing to overpower the guard on the boat if the Confederate boat didn't make its appearance by ten o'clock next morning.

On the cabin deck of this boat were quite a number of Confederate officers, among them General W. H. Fitts Lee, who had been wounded and captured. He was a son of General Robert E. Lee, and to him we communicated our intentions and asked their support. He replied, urging us to make no such attempt, that everything was all right and the object of our trip would be carried out without doubt. I told the men that we could not afford to accept his advice; that we had too much at stake, and I construed General Lee's position to be prompted by what he conceived his duty as a Confederate officer. I urged them, by all means, to carry out our plan.

The next day about noon I was sound asleep under the stepladder leading up to the hatch, when awakened by considerable tumult around me. I discovered about a half dozen men on the ladder, ready to make a charge on the upper deck, where the guards were located. It so happened that the man at the top of the ladder hesitated and by way of encouragement, I called to him, "Don't you stop there; put your shoulders under the hatch and throw it off." He proved to be an Irishman who said, "The divil, you say; you come up here and take my place." There was nothing to do but climb up the ladder and take his place. I soon put my back to the hatch and sent it up, whirling on the deck, and jumped on the deck myself. The guard on duty threw his gun down on me, telling me to go back or he would kill me. I called to the men, "Come on, boys," but none would follow. I noticed General Lee in the front part of the boat, motioning to me, "Go back; go back." It is hardly necessary for me to say that I felt like a fool and went back.

There is a member of our camp here today who states that he was present, close to General Lee, and saw me; his name is J. W. Middleton.

Our boat finally made its appearance and while it moved up very slowly towards our boat for the purpose of throwing a gang plank across, for us to pass over, a party of the Louisiana Guard Battery, a company of highly educated young men from New Orleans, appeared on the upper deck with a Confederate flag belonging to the Seventh Louisiana, tacked on to a piece of scantling in the center. General Lee and Colonel Davis of the Eighth Virginia were at one end of the line. These young men, who were splendid singers, with fine voices, struck up:

"Farewell forever to the Star Spangled Banner,

No longer shall it wave over the home of the free,

Unfurled in its stead to the bold breeze of Heaven,

Thirteen bright stars around the palmetto tree."

These lines constituted the chorus of the song, which was sung with a great deal of spirit, and joined in by many of the men and officers. I forgot to mention that while the boats were coming together the Federal prisoners began to twit our boys about going back to live on corn dodgers and bacon, but when they heard this song they were dumbfounded, ceased their guying and simply stood speechless.

On our arrival at the Rockets, a place of landing in Richmond, we were met by a great many citizens, mostly ladies in carriages, and a company of Richmond cadets, escorted us to the Capitol Square, where we were met by President and Mrs. Davis, who shook hands with every one of us. Mrs. Davis was in tears. We were then regaled by a speech from Governor Smith of Virginia, standing on the platform in front of the Capitol, when among other things he said, "They have called me from the tented field to preside over the destinies of this great commonwealth, because they say I am too old to be there; but I deny the charge and want it distinctly understood that among Yankees and women, I am only five and twenty."

Those who are acquainted with Governor Smith's history, knowing him at that time to be a man about sixty-five or seventy years old, commanding a brigade in the army when he was elected Governor, will not be surprised at his expression. Governor Smith was generally known as "Extra Billy." I will take occasion to mention that when I put my foot on Dixie soil it proved the happiest moment of my life up to that time; I felt like kissing the ground that I stood on.

President Davis, in his speech to us, told us that we were only paroled, and could not enter the service again until duly exchanged. He requested those that lived on the West of the Mississippi not to go home on a visit, pending this exchange, stating that he hoped we would soon be called on to return to our respective commands, as we were greatly needed in the army.

With me, this admonition was not needed, my only ambition was to get back to my command and again mount my horse and resume my duties. For this purpose I sought out Senator Oldham from Texas, who went with me to the War Department and secured me a pass from the Secretary of War, to go to Greenville, East Tennessee, where I learned the Rangers were camped and in due time made my way over there and found them in a deep snow.

CHAPTER XI

THE INHUMANITY OF THE FEDERAL GOVERNMENT.

In reviewing my prison experience and observation, I find that I omitted to mention a case at Bowling Green, which will give the reader a fair idea of the danger of capture in territory occupied by the Federal Army and now take occasion to recall the case of John R. Lisle, a sergeant in Morgan's command, who was permitted to visit his home near Russellville, Kentucky, on a short furlough and was shot down in his own home, in the bosom of his family, by some Tory neighbors, the ball striking him on top of the head, which temporarily stunned him and while on the floor, senseless, they rushed in and secured his capture. He had on a new gray Confederate uniform and when searched, had an order from General Morgan to notify all of their men whom he met or had an opportunity to convey the instructions, to report back to their command, having overstayed their furlough.

I got acquainted with Lisle as soon as I entered the prison and found him a very bright, intelligent gentleman. He was then being tried by court martial on the charge of being a spy and convicted on this order of Morgan's, ordering men back to their command. During the trial he made a pencil memorandum of the proceedings of the court martial and finally, losing his temper one day, blessed out the court martial, telling them that he was satisfied they were after his blood and to stop their mockery of a trial, to go ahead and take his life, lead him out and shoot him. The court martial found him guilty and assessed his punishment at death by hanging. As soon as the findings of the court martial were returned from General Burnside's headquarters, approved, he was taken down into the lower room and had irons forged on him, taken over to the court house under special guard to await the day of his execution. While at the court house his wife and oldest son, a boy about fifteen, were permitted to see him, when he smuggled the memoranda he had made of the proceedings of the court martial to his wife, with instructions to send his boy to General Bragg's headquarters, then near Tullahoma, Tennessee, with this memoranda, satisfied that our Government would demand his exchange as a prisoner of war, putting some Federal officer in confinement, as hostage. After he was taken out of the prison we were not permitted to learn anything more about his fate.

During my imprisonment at Point Lookout, Maryland, a batch of about five hundred prisoners from Johnson's Island were received there. Hastening to the gate to watch their coming in, thinking perhaps I might see some acquaintances, I met John R. Lisle, who had just been released from a dungeon at Johnson's Island, where he had been ever since he was moved from Bowling Green in irons—confined in this dungeon and for the first time then treated as a prisoner of war. There is hardly a doubt but designating a couple of Federal officers as hostages for his safety, had the desired effect and saved his life. I left him at Point Lookout with the balance of the prisoners, from whence he was finally sent around for exchange. I had a letter from one of our prison companions near Bowling Green, about eight years ago, saying that Lisle finally returned South and to his home in Kentucky, where he died only a few years before this letter was written.

In order to give the reader an idea of the intense hatred on the part of the Lincoln Government, it might be well here to note that in the very beginning of hostilities they adopted a policy to degrade the Southern Army in the estimation of their own people, as well as that of foreign countries. In order to carry out such policy the War Department issued an order that all executions of Confederate soldiers convicted by court martial, should be by hanging—a felon's death—which order was never modified and was carried out in its letter and spirit, never in any case permitting an exception.

In this connection I would mention a case in point, which occurred while I was a prisoner and has repeatedly been reported in the papers of the North and South. The case was a Colonel Johnston of the Confederate Army, in conjunction with a lieutenant, whose name I have forgotten, entering the Federal lines as spies. Colonel Johnston was armed with a fictitious order from Secretary of War Stanton to proceed to Murfreesboro, Franklin and Nashville, Tennessee, and inspect the Federal works at these places. They called one evening at Franklin, presented the Secretary of War's order, which seemed to be genuine, when the colonel commanding received them very courteously and rode around with them, inspecting his works. Colonel Johnston also stated to him that he was just from General Rosencranz's headquarters, where he had inspected the works around Murfreesboro. After the inspection of the Franklin works Colonel Johnston told the colonel in command that he was compelled to go to Nashville that night and insisted on leaving at once for Nashville, although dark had set in. The colonel tried to persuade him to spend the night with him but all to no purpose. After Colonel Johnston and the lieutenant had been gone perhaps a half hour the colonel got suspicious and wired General Rosencranz for information, and General Rosencranz replied that there had been no such men there, that evidently they were spies, to not fail to capture them and order a drumhead court martial. The colonel then immediately ordered his horse and with a sergeant, pursued Colonel Johnston and the lieutenant, caught up with them some six or eight miles on the road to Nashville, and insisted that they must go back with him and spend the night, which they did. On their arrival at the colonel's headquarters he immediately had them searched and found ample evidence on their persons that they were Confederate soldiers, acting as spies, notably the sword of Colonel Johnston's was inscribed "C. S. A.," and Colonel Johnston readily admitted they were spies.

During the session of the court martial Colonel Johnston made himself known to the colonel commanding, who then recognized him as a classmate at West Point. He then made an eloquent appeal to the court martial to save the life of the lieutenant, telling them that he was unaware, when they started on this expedition, of its object and finally begged them to have him shot, to permit him to die a soldier's and not a felon's death. He said to the colonel, "When you rode up we both had our pistols out, under the capes of our overcoats and could have killed you easily, thereby saving our lives, but the thought of killing an old classmate without giving him a chance for his life overruled my better judgment and I decided that I might talk out of it, thereby sparing your life," but all to no purpose, his pleadings were ignored and he had to meet his fate by hanging.

After the defeat of the Federal Army at the first battle of Manassas, many wagonloads of handcuffs, put up in barrels, were captured, which were intended to be placed on the entire Confederate Army when captured, and marched into Washington City, wearing these bracelets.

Among Mr. Lincoln's earliest proclamations was the one declaring medicines contraband of war, thus depriving millions of sick of medicines, one of the most brutal and inhuman orders ever published by a civilized Government.

CHAPTER XII.

I REJOIN MY COMMAND.

Recurring to the meeting of my comrades at Greenville, Tennessee, where I found them camped in a deep snow, when they had me relate my prison experience, etc.: They had just received orders to move to Dalton, Georgia, where I, having no horse, proceeded by rail. On my arrival at Dalton I found the largest, best equipped army I had ever seen in the Confederacy, mostly quartered in tents. Our advance line occupied the top of a range of mountains, presenting precipitous fronts towards the enemy. This range of mountains was somewhat in the shape of a horseshoe, largely surrounding Dalton with probably a half dozen gaps, which were strongly fortified by our forces, except Snake Creek Gap on our left, nearly on a line with Resacca, a railroad station immediately in our rear on the only line entering Dalton and our only means of supplying the army and enabling retreat. I found General Joseph E. Johnston in command, with General Hardee, his second in command and General Hood, commanding a corps, immediately in front of Dalton.

Not having any horse and unable to secure one, I met a friend, Captain James Britton from Lebanon, Tennessee, who commanded Hood's escort, who told me that he had several horses in camp, doing nothing, the owners of the horses being sick and confined at the hospital; if I would come and stay with him that I could ride any of the horses. This I gratefully accepted, telling him that I would only do so with the understanding that I would be treated as a member of the company doing duty.

While on this duty, moving out with the escort one morning with General Hood and staff, to his headquarters just in the rear of Railroad Gap, I witnessed the meeting of General J. E. Johnston, W. J. Hardee, General Cheatham, General Hindman, all with their respective staffs, at General Hood's headquarters, which were under an old workshed with a workbench under it. General Johnston and staff were the last to arrive. After dismounting and shaking hands with the different generals and members of their staffs, as also General Hood, he handed General Hood his crutches. General Hood, it will be remembered, lost his leg at Chickamauga and was ever afterwards on crutches. Generals Johnston and Hood then moved up the road about three hundred yards out of our hearing and were soon engaged in a very animated discussion, which lasted perhaps three-quarters of an hour. When they returned Generals Johnston and Hardee mounted their horses with their respective staffs, returning to town, and gradually the rest of the officers dispersed, going to their respective stations.

CHAPTER XIII.

MIDDLE TENNESSEE AND KENTUCKY.

On reflection, I find that I omitted about a year's service in Tennessee and Kentucky, before my capture near Bowling Green and will insert this now.

After destroying trestles and bridges between La Vergne and Nashville, under General Forrest, and capturing a railroad train at La Vergne, on which Colonel Fordyce was captured, we were ordered back across the mountain to Chattanooga, where we commenced scouting and picketing on the Tennessee River. We frequently extended our scouts almost to Guntersville, with the Federal Army massing and camping just across the river. General Mitchell commanded at Huntsville. He gave out that he was building a gunboat, with which to capture Chattanooga, and had the people of Chattanooga badly alarmed about it, but when finally he got his gunboat ready to move up the river, a scout of about twenty Texas Rangers were sent down to meet it with shotguns, taking a position on top of a high bank, opposite the mouth of Battle Creek, which was in plain view of this high bank. The gunboat approached and proved to be an ordinary small river boat, lined with cotton bales on the edge of the decks with the troops aboard, lying around carelessly on the side of this barricade of cotton bales, some of them playing cards. When the boat came very close to our bluff, we turned loose our shotguns on them and drove the boat into the mouth of Battle Creek, where it remained and was utilized by the Federal Army as a bridge for crossing the creek. This proved the end of General Mitchell's famous gunboat, with which he threatened to capture Chattanooga. It was driven out of commission by Terry's Rangers' shotguns and relieved the people of Chattanooga of their anxiety.

While picketing down on the river road with a companion, we stopped at a blacksmith's shop near Nicajack Cave and had our horses shod; just across the river was a camp of Federal infantry and artillery. The river at this point we judged to be about three-quarters of a mile wide, perhaps more; the railroad continued to run on the banks of the river, after passing the Narrows with the first depot out of Chattanooga, Shell Mound. After having our horses shod we rode down to the railroad on the banks of the river, the grade of which was high enough to protect us and our horses. We discovered a soldier at the river, filling some canteens and to see him run, we fired our pistols across, which of course made him run to his camp. Soon after, we heard the artillery bugle and immediately a gun opened on us with shell, which always struck the Nicajack Cave, some three-quarters of a mile in our rear, the country between us and Nicajack Cave being flat and open. We soon moved down to the little brick depot at Shell Mound and opened on them from there, when they perforated it with their shells; we then moved down to a box bridge across the mouth of the creek running into the river and had them make that a target. It is hardly necessary to say that we enjoyed this, somewhat, having a duel with our pistols against their piece of artillery. We were entirely protected and didn't consider that we were under any danger whatever of being hit.

While picketing on this main road, General Morgan ran down on a locomotive as far as Shell Mound, just before our escapade with this artillery and came very near having his engine struck by a shell, but he succeeded in getting back to Chattanooga with his locomotive.

We were soon ordered back to Middle Tennessee, under General Forrest, where we operated around McMinnville, Manchester and along the railroad. After an attack on the outskirts of Manchester one morning, which Colonel Forrest decided was too strong for us, we withdrew further down the railroad, where we charged a block-house, the first we ever attempted to capture and the first we had ever seen. But, although some of our men got right up to the house, we were unable to force them to surrender, and were forced to give it up as a bad job. While engaged in this venture, a large force of infantry, cavalry and artillery had moved out on the road from McMinnville and were about to cut off our line of retreat. When we got in sight of this force, hurrying to get out of this corner, they raised a shout, which I must say made me feel very uncomfortable, knowing that they outnumbered us perhaps five to one, but we succeeded in dashing across the main road, where we wheeled and charged their advance column, bringing them to a halt, permitting others of the command to cross, that were virtually cut off, but they did capture a large fine looking negro man, who was the servant of General Forrest. His name was Napoleon, and he was devotedly attached to General Forrest. In connection with his capture they also captured two fine horses belonging to the general. They carried this negro to Louisville prison and did their best to persuade him to take the oath of allegiance and join them, but he steadfastly refused, as he was devotedly attached to General Forrest and was finally, through some special arrangement, exchanged and returned to the general. The last I knew of him I heard of him in Louisville prison, when he was sent around for exchange.

After operating a while longer in Middle Tennessee without any important captures, we got information that General Bragg had crossed the Tennessee River at Chattanooga and was moving across Cumberland Mountain, driving the Federal Army before him and we were instructed to harass the enemy as much as possible. In accordance therewith we would attack their infantry (moving with their artillery, ordnance and wagon trains by divisions on several of the main roads). We would dash into their rear, forcing them to stop and draw up in line of battle, when they would commence shelling us and we would move out of the range of their artillery rapidly, further up the road, striking another column perhaps in flank, leaving the first mentioned column shelling the woods for an hour or more after we had left. In this manner we kept them harassed and impeded their rapid movements, while General Bragg, with the main army, was moving as rapidly as possible on their flank, crossing the Cumberland River higher up on his way to Glasgow, Kentucky. The Federal Army made a short stop at Nashville, collecting all their forces, and then moved from there towards Mumfordsville, Kentucky, on Green River.

While in pursuit of one of these Federal columns on top of a mountain not far from Woodbury, we struck a point on the pike where it was built across a deep ravine; the crossing protected on the side by a rail fence. Just as we entered the narrow point in this lane, General Forrest, who was riding in advance of our regiment, discovered a vidette of the enemy in the woods on the far banks of the ravine, and he immediately had some men dismounted on both flanks, to drive them in, satisfied that the enemy were going to make a stand on the other side of the ravine. He determined to charge them, horseback, for which purpose we formed fours and prepared for the charge by tightening our saddle girths. Just as we were ready to move on them, a masked battery of four pieces opened on us and drove us back, as we stood no chance of reaching it in massed formation of fours through this narrow lane on the Pike.

The first shell cut off a leg below the knee of D. Rugeley, one of the finest looking young men we had in the company, and one of the best. He was held on his horse by his companions, on our retreat, when the enemy's cavalry charged us and, for the moment, created a little confusion. When Colonel Wharton discovered Rugeley's plight, holding the lower part of his leg by the foot and being assisted by a comrade on each side, holding him on his horse, he was completely overcome with the sight, rode up and fell over on D., with both arms around his neck, crying, when D. said to him, "Colonel Wharton, this is no place to take on in this manner. Leave me and save yourself." This aroused Wharton and wheeling his horse, called on the Rangers to rally and drive back that cavalry and save D. Rugeley, which it is hardly necessary to say, was done in short order. This is perhaps the only instance where Colonel Wharton was seen to lose control of himself and can only be explained by the fact that D. Rugeley's father and he were most intimate friends, and on parting with Rugeley's father had been enjoined to take special care of his boy.

An instance of appreciation of our services was illustrated near Murfreesboro, Tennessee, through which place we had just passed in pursuit of a large Federal column. In passing through a lane a few miles north of town, where a number of ladies had congregated to see us pass, an old lady among them was cheering us and clapping her hands, when she was heard to remark, "Oh, daughter; just look at our soldiers, grand men as they are, all covered with dust so they can hardly be recognized; God bless them! I wish they could stay long enough so I could wash their clothes." This old lady perhaps had never seen a washtub in her life, as judging from the magnificent house which appeared through the woods, and its surroundings, she was no doubt raised in wealth and affluence. It was such expressions as this, on the part of the ladies, that made us good soldiers.

After our army reached Glasgow the enemy had concentrated a strong force at Mumfordsville, which was strongly fortified and which they determined to hold at all hazards. Nashville was not evacuated by them, but a force of ten thousand men, strongly fortified, with Andrew Johnson, demanding of General Nelson to hold this place at all hazards, which was done. While our army was at Glasgow, which was only about twenty-five miles from Bell Station, McDonald, a member of our company, proposed to me to go by and see the Smith family, at whose house he had been sick and to which I agreed, and for this purpose called on Colonel Wharton to give us a pass, which he refused, saying that no one could be permitted to pass our lines unless they had a pass from General Bragg, countersigned by General Polk. We told him, "Colonel Wharton, we feel in duty bound to visit these people," and gave him the reason, telling him that we would make the attempt without a pass. He said, "Graber, if you do and you are caught, Bragg will have both of you shot." I told him, "All right; catching before hanging." We started out at night, telling him "If you miss us you'll know where we are." We started out the main road towards Bell Station; when about a mile we struck an Alabama picket and asked the lieutenant commanding to allow us to pass through, telling him the circumstances that prompted our determination to visit our friends. He said, "Rangers, you know we would do anything we can for you, but our orders are very strict and we cannot disobey them." We then moved back out of sight, struck out into the woods on their flank, passing around them and made our way to the Smith home, about four miles from Bell Station. It is hardly necessary to say the old lady and her daughters, the only ones left at home, were delighted to see us, and especially to hear from the army. They had not heard from their boys, who were in Breckenridge's Brigade, nor their father, who was with them. It will be remembered he left his home with McDonald in a wagon and carried him to Bowling Green, when he was convalescent from his spell of pneumonia. We remained at the house nearly a half day, when we heard heavy firing at Mumfordsville and immediately mounted our horses and started for there.

Arriving at Mumfordsville about night I was unable to get any information of our brigade and we decided to go into the battle with the infantry the next morning, but during the night the Federals surrendered. About daylight we mounted our horses and entered the fort through an embrasure and soon struck the hospital tents, where McDonald dismounted to try to find some liquor. While I never indulged in strong drink, it was hard to keep McDonald from it. While holding his horse, waiting for him to come back, Colonel Wharton rode in, at the head of our regiment, from the opposite side of the fort from where we had entered and on seeing me, simply said, "Hello, Graber; you beat us in," and smiled. I expect we were the first Confederates inside of the fort. It seems that General Chalmers, the evening before, had made a determined attack on the works and was repulsed with heavy loss. The colonel commanding the fort, learning that General Bragg had arrived with the whole army, completely surrounding him during the night, decided it was better to surrender than to risk another engagement the next day, as he had only about four or five thousand men.

After leaving Mumfordsville, our cavalry and Forrest continued on the main road through Elizabethtown and on to Bardstown, Kentucky, out of which place we drove the Federal cavalry. They retreated to Louisville. We were camped at Bardstown several days, awaiting the arrival of the infantry and while there, formed the acquaintance of a number of good people, which means friends of the South. At Bardstown we found the home of Judge Newman, whose daughter, the wife of my old friend, Cannon, then lived at Courtney. Before they had removed from Hempstead, a year or more before the breaking out of hostilities, her sister, Miss Josie Newman, made a visit to Hempstead, where she formed the acquaintance of quite a number of young men that were in the army with us. On our second day's sojourn a Mr. Tom Clay, belonging to Company K of our regiment, whose home was in Washington County, and who had been intimately acquainted with Miss Josie during her stay at Hempstead, proposed to me to call on Miss Josie, to which I agreed. Alighting in front of their house, Miss Josie happened to be standing in the door and recognizing us, rushed to the gate and invited us in. Just then a little boy came along and asked me to give him a little silk Confederate flag some young ladies had presented me with the day before and I had sticking in the browband of my horse's bridle. Fearing the little boy would take the flag while we were in the house, I suggested that I had better take this in with me. Miss Josie then said, "That flag can't come into our house." Up to this time we were unaware that they were Union people. My friend, bowing to her, said, "We will certainly not go into a house where our flag is not welcome," and we declined to go in. By this time her mother had come to the gate, when Miss Josie introduced us. Mrs. Newman having heard my name, through the Cannon family, quite often, she insisted on our coming in, when we told her Miss Josie's objections. She chided her for her discourtesy and told us to come in and bring the flag, when my friend said to Miss Josie, "We will compromise the matter with you and go in, if you will sing Dixie and Bonnie Blue Flag for us," which of course she had to agree to do and, while singing these songs, I sat at the end of the piano with my little Confederate flag in my hand and when she sang the chorus I would wave the flag.

After two days' sojourn we moved on up towards Louisville, part of our force dividing and occupying the town of Taylorsville on our right; the balance of the command camping near Mount Washington on the Bardstown Pike. Here General Forrest received an order from the War Department to personally report to Richmond and turn the command of the brigade over to Colonel Wharton. In about a week the Federal forces advanced out of Louisville. They were said to be a hundred thousand strong, while another force moved out of Cincinnati, about sixty thousand strong, with a view of cutting us off from retreat to Cumberland Gap.

CHAPTER XIV.

BARDSTOWN ENGAGEMENT—I "SWAP" HORSES WITH A FEDERAL.

The object of General Bragg's advance into Kentucky was to form a nucleus for Kentuckians to rally around, our War Department having been importuned by leading Kentuckians to do this, claiming they would have a hundred thousand men to join us as soon as we could reclaim their territory. On this point, however, they were mistaken, as we gathered only about six thousand recruits and they all wanted to serve in cavalry. They joined us largely about half equipped for cavalry service, many of them with citizen's saddles and shotguns or squirrel rifles and, while on the subject, I might mention here that over half of them deserted us before we passed through Cumberland Gap and soon after they found that we were unable to hold Kentucky. Gen. Bragg moved in there with about thirty thousand men, exclusive of General Kirby Smith's force of about twelve thousand, which moved on Cincinnati and fought the battle of Richmond, where they completely defeated the Federal Army of about twenty-five thousand strong, capturing, killing and wounding nearly half, with the balance driven into Covington and Cincinnati.

While at Bardstown, General Bragg, finding that the real object of his campaign was a failure, decided to turn it into a raid; to collect valuable stores and move out again, through Cumberland Gap.

When Colonel Wharton took command of the brigade, succeeding General Forrest, General Wheeler with another brigade occupied the Taylorsville Pike, both brigades holding the enemy in check in their advance as best they could. Our little force at Taylorsville was drawn over to the Bardstown and Louisville Pike, where they met the balance of the brigade at Mount Washington. While at Mount Washington, drawn up in line, eating our lunch, a large force of Federal cavalry made a dash on us but were soon repulsed and driven back. In this engagement a messmate of mine, Roland Chatham, received a pistol ball right in the center of his forehead, just over the eyes, the ball penetrating his skull and burying itself in the brain. This however, did not knock him off his horse and he remained with us until after the enemy was driven back. Passing to the rear with his wound bleeding, he was noticed by some ladies in Mount Washington, displaying his pistol, when they were heard to remark, "Just look at that poor Texas Ranger; shot through the head and still he wants to fight." In this connection I would state that Chatham was sent to the hospital and finally to Texas, never having been completely disabled on account of this wound, and with this ball imbedded in the brain, lived to a good old age, dying only a few years ago at Bryan, Texas, where he raised a large family. Here he started and operated a cotton gin manufactory, which proved a great success and enabled him to amass a considerable fortune. During all his lifetime his wound remained open but never affected his mind. This was, perhaps, one of the most remarkable cases on record.

The Federal advance through Mount Washington and Taylorsville continued daily as soon as it was light enough to discern anything. The enemy's skirmishers would advance and, supported by their line of battle and artillery, would drive us from positions we had taken up. We would then fall back to another good position, perhaps a mile, and defend that as best we could, again to be driven from it in the same manner. I forgot to mention we had with us in this brigade, the First and Second Georgia and the Tennessee Battalion, under Colonel Baxter Smith, who is still living at Nashville, Tennessee.

When within nine miles of Bardstown, one morning (dark and drizzling rain) the enemy failed to make its appearance at daylight. Waiting until about nine o'clock, Colonel Wharton got suspicious, and sent a scout in our rear, who struck a large cavalry force of the enemy of about eight regiments, occupying the pike near the Fair Grounds. Returning, full speed, the scout reported to Colonel Wharton this condition. Immediately placing himself at the head of our regiment, drawn up immediately across the pike, Colonel Wharton sent couriers to the balance of our regiment and to a section of little brass six-pounders (originally the property of the Arkansas Military Institute) commanded by Captain Pugh of our regiment, a western Texas cowman, instructing them to come on and catch up with our regiment as fast as they could. Wharton at the head of the regiment in column of fours, struck a lope and soon arrived in sight of this body of the enemy's cavalry. He then ordered a charge and when at a junction of a dirt road with the pike, about two companies of this cavalry formed in an orchard behind a rail picket fence, which are rails stuck in the ground, picket fashion, and fired on our flank point blank. About thirty or forty of us turned on them, halting in front of this picket fence with our bridle reins thrown over the horns of our saddles, and with a six-shooter in each hand, began to empty saddles. This caused them to break and enter a lane in their rear, having already let down the fence to provide for such an emergency, and fled up the lane in a northerly direction from whence they had come. Colonel Wharton with the balance of the regiment dashed into the solid body of the enemy in his front and scattered them. It soon developed that they were panic stricken and were driven over the open country, interspersed only by rail and rock fences, in detached bodies of twenty and fifty, and so on, by only a few Rangers, driving them like cattle on the prairies. Here was one of the most brilliant cavalry engagements we were ever in and resulted in our capturing a great many prisoners.

When the regiment passed through Bardstown somewhat hurriedly, passing by the Newman residence, Miss Josie Newman, who was standing at the gate, watching them go by, saw a Major Jared Gross, a former acquaintance, loping up the column. She recognized him, clapping her hands and calling out, "Good-bye, Jared; I'm glad to see you running," when the next moment she recognized a Federal, Major Watts, riding behind one of our boys, a prisoner, his face badly bruised and his clothes torn and soiled, having had his horse killed under him. This sight immediately brought her tears and she went back into the house, crying. She was a kind hearted, good young lady, full of spirit in her Union sentiment.

Now, to go back to the party of Federals in the orchard, fleeing up the lane from the direction whence they came: Captain Mark Evans, commanding one of our Western companies, and I, were the first ones to enter the lane and drive these fellows. We were followed by quite a number of others, who stopped at the fence with us when first fired into. In running up the lane we ran over a number of six-shooters and belts with sabre and six-shooters attached. The six-shooter was always a valuable capture for us, as we could readily sell it to men in the army who had money, which we were always in need of, and although we were virtually maintaining ourselves without the aid of the Government, we could not afford to stop and pick up these pistols, as everything depended on crowding these Federals, who outnumbered us at least ten to one; but, as before stated, they were panic stricken, which sometimes happened to the best of troops.

After passing about a mile up this lane, I noticed a very fine pistol. I recognized it as a Tranter, an English pistol, self-cocking, of which Colonel Terry had four, and I was always anxious to secure a pair of them. My first impulse was to stop and get this pistol; then again concluded not to stop, as so much depended on our crowding them, but, after passing it perhaps thirty or forty yards, I decided I would go back and pick it up, anyway. For this purpose, I wheeled and as my horse's position was across the lane, in turning, one of our men just behind me, struck my horse's neck and broke the headstall of my bridle, dropping the bit out of the horse's mouth. He wheeled and ran after Evans and the Federals, running faster than ever I had known him to run before, and he would soon have carried me right in among them. But, when near Evans I called to him to stop my horse; at the same time one of the Federals dismounted from his horse and surrendered. He and Evans together stopped my horse, and as there was no time for swapping bridles, I slipped over on his horse, handing him my bridle rein which was still around my horse's neck with the bit attached; grabbing his pistol, I went on my Federal horse and told the Federal to wait and turn mine over to some of the boys behind.

Continuing up this lane we discovered a bunch of about twenty-five or thirty, some hundred and fifty yards to our right, in a field, headed by an officer riding a magnificent horse and in magnificent uniform. We soon arrived at a big gate on our right, just beyond where another fence connected with the lane fence, this fence running due east, and which this bunch of Federals had to cross. When we reached this gate Evans said to me, "Run through that gate and head off this bunch," which I did. I forgot to mention that this party was driven by only about a half dozen of our men. After passing through the gate I stopped, took position almost immediately in front of them and when the officer got near the fence I threw my pistol down on him and demanded his surrender, to which he paid no attention, but threw off the top rail, the rider of the fence, and made his horse leap the fence, passing right in front of me, running through an orchard and I have never been able to understand how he succeeded in avoiding the limbs of the trees without butting his brains out.

When the balance of his men came up and attempted to jump the fence, the first man broke it down and furnished an easier way for the balance to cross but, being headed off by me, they were forced to take right down the fence east, followed by our boys, whom I cautioned several times to hold their fire until the Federals would bunch up. To this, however, very little attention was paid and with my additional pistol, my shots held out longer than theirs.

Now, it must be understood that having to load our pistols with loose powder from the powder flask, which had a gauge attached, then ramming down the ball with a ramrod attached to the pistol, then putting a cap on the nipple, it was necessary to stop and reload, as an attempt at reloading, running, would have spilled the powder and caused confusion; hence, one after another of our boys dropped behind to reload. This found me alone, just after the Federals and I had turned the corner of a stone fence, starting due north again. When about a hundred yards from this stone fence I fired my last shot, when one of them looked around, discovered I was by myself, called on the others to "turn on him; there is only one by himself; give him h—." I wheeled and the Yankees wheeled. When we had run back only about fifty yards, two of our men, who I think were Geo. W. Littlefield and Beardy Miller, turned the same corner of the stone fence. When this bunch of Federals saw this, they again wheeled, running north. When Littlefield and Miller came up to where I was they said, "Come on; come on." I said, "No, I have got to stop and load my pistol," which I proceeded to do, they continuing after this bunch of Federals. Having about three or four chambers of my pistol filled with powder and standing about fifteen yards from the fence, seven more Federals came around the same corner of the fence, running between me and the fence, after I had drawn back my horse about ten steps, giving them more room. If I had had one load in my pistol, I would have demanded their surrender, which I believe they would have done, but they never said a word to me nor I to them, and went flying after Littlefield and Beardy Miller, who were after the first bunch.

I forgot to mention that before we had reached this far, we heard heavy firing of infantry and artillery. We knew it was infantry by their first volley; then a very rapid, scattering fire, as also rapid cannonading in the direction of the Fair Grounds, which we concluded to mean that the balance of our brigade were passing down into Bardstown, around this infantry and artillery, which had been sent in support of their cavalry.

After having completed the loading of two of my pistols, I discovered a bunch of about eighty or a hundred Federals running towards me, cut off by the long fence running east. When they struck the fence, in place of crossing it, continuing in their course north, they turned right down the line of fence east, on the south side of it. By this time the firing at the Fair Grounds had become more scattered and distant, and the artillery had ceased firing, but I was afraid to venture back the way I came, by myself, therefore, decided that I would let down the fence, getting on the south side of it, follow this last bunch east, until I was about four or five miles east of Bardstown, then turn due south and strike the Springfield Pike, on which I knew our infantry were moving from Bardstown to Perryville. I finished loading my pistols, then crossed the fence and started east in the wake of these Federals, keeping a sharp lookout ahead and, after riding about three or four miles, passing through woods-lots and fences, I emerged from the woods, up on a ridge, and discovered these fellows about a quarter of a mile below me in a field, drawn up in a line, facing in my direction. I resorted to a ruse, taking off my hat and waving it behind me, then started at them, but this would not work and immediately they started after me. I turned south and put my Federal horse to his best and soon got out of sight.

Having run in this direction some three or four miles, coming out of a woods-lot through a big gate to a large, white house I stopped and called, hoping to get some information about the best way to get to the Springfield Pike. After calling some little time, an old gentleman came out of the door, to the front porch, when I called to him that I was a Confederate soldier and wanted some information about striking the Springfield Pike, four or five miles east of Bardstown. Having heard the firing of the infantry and artillery, which no doubt greatly alarmed him, he talked so fast and rambling that I was unable to understand him, and I begged him to come to the gate, which he started to do. When about half way, I heard the woods-lot gate creak, looked around and here were my Federals, coming single file, which of course started me again, running south into a short lane running east, and when at the mouth of this lane, only about three hundred yards long, I looked across the corner of this man's field and found about a dozen or more of these fellows bunched up at his gate, talking to the old man. I immediately turned south again, putting my horse to his very best. When about three miles from there, I struck a lane with a dirt road running towards Bardstown. I kept a sharp lookout for the Federals behind me, whom I never saw again and don't believe they followed me any further. Looking up the lane east, I discovered five Confederate cavalrymen coming in the direction of Bardstown and when they got up to where I was waiting for them in the lane, having crossed the fence, I found that they were three Georgians and two of our own regiment. I then tried to get them to go back with me, telling them that I believed that we could pick up quite a number of prisoners, but the Georgians were unwilling; they too, had heard the firing at Bardstown and did not think it safe for us to go back in the direction of where I left these people scattered over the different fields.

I now suggested we strike south again until we reached the Springfield Pike, which we did in due time and struck Anderson's Division of Infantry, reporting to General Anderson our engagement and telling him I was satisfied we could pick up many prisoners if he would only send back with me a couple of companies of cavalry. He stated he did not have a man to spare and was unable to do so, but told me to wait there, that General Hardee would come up pretty soon and might act on my suggestion.

In about half an hour General Hardee, with his staff, came up, and I reported the engagement to him and found he had had no particulars. Being unable to tell him whether the balance of the brigade with the two little popguns had got through safely to Bardstown, made him somewhat apprehensive, but he was, nevertheless, gratified to know that the Rangers had come through all right.

General Hardee, in response to my request to send some cavalry with me to pick up these stragglers, said that he did not have a man to spare and told me we had better stay at his headquarters that night. The next morning we would find our command at a certain point on this pike, he said. This we decided to do, being very hungry and tired. The next morning we started for our camp and, on my arrival there, found my horse with the saddle, everything all right, but no one in the company could tell who delivered him or where he came from. Captain Evans, I suppose, being too much engaged in collecting his scattered forces, had not made any report on my exchange of horses. I never found out what became of my good Federal who held him for me and swapped with me. My comrades, who had concluded that I was perhaps killed, shot off of my horse, had given me out and, when I rode in on my Federal horse with the Federal overcoat and other equipments, you can imagine their surprise.

Miss Josie Newman, just before Major Gross passed her house, had called to some members of our company to know where I was and their answer was that I was left on the field, either dead or wounded and this caused her and her mother, with friends, to look over the field for several days, hunting me or my body, so Mrs. Cannon reported after a visit to her home, several years after the war.

CHAPTER XV.

THE BATTLE OF PERRYVILLE.

Referring back to the balance of the brigade we left formed on the pike, nine miles from town: Couriers were sent them and to our little battery, to follow us and catch up as fast as they could, which they tried to do. When near the Fair Grounds they fell into the enemy's infantry and artillery support, but successfully moved around them, losing only a few killed and wounded and taken prisoners; our loss in killed and wounded was very small.

The cause of our being cut off was through General Wheeler, who had occupied the Taylorsville Pike, moving into Bardstown the night before, sending a courier to Colonel Wharton with a dispatch ordering him to move in also. This courier was captured, which of course, proved valuable information to the enemy and on which they acted by throwing this heavy cavalry, infantry and artillery forces across our line of retreat.

This brilliant achievement of Wharton's extricating his brigade from this trap, secured his promotion to that of Brigadier-General, the same as Forrest's exploit in the capture of Murfreesboro had secured his commission as Brigadier-General.

After leaving Bardstown our army continued its movement towards Perryville, its rear covered by our cavalry, all under the command of General Joe Wheeler. We pursued the same tactics that we did between Louisville and Bardstown, taking up favorable positions only to be driven from them by the large force of the enemy, usually by their superior artillery and heavy flank movements, thereby retarding their advance and giving our infantry, artillery and wagon train ample time to keep out of their way, also enabling some part of the cavalry to collect valuable army stores, such as provisions, stock, etc.

At Perryville we were forced to call a halt and give battle, our right wing, commanded by General Polk, becoming actively engaged about two o'clock in the evening.

The battlefield selected was one of the most favorable to both armies that could have been wished for, except that the extreme left wing of the Federal Army was caught without water until they succeeded in reaching a spring. Both lines of battle were on wooded ridges, intervened by a gentle valley from one and a half to three miles wide, these ridges terminating not far from Doctor's Creek where there was considerable water, and which was commanded by our lines. At the head of the valley another wooded ridge sprang up about equidistant between the terminations of the two first mentioned ridges.

About ten o'clock we were ordered to our extreme right, commanded by General Cheatham and our line of march in the rear of the infantry line was discovered by the enemy, causing a concentration of their artillery to such an extent that we were forced to drop to the rear out of their sight. Finally we were ordered up on this wooded ridge commencing in the center of the valley, as a corps of observation, to watch the enemy's extreme left and frustrate any flank movements they might undertake.

I forgot to mention that the artillery on both lines opened about daylight and gradually developed on both lines to about one o'clock, the infantry of both lying down and keeping out of sight. While on the ridge as stated, acting as a corps of observation, General Wharton, with his field glass, discovered a body of Federal cavalry, loaded with canteens, at a spring at the foot of the mountain they were occupying and called to the command, "About a half dozen of you get off your horses and drive that cavalry away from the spring." As the mountain or ridge we were on, on the side next to the enemy, was very rocky and precipitous, the necessity of dismounting was apparent. I, with five or six others, obeyed the order and we were soon down in the valley, charging this spring, when this cavalry, with their long range Spencer rifles, took position behind a rock fence and opened on us. We had only one long range gun, in addition to six-shooters and knowing that the eyes of our own command, as well as Cheatham's Division of infantry were watching us, we never considered a halt, but charged right on to them and, with our pistols, drove them away from the spring. We followed them around the foot of their ridge, past a house in the rear of the ridge, then down a line of fence, while they passed into the field and finally into a cedar thicket. We decided that we had better retire. We had started to do so, when one of these fellows came out of the thicket, riding a gray horse and called to us, waving his pistol. We turned loose on him with our pistols and drove him back into the thicket. We again started to retire, when he made his appearance again, pursuing the same tactics, when one of our boys, who had an Enfield rifle, the only gun in the party, crept down the outside line of the fence, unseen by them, until about even with the thicket and when the fellow made his appearance again, the third time, he fired on him, tumbling him off his horse. This brought a shout from our party, when simultaneously with our shout, a battery opened on the extreme left of the ridge, almost right over us, but they were not shooting at us. Still we knew unless we hurried out of there, we would be caught, and immediately proceeded to do so. When we got in sight of the ridge occupied by our cavalry, we discovered the object of their artillery fire, which was shelling a party General Wharton had sent around, leading our horses, to bring them to us. Before we got half way across we found our regiment sweeping around the foot of the mountain, across the valley, up on the enemy's ridge and as soon as they were out of sight in the dense woods on the ridge, they fell into the enemy's infantry behind a stone fence, which poured volleys into them and it is hardly necessary to say, badly scattered them, and they left a number of killed and wounded on the field. In the meantime, General Cheatham and staff had been seen crossing the valley to the point where our regiment was engaged, followed by his strong line of infantry. General Cheatham called to our scattered forces to "take this cavalry out of here and let my people take a hand," which they did as soon as they got within range of this stone fence. This fence was defended by the enemy's infantry at close quarters with clubbed guns and bayonets, but they finally yielded and were driven, inch by inch, off the mountain to their rear. This was the opening of the battle of Perryville and occurred about two o'clock in the evening. Among the dead left temporarily on the field was Captain Mark Evans, shot through the center of the head. The reader will remember that a few days before he saved my life and assisted me in swapping horses with the Federal in the Bardstown fight.

After rallying his forces General Wharton moved around in the rear of this wooded ridge and, while moving parallel with this ridge in the valley beyond, discovered an ordnance train in a lane about a quarter of a mile to our right, and prepared to charge it. Immediately a battery of four pieces opened on us on our flank, compelling us to withdraw, as we were satisfied that this battery was supported by a heavy force of infantry. Under this fire of artillery we had a complete set of fours cut down by one cannon ball or shell that passed through the bodies of four horses, cutting off both legs of one man below the knee, but not injuring the three other men, who mounted behind other comrades and rode off the field. This set of fours was just in front of the set of which I constituted a part and, on the spur of the moment, I stopped with our wounded friend to assist him. When attempting to hand him my canteen, to give him water, my horse pulled back completely out of his reach, preventing giving him water, which I could not throw to him, as the stopper of the canteen was lost, when Jared Gross, seeing our predicament, came back to assist me. Our command, in the meantime, had gone forward into a piece of timber, out of sight of the artillery. When Jared rode up pretty close to me I suggested that we had better keep apart as this artillery had the range on us, and we had barely separated when they fired another shot which cut the side of the mountain and would certainly have got us both if we had failed to separate. We were compelled to leave poor Duncan on the field, where he was afterwards attended by our surgeon and taken to a house and left inside of the enemy's lines the next day. We never heard of him any more, assuming that he died, as the shock was too great, in connection with the loss of blood, for him to survive.

CHAPTER XVI.

I REFUSE TO BECOME A TEAMSTER.

While at Corinth, immediately after the battle of Shiloh, we were ordered to furnish two wagon drivers and called for volunteers, having two wagons to the company. There was not a man in the company that would agree to drive wagons and we were instructed to draw lots, when, with my usual luck, I drew lots to drive wagons, which was a four-mule team; and I had never done any driving before. The other party was Jared Gross, who also objected to driving mules. I told General Wharton that I didn't leave my home and everything I had to come out there and drive a mule team and that I wouldn't and couldn't do so. He said, "Now, Graber, you know you agreed to this drawing and it is not right or fair for you to refuse." I told him that I knew it was mean, but I did not expect that it would fall to my lot to drive this wagon, when he finally told me, "If you do not obey this order I will have to have you court martialed." I told him, "All right, Colonel Wharton, you may punish me as much as you like, but I am not going to drive that wagon."

Some one then proposed to hire a couple of men and pay them fifty dollars a month each, which was done, and Duncan, with another man from Brazoria County, whose name I have forgotten, volunteered to take the job.

After crossing the Tennessee River at Lamb's Ferry, we left our wagons and considerable private baggage with cooking utensils and tents, at Bear Creek. A few days after, the Federal cavalry crossed the river and captured the whole outfit, except the men in charge of the same. This was the last of our luxuries, tents, cooking utensils or wagons never being issued after that, except to our headquarters or the commanding general and his staff, who employed Duncan to drive the headquarters wagon.

Having been engaged in this, and fearing that the war would end and he would have to go home and report he had never been in any engagements, Duncan decided that he must go into the battle of Perryville with us, where he lost his life, as stated.

After our experience with the ordnance train and battery, our command followed in the rear of our infantry line, which slowly, but gradually, drove the enemy until dark, capturing several batteries of fine guns. By one of the batteries we found the body of General Jackson, a Federal general from Kentucky, who, when he found his infantry had abandoned the battery, seemed determined to throw away his life and, single and alone, dashed up to one of our infantry men, cutting at him with his sword, when the man shot and killed him.

After dark we tied our horses in the edge of a woods, to a rail fence which enclosed a large corn field, where the desperate fighting stopped. We then went into the field and secured some corn for our horses. As the most of the corn was destroyed by the lines of battle, we had to pass over a good deal of ground to get sufficient corn for our horses. At the point where I stopped gathering, having secured as many ears of corn as I could carry in my arms, the dead lay so thick I believe I could have stepped from one to the other within a radius of ten or fifteen feet. Among them I noticed the dead body of a magnificent looking man lying on his back with his eyes open, seemingly looking at the starry firmament. Noticing that he wore an officer's suit, I turned up his collar which disclosed two stars, denoting his rank as lieutenant-colonel. I afterwards learned that he commanded a Tennessee regiment in Cheatham's Division.

During the night an armistice was had by mutual consent, for the purpose of taking care of the wounded and burying the dead. We were ordered to destroy the small arms left on the field, which were very thick, by breaking the stocks on the trees, which job we soon abandoned because many of the guns were loaded. The batteries captured by our people were exchanged for our own guns, as we only had horses to carry off the number captured, leaving our inferior guns spiked on the field.

The battle of Perryville, for the number engaged, has always ranked as one of the most desperately fought battles of the war, equal to Shiloh, Chickamauga and others for desperate fighting, and which the respective losses of the two armies fully sustained.

The battle of Perryville proved such a blow to the Federal commander that it made him more cautious in his rapid advance. Our infantry during the night commenced their retreat with the wagon train, artillery and everything belonging to them, moving towards Harrodsburg, where we were met by General Kirby Smith and his army, coming back from Cincinnati. At this point we found a very large amount of pickled pork in barrels, that had been collected for removal with our army, but had to be abandoned and was largely destroyed by our cavalry, still covering the retreat, as heretofore.

The enemy at this point crowded us pretty close and came very near forcing a general engagement again, which no doubt would have proven disastrous to our arms, because they outnumbered us at least four to one. Our cavalry service continued to cover the retreat except with occasional branching out to different points where army supplies were stored, notably

Lebanon, where I was sent with a detail of three others to a man's house by the name of Penick, who had a large plantation and owned a great many negroes. He was said to have a great deal of bacon, which we were instructed to have carried to Lebanon. On arriving at the house I went in and told the gentleman our business. He met us in the hall, joined by his wife and daughter and in answer to our demand that he have his negroes hitch up his wagons and load the meat, he spitefully told us that he had hid out his mules, negroes and bacon and said, "Get it, if you can." In reasoning with him, trying to persuade him that we would certainly find his hidden stuff, he became very insulting, when I finally told him he was taking advantage of us, knowing well that his gray hair and the presence of the ladies would protect him from our resenting his insults, but told him if he had any boys to bring them out and we would settle the matter with them pretty quick. He said, "I have two boys, but they are in the army and if ever they meet you, they will meet you like men." I asked him what branch of the service they were in, when he told me they were in the cavalry. I then told him that we had a cavalry fight a couple of weeks before at Bardstown, where no doubt his boys were engaged, when on his further enquiry about the engagement, I told him how we scattered them all over the country, killing and wounding a great many. The ladies burst into tears and went back into their room, and the old man had nothing more to say about his boys.

I then again tried to persuade him to give us at least one wagonload of bacon, promising him that if he would send his team and a boy to drive it to Lebanon, he would surely have them returned, when he again refused in a spiteful, insulting manner. I told him that we had understood he had some six or eight yoke of work-oxen and in Texas we knew all about handling oxen and we would go into his pasture and drive them up and hitch them to the wagons that were at the house, but this was only a threat. We gave him up as a bad job and when we reached the pike about three miles from there, we met a citizen who told us that Wheeler's cavalry had evacuated Lebanon and burnt all the meat stored there, which we were induced to believe, and decided to ride back to the Harrodsburg Pike and get with our command, which we did.

Our army then continued to retreat, the main part of the army moving towards Crab Orchard, where we struck the Cumberland Gap road, while the army, under Kirby Smith, was struggling over Big Hill, and had still to join the main army at the junction of the roads at Pitman's. The army then moved into the mountains on the Cumberland Gap road, which, owing to the character of the country, was generally restricted to a single wagon track. This stretched out our columns of retreat for perhaps twenty miles or more and cut up the road very badly, frequently causing wagons to stall.

Two infantrymen consequently were detailed with every wagon, of which we had thirty-eight hundred, laden with provisions and valuable stores. This detail of two with each wagon was ordered to assist any wagon that was stalled by taking hold of the wheels, thereby helping the team to pull the wagon out of the rut.

A division commander was detailed every day to take charge of the wagon train and artillery and keep it moving. When a wagon stalled, the whole line of retreat, infantry, wagons and artillery behind it, would have to wait until it would move again, thereby seriously impeding our line of march and causing the cavalry in the rear desperate fighting sometimes to hold off the enemy.

It was reported of General Cheatham, when he had charge of the train, that one of his wagons was stalled, and he put spurs to his horse and rode up the line and reached the wagon. The driver was whipping his mules and the two infantrymen were standing by the roadside, resting on their guns. At the sight of this, he jumped off his horse, took hold of the spokes of the wagon wheel and tried to turn it, but all to no purpose. The two guards still stood resting on their guns. General Cheatham lost his patience and turned around and slapped one of the guards in the face. This happened to be an Irishman, who said, "Be God; if you were not Gineral Cheatham you couldn't do this." General Cheatham pulled off his sword belt, coat and hat and threw them down by the side of the road and said, "Now, there lies General Cheatham and here is Frank Cheatham; now light in." They say that at this invitation the Irishman lit in and got the best of the bargain, of which General Cheatham never made any complaint. The two men then took hold of the wheels in conjunction with General Cheatham, and started up the wagon, and with that the whole line of retreat.

This incident was currently reported and generally believed by all who knew General Cheatham, but I would not be willing to vouch for the same, as it is almost past belief.

After leaving Crab Orchard, General Buell dispensed with his cavalry, as they were unable to cope with ours and moved only with his infantry and artillery in advance. To enter into the details of the rest of this campaign, would require too much space and will only say that the brigade of General Wharton, which always includes the Terry Rangers, in conjunction occasionally with other cavalry, were expected to and did succeed in retarding the pursuit of the enemy, restricting his advance to from six to eight miles a day only, thereby protecting our infantry column, as well as the artillery, ordnance and thirty-eight hundred wagons loaded with valuable army stores. On this retreat the infantry were called on only one time to fire a gun. We met the enemy in a general engagement at Mount

Vernon, Barren Valley, Rocky Hill, Bushy Mound, Wild Cat, Pitman's Road, Little Rock, Castle River and many other points, inflicting on them considerable loss. This mountain service on the part of the Rangers proved a most severe tax on their endurance, on account of being deprived of rations. At one time, for nearly two days, we depended on picking up raw corn left in the camps of artillery and wagons, where the horses and mules had been fed. A number of times, after fighting all day long, we had to go out into the hills ten or twelve miles to find forage for our horses before we could retire to get a little rest. Our camping places were frequently by the light of the enemy's fires.

To give the reader a better idea of the valuable service we rendered, I will quote an order issued by General Wheeler, read to us at Cumberland Gap, October 23, 1862.

GENERAL ORDER NUMBER THREE:

"Soldiers of the Cavalry Corps, Army of Mississippi:

"The autumn campaign in Kentucky is over, your arduous duties, as the advance and rear guard, for the present, are finished. Your gallantry in action, your cheerful endurance in suffering from hunger, fatigue and exposure, render you worthy of all commendation. For nearly two months you have scarcely been for a moment without the range of the enemy's musketry. In more than twenty pitched fights, many of which lasted throughout the day, you have successfully combated largely superior numbers of the enemy's troops of all arms. Hovering continually near the enemy, you have engaged in no less than one hundred skirmishes. Upon the memorable field of Perryville, alone and unsupported, you engaged and held in check during the entire action, at least two infantry divisions of the opposing army. By your gallant charges on that day you completely dispersed and routed a vastly superior force of the enemy's cavalry, driving them in confusion under their artillery and infantry supports, capturing in hand-to-hand conflicts many prisoners, forces and arms. Your continuous contact with the enemy has taught you to repose without fear under his guns, to fighting wherever found and to quietly make your bivouac by the light of his camp fires. On this continued series of combats and brilliant charges, many great men have fallen. We mourn their loss. We commend their valor. Let us emulate their soldierly virtues.

"JOSEPH WHEELER,

"Chief of Cavalry."

CHAPTER XVII.

OMISSIONS IN PRECEDING CHAPTERS

After leaving Cumberland Gap our army again moved into Middle Tennessee, with headquarters at Murfreesboro. Our cavalry in the advance camped near La Vergne, at Nolandsville and Triune. The enemy concentrated at Nashville, from whence they sent out foraging parties, supported by large infantry forces with which we had daily engagements, restricting their foraging within a small area of country. At Nolandsville, where General Wharton made his headquarters, we camped nearly a month, when Lieutenant Decherd was instructed to select about fifteen men and cross the Cumberland Mountain, for the purpose of buying fresh horses, which were very much needed. I was ordered to go with this party.

While camped near Winchester, Tennessee, intending to cross the mountain the next day, we heard the distant roaring of the guns of the battle of Murfreesboro, which was not expected so soon when we left the command, and which proved a great disappointment to our party, as we felt that every man was needed for such an event. We, therefore, hastened back to the army, which we found evacuating Murfreesboro, and reported. Of the Rangers' part in that great battle I will not mention in this, as that is of record in the general reports of General Bragg and others, and will only say that they fully sustained their character as one of the leading regiments in this army, capturing prisoners, artillery, wagon trains, etc., and finally covering the retreat of the army off the field.

Our army then continued its retreat through Shelbyville to Tullahoma, our cavalry still operating on the north side of Elk River. Before crossing Elk River a courier reached General Wheeler from General Forrest, after Wheeler had crossed the bridge, requesting him to hold the bridge until he (Forrest) could cross with his command. Promptly on receipt of this information, General Wheeler, with a portion of his command, notably the Fourth Alabama Cavalry, recrossed the bridge to the north side, determined to hold the same until General Forrest had crossed with his command. Before Forrest reached Shelbyville, however, General Stanley, with a heavy force of cavalry, outnumbering Wheeler's little force ten to one, charged and forced them back across the river, cutting General Wheeler off from the bridge. General Wheeler spurred his horse to the bank and over it, into the dangerous river, which had been swollen by excessive rains, making a leap of not less than twenty feet, with Stanley's cavalry shooting after him and continuously firing on him until he reached the opposite bank. This was, perhaps, the most miraculous escape he had during the war.

Before reaching Tullahoma, a Captain Gordon, who had distinguished himself near Bardstown, where he held in check a whole brigade of the enemy's infantry on the Bloomfield Road for a whole day with only twenty men, was ordered to select twenty men from the Rangers and enter Kentucky, for the purpose of gaining information of the disposition of the enemy's forces, preparatory to a general raid by our cavalry. The history of this trip, which resulted in my being wounded and captured and held a prisoner just one year, lacking a day, I have already recorded, and by an oversight, it crept into this history ahead of the proper time.

Recurring to the hard service sustained by us in the mountains between Crab Orchard and Cumberland Gap: The last night we were on picket duty our company had dwindled down to seven men and I happened to be on vidette with a messmate, John Cochran. Just at daylight, when the enemy usually made its appearance, we were relieved by two others of the command and when we reached the reserve picket, discovering a grassy spot in the middle of the road, I told Cochran I must try to steal a little nap, and laid down on this grassy spot, holding my horse by the bridle, when I was awakened, only about ten minutes after, by Cochran stooping down from his horse and jabbing me with his pistol. The reserve picket had formed a line across the road, just a little back of where I was sleeping and were firing on the enemy's advancing skirmish line, the noise of which failed to awake me and it was only his prodding me with the end of his six-shooter that got me awake. I had just time enough to swing on to my horse and get out of there. Here Cochran's prediction, frequently made, that he would bet Graber would wake up some fine morning with a Yankee bayonet sticking in him, came very near being verified. I merely mention this to give the reader a fair idea of our complete exhaustion for the want of sleep, continuous hunger and arduous duties.

CHAPTER XVIII

GENERAL JOHNSTON'S FAILURE TO STRIKE—SHERMAN

Recurring to my service in Captain Britton's company, acting as escort to General Hood at Dalton, Georgia, where I described the meeting of the several generals with General Hood at his headquarters in the rear of Railroad Gap: On our return to camp that night after supper, Captain Britton suggested he should go up to headquarters and pump Major Sellars on the meaning of the meeting that morning. He reported on his return from a visit to headquarters that General Mower, commanding Hooker's old corps, had moved down to Snake Creek Gap during the day, which was located about nineteen miles in our rear and about ten miles west of Dalton.

General Hood plead with General Johnston that morning for permission to move out of his works through Railroad and Rocky Face Gaps with his corps and defeat Sherman's Army before Mower could return to reinforce them. Captain Britton said that he would bet our army would be in full retreat that night, falling back to Resaca, which prediction was verified, as, by daylight next morning, our infantry and artillery were engaged with the enemy at Resaca, where we came very near losing a large part of our army by having their retreat cut off.

Had General Johnston yielded to General Hood's plan, there is no question but what he could have destroyed Sherman's Army; here was a golden opportunity lost by General Johnston, and was the beginning of the downfall of the Confederacy.

After about two weeks I succeeded in getting a horse with the regiment and continued with the regiment during the whole of the North Georgia campaign, the details of which I will not venture to insert, as they will be recorded fully in a history now being written by Colonel Ben F. Weems of Houston.

During the siege of Atlanta General Sherman started out two cavalry expeditions, one under a General Stoneman to move around the right wing of our army, and one under General McCook around the left wing of our army, both to unite on the Macon line of railroad, and to destroy and tear up the same, then move on to Andersonville and release our prisoners. Had these expeditions proven a success, with an army of probably twenty-five or thirty thousand released prisoners turned loose in our rear, it would have wound up the Confederacy. At Atlanta, General Hood took command of our army, not exceeding thirty-six thousand muskets and, to use his words, "This army through General Johnston's retreating from Dalton, had become an army of laborers by day and travelers by night," while the army at Dalton, including Polk's corps at Rome, numbered eighty-six thousand muskets, and was better equipped and organized than any army the West had ever had. The North Georgians and Tennesseans, largely constituting this army, with their families inside of the enemy's lines, were anxious and eager for an advance, and there is no question of doubt had General Hood been permitted to give battle at Dalton, our army would have recaptured Tennessee and Kentucky.

Referring back to the enemy's cavalry expedition out of Atlanta: General Stoneman, with a large part of his force, and a lot of convalescents in the town of Macon, Georgia, were captured near Macon by General Iverson, commanding Georgia cavalry. General Wheeler with our brigade, Ross' and Roddy's, forced McCook to a general engagement on the evening of the second day between Noonan and Philpott's Ferry, where they finally surrendered, with the exception of himself and staff, and Colonel Brownlow and some other line officers, who swam the river that night and made their escape.

General Wheeler issued an order that night for no man to cross the river after these fellows, when I, with several of our regiment, decided there must be some mistake about it and crossed the river to try to catch these fellows, specially anxious to capture Colonel Brownlow. Immediately after crossing the river we found a quartermaster's clerk, so he represented himself to be, left wounded at a house. His wound, however, was not very serious we thought. He had on a magnificent pair of boots, which just about fitted me and I had been unable to secure boots, only wearing shoes, when I proposed to him to exchange with me, which he readily did. While he was pulling off his boots, the lady of the house came in and opened a tirade of abuse on me for taking a poor, wounded man's boots. I told her I had but just come out of a Federal prison where they treated us worse than that and I was satisfied that my shoes would prove more comfortable to this man at Andersonville, than the boots, to which our prisoner agreed. We then continued our pursuit on the main road to Wedowee, the county seat of Randolph County, Alabama, occasionally taking a prisoner, whom we would turn over to reliable citizens, to be taken to West Point where we had a garrison. We were unable to secure many prisoners, probably not exceeding eight or ten, as those afoot would hear us coming in the road and dart into the brush, while their officers impressed every horse they could lay their hands on and soon outdistanced us with their fresh horses.

At Wedowee we found a tanyard, where I purchased a lot of good leather, sufficient to rig a Texas saddle. We had some men detailed to make saddles, who were experts in such work and moved down with the army as fast as it retreated. Our first shop was at Ackworth, Georgia, where they did a good deal of work, but were prevented from turning out anything extensive ever after, for the reason they were unable to get leather. I paid one hundred and twenty-five dollars for the leather I got at this tanyard. Colonel Harrison promised me, after my return from prison, that if I would furnish the leather he would have rigged for me one of the finest saddles that could be made, which was the inducement for me to carry this roll of leather on my horse's back.

Going back into the town from the tanyard, we stopped at a hotel to get some dinner. This was one of the ordinary country hotels with a porch in front and large square columns under the porch. While eating dinner, I had a seat at the end of the table where I could see out on the street. The hotel was located somewhat under the hill, away from the square, when I discovered Carter Walker, one of our party, who had finished dinner, behind one of the posts with his pistol out, talking to some one on the street towards the courthouse. Having his pistol out suggested to me that there was trouble ahead, so I jumped up and told the boys to come on. As we got out on the porch we discovered about fifteen or twenty men on their horses near the courthouse, with one of them talking to Carter Walker, about fifty yards distant from us. As soon as we came out, he retired and when he got back with his crowd, said something to them and immediately they wheeled and left town. This proved to be a party of bushwhackers, who were not anxious for a fight with us. We now decided to return and when a few miles from town, we heard of an old gentleman, whose name I have forgotten, the only Rebel citizen in that section, whom we decided to go and see and get some information from.

After reaching his house and getting acquainted, we decided, on his urgent request, to stay with him that night, as we were very tired, as were also our horses, and we did not suppose there was any great need for our services immediately after the destruction of the enemy's cavalry. This old gentleman had had considerable trouble with his Tory neighbors, who came to his house several nights and opened fire on him, which he, his old lady and his daughter, a barefooted girl of eighteen, returned with their squirrel rifles through port holes cut in the logs of his house.

On the information of our old friend, we decided to visit the house of a Tory neighbor of his, across the mountain, who belonged to the Tory regiment in camp at Rome, which we did. Riding up to the house in blue overcoats, we called for a drink of water, when a lady invited us in, supposing that we were Federal soldiers. In our talk with them, there being two other ladies in the house, we represented that we were Federal spies on our way to Andersonville to make arrangements about the escape of our prisoners there, which created quite an interest with these women, who told us that a large number of young men of the neighborhood belonged to the First Federal Alabama Cavalry, stationed near Rome, and quite a number of them were expected home pretty soon on a furlough. We then arranged with them to tell their boys about our visit and tell them that we expected to return there in about ten days, as we would probably need their assistance and we wanted to confer with them. Our idea was that we would return there at that time, with our company, and capture the whole outfit.

After making complete arrangements, we started back towards Philpott's Ferry, where we again recrossed the Chattahoochie and, on our arrival at Noonan, found that Wheeler had moved over to Covington, on the Augusta road.

Riding all that day in a drizzling rain, we called at a house for the purpose of getting some feed for our horses and something to eat for ourselves. Night had already set in. We asked the gentleman if he could take care of us that night, give us a place to sleep on the floor, as we never slept in a bed, and get something to eat for our horses and ourselves. His answer was, "Certainly, gentlemen; light and come in." I told him before we got off our horses that we were about out of money and did not have enough, perhaps, to pay our fare, when he stated that if his wife had anything left from supper we could have it and he would give us some shattered corn for our horses. We, of course, didn't feel very comfortable under such liberality, but decided to stay, nevertheless, and sleep down in his barn, some distance from the house.

While we were waiting for his wife to gather what she had left from supper, he asked us if we were that command the other day that fired on the Federals when they were tearing up the railroad near his house. I told him that we were, and he said, "They were in my pasture trying to catch my horses, when they heard the guns fire and you ought to have seen those devils run." When we went in to supper we found a little piece of cornbread and a little butter, all they had left from supper, so the woman stated, not enough to satisfy one man's hunger. We did not sit down at the table, didn't touch anything they had to offer us, and went down to the crib to get the shattered corn for our horses, which he consented for us to take, fed our horses and laid down to rest for the balance of the night. Next morning we got up early and without going to the house, proceeded on the road towards Covington. Here now, was a fair illustration of the want of appreciation of a Confederate soldier, with a selfish lot of people, whom we occasionally met. Rest assured it was very discouraging to us. The idea of coming all the way from Texas to fight for and protect these people! He had told us that we saved his horses from capture by engaging the enemy near his house; you can imagine our disgust at such treatment. We now proceeded on the Covington road. When about two miles from there we came to a large, white house, a magnificent place, and rode up to the gate. A man about twenty-five years old, well dressed, wearing a white starched shirt, the first we had seen in a long time, came out to the gate. When within twenty feet of us, espying the leather on my horse's back, tied to the rear of the saddle, he called out, "I want that leather." I said, "If you need it any worse than I do, you are welcome to it." He said he did, he wanted to make shoes out of it. I told him that I wanted to make a saddle out if it, to ride to keep Federals off of him, when he insisted that he needed it worse. I then told him that we wanted some breakfast and some feed for our hoses. He said, "All right, gentlemen; light and come in." Before getting down I said, "I had better tell you that we are nearly out of money, not enough to pay for breakfast and feed, away from our command unexpectedly, but as soon as we get with them and we have an opportunity, we will send it to you." He stated that he couldn't afford to feed us without pay, that the armies had been around him for some time and had nearly eaten him out of house and home. I told him that he needn't say anything more, that we didn't want anything he had, although our horses were hungry, as well as ourselves. As we rode off he called after us, "I'll feed you for that leather," thus adding insult, but we decided not to notice him.

About three miles further down the road we came to another house, a somewhat humble cottage, and stopped to make some inquiry, when a lady came out to the gate and we asked how far down the road we could find a house where we could get something to eat for ourselves and feed for our horses. She asked us if we had tried at the big, white house we had passed on the road. We told her that we had and were refused because we had no money. She then insisted that we come in and partake of such as she had, telling us that she had very little left, as the commissary from Atlanta had visited her and taken all the corn she had, except five barrels, which in Georgia, means twenty-five bushels. This, she and her two daughters had made with their own hands, her husband being in the Virginia army. She then told us about this man at the big, white house, who had never been in the army, but had an exemption on pretense of working in a saltpetre cave and had never had any forage taken by the commissary from Atlanta, as he had protection papers, so she called them, from his general at Atlanta. I merely mention these cases to show you the condition at that time, of the State of Georgia, the worthy people submitting patriotically to all manner of abuse by some of our army officials, while some of the rich, through nefarious practices, escaped the weight of war. Thanking this lady for her kind offer, which we could not afford to accept, we continued on this road and two miles further on struck a large cornfield with tempting roasting ears and decided to stop, build a fire, dry our clothes and roast corn for our meal, feeding our horses on the same, in moderation. We had to build our fire of rails taken off the fence and very soon were enjoying our roasting ears and the warm fire, being somewhat chilled by the rain. The proprietor of the place came up the road and, judging from his manner and looks, was pretty mad, when he said, "Gentlemen, if you had come to the house I would have gladly given you a good meal and fed your horses, rather than to see the destruction of my rails." I told him that we didn't believe it, that we had tried several places up on the road and were refused because we had no money and he, no doubt, noting that we were in no mood for argument, decided that he had better say no more. We then proceeded on our road to Covington. When on our arrival there we found that Wheeler, with all the cavalry having horses fit for service, had gone on a raid into Middle Tennessee, by way of Dalton, tearing up the railroad in Sherman's rear for many miles, and finally entering Middle Tennessee, returning by way of Mussels Shoals, rejoining the army below Atlanta.

After the battle of Jonesboro, Hood started on his fatal Middle Tennessee campaign, his march to the Tennessee River being covered by our cavalry, making a feint at Rome, Georgia, to which point General Sherman had followed, confidently expecting to give Hood battle at Gadsden and never suspecting his move towards the Tennessee River. While concentrating his army at Rome, Harrison's Brigade, under Colonel Harrison, commanding our regiment, made a feint on Rome by dismounting, hiding our horses in the rear in the woods, out of sight, and advanced on the outer works of Rome, preceded by a line of skirmishers. For this purpose, not having our battle flag with us, we used a new flag, sent us from Nashville, made by a couple of young ladies from their silk dresses, with the name of Terry's Texas Rangers worked in gold letters and some Latin words on the other side. After skirmishing with Sherman's infantry a short time, we retired down the valley, which at this point was perhaps a couple of miles wide, from the hills to the bottoms.

Falling back that night some six or eight miles, we struck a wooded ridge, running from the hills to the bottom, perhaps nearly three miles long. This ridge overlooked the country in front towards Rome, several miles. General Sherman coming out in person with a corps of his infantry, expecting to give Hood battle the next morning, discovered there was only a handful of cavalry in his front, which was Harrison's Brigade, and which he was specially anxious to capture. For this purpose he sent a heavy cavalry force, perhaps three times our number, into our rear, flanking our position by moving through the hills on our left, then occupying nearly every road in our rear, for eight or ten miles. During the night we received reinforcements of Pillow's Brigade, a new command, which had been in only one engagement, at La Fayette, Georgia, where they were badly handled, causing the loss of a great many killed and wounded and in consequence, they were a little demoralized. We also received a section of artillery, two pieces, under a lieutenant, whose name I do not remember.

This artillery was stationed on a hill to the left of our position, under an old gin house.

Immediately after taking position the artillery opened on the enemy, a heavy line of battle making its appearance in the edge of the woods, about a mile distant. The Rangers were kept mounted, drawn up near this old gin house, supporting the battery, when all the rest of the two brigades had been dismounted with their horses immediately in the rear, out of sight of the enemy.

Very soon a courier from the right of our line, dashed up to Colonel Harrison and reported that the enemy were flanking us, down in the bottom, with a heavy force. Harrison abused him, told him to go back and tell his colonel if he sent him another such message he would have him court martialed, but very soon a lieutenant dashed up from the extreme right of our line, reporting the enemy advancing in the bottom, and about to outflank us, when Colonel Harrison decided to ride down in the rear of our line and ascertain conditions for himself. Immediately the enemy raised a shout and charged. The lieutenant of the battery, concluding that his guns were in danger of being captured, limbered up and ran down to the road, where he met Colonel Harrison returning and was by him ordered to unlimber and open again on the enemy, when he succeeded in firing one shot and was sabered right over his guns by the enemy's cavalry. In the meantime, through some misapprehension of orders, the Alabama Brigade broke for their horses, followed by the balance of our brigade, when our regiment was ordered to charge their cavalry, which we did, striking them on their flank, using our six-shooters, to which they paid no attention, simply calling out, "Clear the road for the Fourth Regulars!" This Fourth Regulars was commanded by a Captain McIntyre from Brenham, Texas, who was in the United States Army, a lieutenant, when the war broke out, having just graduated at West Point.

It is hardly necessary to say that finding the enemy's cavalry in our rear for a great many miles, resulted in a general stampede, everybody trying to make their escape out of it. In recording this engagement I regret to have to mention the loss of our beautiful flag which, encased in a rubber cover, slipped off its staff and was found by a Major Weiler, commanding a battalion of the Seventeenth Mounted Indiana Infantry, and after many years, returned to us at Dallas, Texas, by Governor Mount and staff, instructed to do so by a joint resolution of the Indiana Legislature, in response to a memorial, drawn up and sent by me.

In this engagement the Terry Rangers lost no prisoners, had only a few wounded and none killed, while the Alabamians' loss was quite heavy in prisoners and the balance of Harrison's Brigade had very few men taken prisoners. I made my escape by crossing the big road, being joined by about eight or ten Alabamians, one of whom was shot in the fleshy part of the thigh, which somewhat demoralized him, when he called on me, "Texas, can you take us out of here?" I told him, "Yes, follow me; I'll take you out." I struck out straight for the river bottom, the Federal cavalry not following us, and when out of sight of the main road, in a little branch bottom, I called a halt and told the men my plan of trying to swim the river, as the road ahead of us seemed to be occupied for many miles, judging by the scattered firing a great distance ahead of us. The wounded man straightened up in the saddle and asked me if I was an officer. I told him, "No," and he said that he was a lieutenant and would take command of the squad. I told him he could take command of his own men, but he couldn't command me, and told his men, "Now, all of you boys that want to go out with me, come on," when they all followed me, including the lieutenant.

Reaching the high ground on the other side of the branch, I discovered a house, with a lone cavalry-man at the front gate, and, getting a little nearer, I recognized him as one Joe Harris, of our company, who was well acquainted in that section, having married, near Cedartown, the daughter of a Doctor Richardson, just on the other side of the river. He suggested to me that he knew of a batteau about seven miles this side of Rome; that we go up there, put our saddles and equipments into the boat, swim our horses across, then go to Doctor Richardson and get a good dinner; to which I, of course, readily consented. On our way to this batteau, following the river in the bottom, we struck hundreds of Alabamians trying to find a crossing place. These men we took along with us and when we reached the boat we were the first ones to cross, leaving the Alabamians there to cross as fast as they were able. Joe and I then rode to Doctor Richardson's, about ten or fifteen miles, and by three o'clock sat down to a sumptuous dinner. Here we stayed all night and the next morning recrossed the river, finally striking the main Gadsden road and finding our stampeded forces gathering at some gap, the name of which I have forgotten. Here we met General Wheeler, with the balance of his command. We then moved down to the town of Gadsden, where we recrossed the river and spent several days resting our horses and ourselves.

General Hood, in the meantime, with his army, crossed the Tennessee River, and General Sherman returned to Atlanta, leaving Thomas' Corps to follow Hood into Middle Tennessee. Wheeler and his cavalry returned to below Atlanta, where we struck Sherman's forces moving in the direction of Macon, Georgia, by way of Augusta to Savannah. We then had daily engagements with Kilpatrick's cavalry, often driving them into their infantry. Sherman used his cavalry to forage for the army, depending altogether on the country for his commissary. To enter into detail of the many engagements had on this trip would occupy too much time and space. Our service was largely, as stated, to keep his cavalry from foraging, burning and destroying the country. In connection with this I would mention an incident at Macon:

I was at a blacksmith's shop with a comrade by the name of Freeman, who was about seven years my senior in age. While waiting to get our horses shod we heard artillery, supported by small arms, open at our works, about a mile across the river. We immediately mounted our horses and dashed over there and just as we got in sight of the roadway through the breastworks we witnessed a lone trooper of Kilpatrick's cavalry coming up the road through the works, having his horse shot just as he reached inside. His horse fell on his leg, from which position he was trying to extricate himself and was about to be shot by an excited militia of young and old men, who had never been under fire before, when Jim put spurs to his horse and with his pistol raised, dashed up to where this man lay under his horse, and drove off the excited militia, I, of course, following him. He called up a lieutenant, asked his name, company and regiment; told him to take charge of that prisoner and see that he was well treated, that he would hold him personally responsible for his safety, and immediately wheeled his horse, I following him, and returned to town without giving the lieutenant a chance to ask questions. On our return I asked Jim Freeman his reasons for doing as he did, risking his own life, by being shot by the excited militia, in order to save this Federal. He answered, "He is a brother Mason." I asked him if he ever met him before. He said, "No, but I saw him give the grand hailing sign of distress, which obligates a Mason to save the life of a brother, at the risk of his own." Here was a beautiful illustration of the work of Masonry, and I told Jim Freeman the first opportunity I had of joining the Masons, if I lived through the war, I intended to be one, which resolution I carried out, joining the Masons at Rusk, Texas.

General Kilpatrick with about four thousand picked cavalry, armed with Spencer repeating rifles, which they were expert in handling, was detailed by General Sherman, after leaving Jonesboro, to forage and destroy property, under pretext of burning gin houses. They also burned a great many fine houses, the homes of rich people, on their line of march, and got their operations down to a system. He would have his engineers select a strong position along the line of march, fortify it with rails and logs and place about one thousand men in such works. His engineers then would advance some two or three miles and direct another line of fortifications in a similar manner; the balance of his command would scatter out on both flanks inside of these lines, collect provisions and forage, burn gin houses and homes, the latter of which, of course, were plundered before being consigned to the flames. In this manner he continued his operations to very near the coast.

CHAPTER XIX

GEORGIA SERVICE—A NEGRO'S PREFERENCE—A HAZARDOUS UNDERTAKING.

At this time General Wheeler would detail a fresh brigade every morning to take the advance and move on the enemy.

When a few miles from Buck Head Creek, Harrison's Brigade was placed in advance. Striking the first line of works, we formed a line and prepared to charge, when General Felix Robertson was seen immediately to the right of our line on a magnificent horse. At the time, he was acting as chief of staff to General Wheeler, and he gave the order to forward, waving his hat and led the charge. We drove them out of their works and it became a running fight down the road with General Robertson leading, having a better horse than the balance of us. We soon struck a branch where the enemy had lined up on the other side, and they poured a galling fire into our advance. General Robertson had his arm badly shattered by a bullet and being alone drew his horse to one side at the ford of this branch. When I saw him he appeared deathly pale, reeling in his saddle, and a couple of the men behind me started over to assist him, but he called to them, "Never mind me, boys; crowd 'em, crowd 'em," which we did, and again started them on the run. They made another stand across Buck Head Creek near the church and set fire to the bridge, covering the fire with a piece of artillery. Wheeler then sent down a few men with long-range guns, dismounted, who soon drove the artillery away. We then repaired the bridge floor with benches out of the church and were soon across the creek, after them, with the Third Arkansas in advance.

As we were riding rapidly in pursuit, General Wheeler passing our column to reach the advance called to us, saying, "We've got them this time; Dibrell is in the rear." General Dibrell commanded Tennessee cavalry. We soon got into an old sedge field, an open country for several miles, where Kilpatrick had established a fortified camp, built a line of breastworks perhaps two miles wide, his left flank touching the road.

The Third Arkansas had formed a line of battle and was charging the breastworks perhaps two hundred yards ahead of our regiment, which emerged from the woods in columns of fours, moving rapidly to the support of the Third Arkansas. The enemy had planted four pieces of artillery in the road on our right, which poured a galling fire into the Third Arkansas, as well as our flank. The Third Arkansas finally reached the breastworks under a galling fire of four thousand Spencer rifles and drove the gunners away from their artillery, thereby silencing the same, but they were unable to cross the works and not being supported promptly, had to withdraw. The reason of our failure to support promptly was that when we reached about half way across the open, an order came to us through Adjutant Billy Sayers for the Rangers to file to the right into the road. This divided our regiment, a part continuing ahead, the other part moving into the road and, as soon as we struck the road, a hail of grape and cannister swept it and drove us into the thick woods across the road and finally forced us to give up the attack, which was most unfortunate, as the Third Arkansas lost a good many men. Our regiment lost a few, too, and nothing was accomplished. General Dibrell was seen in our left front in the woods, unable to strike Kilpatrick in the rear on account of not being able to cross the creek. General Wheeler now brought up his entire force, making disposition of them for a final charge on Kilpatrick's flank and rear, as well as in front, and when we moved forward we found the bird had flown; Kilpatrick had abandoned his works and fled.

We next had quite a severe engagement with the enemy's cavalry near Griswoldville, said to have been one of the most beautiful towns in Georgia, which the enemy had burned. As soon as we caught up with them we charged and drove them into their infantry, which proved in heavy force and forced us to retire.

At Waynesboro, Georgia, we had considerable fighting in order to save Augusta, Georgia, which had one of the largest arsenals in the Confederacy and no doubt was a tempting prize for General Sherman's torch.

General Braxton Bragg happened to be in Augusta, when he conceived the idea of resorting to a ruse, which proved quite successful. He called up General Wheeler by telegraph at Waynesboro and instructed him when he was forced to give up the town, to leave the telegraph office intact, but give it the appearance of having been abandoned precipitately, then advise him promptly when the enemy entered town. Waiting a reasonable time for the enemy to take charge of the telegraph office, General Bragg called General Wheeler, when a Federal officer answered. General Bragg said, "General Wheeler, hold Waynesboro at all hazards. Longstreet's corps is arriving. I will take the field in person tomorrow. Signed, Braxton Bragg." This had the desired effect. General Sherman, satisfied he would have to give battle before Augusta was surrendered, decided he had better pass by and move on to Savannah as fast as possible. There is no question but this ruse saved Augusta, Georgia, though General Wheeler with his corps put up a strong defense, never permitting the enemy to cross Brier Creek, which was between them and Augusta.

About ten or twelve years after the war, when General Sherman was a resident of St. Louis, he gave an interview on the reason he spared Augusta, Georgia. This had been a subject of discussion by historians and especially friends of the North and was frequently attributed to General Sherman having relatives living in Augusta, Georgia. Another story was that Mrs. Lincoln, through a relative or friend, had stored in Augusta a large amount of cotton. There were various other stories, which General Sherman finally set at rest, giving his reasons for sparing the city. He claimed that one of his officers intercepted a telegram from General Bragg to General Wheeler at Waynesboro, instructing him to hold Waynesboro at all hazards, that Longstreet's corps was arriving and he would take personal command the next day. He further stated that on account of his depleted commissary, having to depend on the country for the rations of his army, he was in no condition to give battle, satisfied that Bragg would defend Augusta to the last, therefore passed it by and hastened to the coast. "But if the people of Augusta think that I spared their city through any love or affection for them, if the President will give me permission, I will take a hundred thousand of my bummers and go down and burn it now." I read this interview in a St. Louis paper.

When near Savannah, Georgia, the place having been evacuated by our forces, who crossed the river at Pocatalego, Wheeler's cavalry was ordered to cross the Savannah River at a point about fifteen miles above Savannah. For this purpose we had only one steamboat, and Harrison's Brigade was ordered to cross last, necessitating our camping in the river bottom for several days, during which time details were sent out of our brigade to collect provisions, as we were without commissary. I had charge the second day of a small detail, and after riding about twenty miles, we scattered out, each man to bring in as much as possible. On my return to camp that evening late, without having succeeded in securing anything, only a piece of cornbread and a slice of bacon for myself, I was feeling disgusted. When about a mile from our camp, following a well-beaten path, I spied a negro man on another path crossing the one I was on and when within a few yards of me, I stopped him and asked if he couldn't tell me where there was something to eat, telling him that I had ridden all day long, trying to get something for our command and had signally failed.

The country through which we had passed for several days is the greatest sweet potato country perhaps in the South; large fields all over the country had been devoted to sweet potatoes, which had fallen a ready prey to Sherman's army and the whole country seemed to be eaten out. I told this negro, after he told me where he lived, about a half mile from there, that I was satisfied he knew where there were sweet potatoes and where there was corn for our horses. He assured me he did not and said that the

Federals had taken everything that his old master had and didn't leave him a thing. I continued to talk with him, trying to arouse his sympathy, told him of our poor fellows not having had anything to eat for several days and I had been riding all day long without securing anything, thereby working on his sympathy. Finally he broke down and said, "Young Marster, if I were to tell you where there are sweet potatoes, old marster would kill me." I told him that his old master never would know anything about it, and he finally said he didn't think it was right, that his old master had given these Yankees everything they wanted, had plenty of potatoes left and refused to give our own folks anything at all. "Now," he said, "if you will strike across this way," pointing in the direction of his house, entering a lane leading to the house, "about a hundred and fifty yards this side of the house, on the left across the fence, you will find some haystack poles standing, with a lot of shattered hay in the lot and if you will dig down about two feet you will strike more potatoes than you will need for several days. Up the river, in the bottom, about two miles, you will find a couple of pens of corn, enough to feed your horses for several days." He had just finished telling me, when I noticed an old man, who proved to be his master, coming our way, and as soon as the negro saw him he said, "Fo' Gawd, marster; there he is now; he'll kill me; he'll kill me." "No," I said "he will not; he never will know that you told me; you stand perfectly still and don't get scared." I jerked out my pistol and threw it down on him, telling him within hearing of his old master, that if he didn't tell me where there was something to eat, I would kill him, and the old man called, "Let that man alone; he don't know where there is anything to eat; there is nothing on the place, the Federals just took everything I had." I still insisted on killing the negro if he didn't tell me where there was something to eat, and finally let him off, satisfying the old man that he hadn't told me anything.

As soon as I reached camp I told Colonel Harrison to get out a detail of fifty men, with sacks to carry potatoes in, when he ordered Major Pearrie, our commissary, to get out the detail and follow my instructions. I told Pearrie that I was satisfied the people at the house about a half mile from there had plenty of potatoes, but did not tell him the source of my information, determined not to tell anybody. When we moved up the lane near the house. Major Pearrie halted us, went to the house to talk to the old man and negotiate for the potatoes, when the old man satisfied him there were no potatoes on the place. In the meantime I had no trouble in finding the lot just as the negro had described to me and when the major returned and ordered us, "About face; move back to camp; there is nothing to be had," I dismounted, crossed the fence into the lot and commenced digging with my hands and in about two feet, struck potatoes, then called to the men to come over with their sacks, which, it is hardly necessary to say, we filled up to the top. We thought we left potatoes enough to last the old man and his family for another year, and perhaps more. We then sent up the river bottom and found the corn, on which we fed our horses. Here is another instance of the attachment of the negro to our own people, his sympathy for us controlling his actions, and I always regretted not taking this negro along with us, fearing perhaps that his old master might have suspected him of giving us information about these potatoes and corn.

After crossing the river and reaching Pocatalego, we found General Hardee and General McLaws, with the infantry out of Savannah and also artillery organizations, which were turned into infantry. General McLaws made a request on General Wheeler for a company of cavalry, preferring a company of Texas Rangers, to scout and act as escort for him, when Company B, to which I belonged, was detailed for this purpose.

One night, Captain King, inspector general on McLaws' staff, came down to our campfire and requested me to accompany him on a ride across the swamp, to find Wheeler's cavalry, which I consented to do. We proceeded into the swamp on a corduroy road, the night being one of the darkest we had ever been out in, the only light onto the road was the sky appearing between the tall trees on both sides, which governed us in keeping about the middle of the road and kept us from riding off the logs into the deep mud and water. After riding perhaps a half mile, expecting every minute to be fired on by Sherman's advance pickets, our horses necessarily making a great deal of noise by stumbling over the logs, Captain King stopped and asked did I not think one of us could get through easier than both, as it would reduce the noise considerably. I told him that it certainly would. He then asked me if I would carry a written order to General Wheeler, which was for Wheeler's cavalry not to fail to cross the swamp that night in order to be on hand by daylight in the morning, when General Hardee expected an attack by the enemy's infantry. I told Captain King that I would carry the order, which he asked me to show every brigade commander that I might find, until I reached General Wheeler. Captain King then returned to General McLaws' camp, as he would be needed the next morning.

I rode through the swamp, crossed the bridge and after about a twenty-mile ride, found Wheeler's cavalry, first striking a Georgia brigade, to a colonel of which I read the order, when he immediately ordered his brigade to saddle up; the next I struck Harrison's brigade, who also followed suit; the next I struck Colonel Ashby's headquarters, commanding Tennesseans. I found him lying on a pallet in front of a fireplace, surrounded by his staff, all asleep. I showed him the order; after reading it and noticing that I was wet, having ridden in the rain part of the time, he made me step up to the fire, then after drying my clothes, take his pallet and sleep until it was time to cross the swamp, his command being very near the swamp. He promised me that he would send the dispatch direct to General Wheeler, who was not far off and would have me awakened when the last were about to cross, thereby giving me as much sleep as possible. This kind treatment of Colonel Ashby's was much appreciated, but was not a surprise to me, having known him as one of the most gallant officers and gentlemen I ever got acquainted with.

Some time after the war, meeting Lieutenant Fulkerson, the commander of our company, at Bryan, Texas, he told me that General McLaws told him a few days after this engagement that Graber's ride that night, finding Wheeler's cavalry, who crossed the swamp in time to cover the retreat of our infantry, no doubt saved our little army, only about seven or eight thousand strong. This army was composed of the infantry and artillery that were stationed at Savannah and Charleston and at different points along our line of retreat and was joined at Bentonville with the remnant of Hood's army, out of Tennessee, after the disastrous Hood campaign in that State.

While this humble individual service was nothing extraordinary, nothing more than performed by individual members of our company frequently, yet the result was such that I always had cause to feel proud of it. I forgot to mention that I crossed the swamp without being fired on by the enemy, as they had not reached that part of the crossing when I passed through.

The following letter from General McLaws was received by me more than thirty years after the incident just related, as the date indicates:

Savannah, Ga., April 9th, 1897.

My Dear Graber:

Your letter of the 5th reached me yesterday evening, and it gave me great pleasure to receive it, for I have very often spoken of the Texas company which formed my escort for a great deal of the time during that campaign, and always in praise of its daring spirit and its devotion to our cause. And there is no one in the company whose name I have mentioned more often than yours, for I saw more of you personally than of most of them, as you were sometimes connected with my scouting party.

When the Federal Army, which crossed at Fort Royal ferry, commenced its movement northward to meet the column under General Sherman, which came from Savannah, it was your company scouts which gave me notice of it, and I commenced following their movement along one side, which was the left bank of the Salkatchie. The night I left my headquarters was a very cold one, and the troops suffered considerably. I had an A. D. C., a relative of mine, whom I had found in Colcock's regiment of cavalry, and, not being accustomed to campaigning, he grumbled some as we rode along and my other A. D. C., Mr. Lamar, hearing him, asked what was the matter. He replied, "Lamar, if this is liberty, I would rather be a slave." We arrived in time to successfully defeat the crossing at Braxton's Bridge, and I then rode on that night to Reeves' Bridge, some eight or ten miles above, and, finding everything in readiness, rode on to the bridge above. When I started from Braxton's Bridge, I had some seven or eight of Colcock's cavalry, who professed to know the country, and I had sent several of them to find Wheeler's cavalry, in order to get a force from him to help defend the crossing at Reeves' Bridge the next day, but I heard afterwards it was not done and in some unaccountable way my escort from Colcock's cavalry disappeared, every one of them. Fortunately I came across my inspecting officer, Captain King, a very energetic and fearless soldier, and I directed him to go on and bring over a division of cavalry under Wheeler, have them dismounted and placed in line close to the swamps on the right of the infantry force at Reeves' Bridge. I went on to the bridge above where General Hardee was in command, and he, seeming confident of holding his position, I started back to Reeves' Bridge alone, my escort having disappeared, as I have stated. On my way back, I came across a camp of a single teamster with his team and wagon. I dismounted, told him who I was, and asked him to feed my horse and let me lie down by his fire and to wake me before daylight, all of which he consented to. Before daylight the next day, I was on my way and arrived at Reeves' Bridge very early and found that Wheeler had sent me a division of cavalry which was placed as I had directed. I met Captain King, who told me of the daring ride of you and himself, and of your desperate venture to find the cavalry, and for which I was very grateful, for, had it not been for additional force thus acquired, the enemy would have crossed above me early in the day, for the Salkhatchie had fallen so much that it had become fordable and the enemy were crossing not only above, but parties crossed between Reeves' and Braxton's bridges, and after crossing in sufficient numbers to warrant it they would have come down on my flank at Reeves' bridge, and I would have had to retire. The presence of the cavalry prevented this. The cavalry late in the day, having exhausted its ammunition, I directed that they be formed mounted in the woods in the rear, and to charge any body of the enemy attempting to make a flank attack of the force at the bridge. This condition continued until sundown, when I directed the officer in command at the bridge to increase his force in the fortifications protecting the bridge and then to withdraw his artillery by hand, and as night approached the troops were withdrawn and I directed them to march directly to the rear and bivouac after going four or five miles. I then rode towards Braxton's bridge alone, my Carolina cavalry escort never returning to me. As I rode along I saw a mounted man sitting on his horse looking intently down the road. As I approached he heard my coming and turning recognized me and spoke quickly, telling me that the enemy had crossed and were between us and Braxton's bridge. I told him to go ahead and act as scout and keep a good lookout. So on we went until we saw a man on horseback. His horse was half hidden in a blacksmith's shop. He also was looking down the road intently, and, as I came up, he also said the enemy had crossed, and were occupying the road. I told him to join the other man and go ahead. We had not gone far when I heard the rapid gallop of a number of horses, and I thought to myself if the enemy have crossed cavalry I may be captured, so I withdrew a little off the road, so as to have a chance of running quickly to my infantry in the rear. A considerable body appeared, dashing wildly on, each man having his pistol drawn, and, as they came near, I was saluted with wild hurrahs. It was the lieutenant with his Texas company, who told me that he had heard I had been captured, and he had determined to rescue me at the risk of the lives of all, and the men demanded it. Of course, I was much gratified, and, feeling myself secure, we rode on rapidly to find out what had been done at Braxton's bridge. As we went, the first of the parties who had crossed the river were visible but a short distance away, three or four hundred yards along the edge of the river swamp to which they had retired. We halted where the Braxton bridge road joined the one I was on, and I sent in my staff officer, Captain King, to tell the officer to march his command in my direction. After waiting a long time, word came that he had started his command on another road. He had become alarmed, because parties of the enemy had been seen by his command to cross the river above him, and he was apprehensive of being intercepted. I let him go, although his scare cost his men a good many more miles of marching. My escort, with myself in charge, rode on towards the

Ediste, bringing up the rear. I would very much like to read your account of what took place when you were with Paysinger. He would come in after a scout between twelve and daylight at night, and would report to me at once, and he gave valuable information as to the movements of the enemy.

The morning after the Battle of Bentonville he came to my tent about three o'clock a. m., and told me that the enemy were moving on our left. I so reported to General Hardee, but he had been notified by General Hampton that the enemy were marching on my right, and I was sent with my command on the right. I then told General Hardee that I was apprehensive that there was a mistake, that I was so certain that our left would be attacked and not the right, I would not fortify it, but wait for the order to return to the left. We had not been on the right an hour before General Hardee came himself in great haste, calling for my command to hurry to the left, and we did get back just in time to check the enemy. Of the things done in these days there are many that I would like very much to have related again by those who were participants, but it would hardly do to put them in print. The conduct of the enemy was, however, so exasperating that there was no treatment too harsh as a punishment for their misdeeds, and I have always regretted that there had not been more scouting parties organized to follow in the wake of Sherman's army and circulate on his flank. Your company acting as scouts, as well as escort, working in small parties, encouraging individual daring and enterprise, was equally as efficient as a much larger body moving in compact mass under one head.

I shall always remember with pleasure the duties you performed while acting as my escort and also the pleasure I had in my personal intercourse with you, as individuals. I always kept in my mind that the individual soldier was entitled to be treated with the respect due to a gentleman, if his behavior warranted it. This in our Southern army. You will oblige me by assuring all of Company B of my high regard and respect for them individually as brave and honorable men, and collectively as an organized company, for I gave them a chance to show their characters in both ways, and was sorry to part with you all.

Very truly your obedient servant,

L. McLAWS.

We served with General McLaws until after the Battle of Bentonville and to the time of surrender of Johnston's army at Jonesboro, North Carolina, never uniting with the regiment again, though occasionally meeting with them, notably at the Battle of Bentonville, where they distinguished themselves by one of the most brilliant charges ever made by cavalry. This charge was made without our company (as we were with General McLaws and the infantry) and resulted in the safety of the whole army by saving an only bridge across a deep river, the only means of retreat of the army. It seems this bridge was guarded by some of Hampton's cavalry, when General Sherman ordered Mower's corps to make a dash around our left flank and capture this bridge and destroy it. While Mower was proceeding to do this by a rapid advance in the rear of our army, he had his pioneer corps with their spades and picks ready to entrench, and when in sight of the bridge, he poured a volley on the South Carolina cavalry, who immediately abandoned it. General Hardee dashed up to where our regiment was formed, at the time perhaps not numbering two hundred men, and asked, "Who commands this regiment?" A Lieutenant Matthews spoke and said he was in command of the regiment this morning. The general asked, "Lieutenant, can you hold those people in check until I can bring up the infantry and artillery?" He answered, "General, we are the boys that can try," and called to the Rangers to "Come on."

Right here I would mention a sad incident in connection with this charge. General Hardee had an only son, a boy about eighteen years old, who importuned him for a month or more, to allow him to join the Texas Rangers, and he had only given his consent that morning for the boy to join the regiment and he had fallen into rank with Company D. Another case: Eugene Munger, a cousin of our Dallas Mungers, who had borne a charmed life from the time he joined the Rangers after the Battle of Shiloh, and had never had a scratch, happened to be on a visit to the regiment, talking with some friends, when this charge was ordered. As they went in, passing by General Hardee, his son saluted him. The Rangers went into a thick woods, hardly suited for a cavalry charge, raising their accustomed yell and with their pistols, dashed into the first line of infantry, who on account of the sudden, unexpected onslaught, must have overshot them in their first volley. The Rangers were right among them, drove them into the second line, which became demoralized and fell back in confusion, the Rangers immediately withdrawing with quite a number of prisoners, bringing out their dead and wounded. Among the dead were Hardee's son and Eugene Munger. But they accomplished what was intended. General Hardee had brought up his infantry and artillery, which held the enemy in check until night, when the army crossed the bridge and was saved.

About an hour before the Rangers' desperate charge, General McLaws sent for me, when I found him immediately in the rear of his breastworks. He instructed me to take two or three men of the company and move around in the rear of Sherman's army and ascertain if Schofield's army, who had headquarters at Goldsboro, was moving to the support of Sherman, telling me that our army would fall back that night on the road to Raleigh and I would find him somewhere on that road. Taking three other members of the company, among whom was Virge Phelps, an old Mexican and Indian fighter, a man of extraordinary nerve, we proceeded across the bridge, then up Mill Creek towards Little River, where we found a division of the enemy camped about fifteen miles towards Goldsboro. We then proceeded on towards Goldsboro and found everything quiet outside of the enemy's camps. We ran in vidette pickets on several roads leading into Goldsboro, when finally we reached the town of Pikeville, the first station on the Goldsboro and Weldon Railroad. Here we stopped to make some inquiries, wearing our Federal overcoats and drawing up at a house for this purpose we asked for a drink of water. A very good looking, intelligent lady came out with a bucket and dipper and handed us water. On inquiry we found the enemy had never entered the town and none had been seen there. Finally this good lady asked us what command we belonged to. We told her that we belonged to the Fourth New York Cavalry, which claim we had made at several places where we had stopped for information. This woman kept looking at us and finally said, "Young man, you can't fool me; you are no Yankees, you are some of our own folks." I asked her why she thought so. "Well," she said, "I imagine Yankees don't talk like you do," which caused us to laugh, and as we then had decided to return and make report to General McLaws, I thought it wouldn't make any difference to tell her who we were and stated that we belonged to Wheeler's cavalry. This brought forth a tirade of abuse from this woman. I said Wheeler's cavalry purposely to ascertain if the terrible name of Wheeler's cavalry had reached there. Wheeler's cavalry, through misrepresentations and frequently through the acts of Yankee scouting parties claiming to belong to Wheeler's cavalry, had gained a very unenviable reputation, so when we claimed to belong to Wheeler's cavalry, this woman said, "I wish I was a man; I would shoulder a gun and help put you down and only wish the Yankees would come in here right now and kill the last one of you." I said, "Madam, you needn't wish for the Yankees, you will have them soon enough and get a taste of some of their deviltry." We then proceeded back in the direction of the Raleigh road from Bentonville.

CHAPTER XX

I SELL A TEN DOLLAR GOLD PIECE FOR FIFTEEN HUNDRED DOLLARS.

I will recite an incident occurring while we were camped about six miles on a plank road from Fayetteville, North Carolina, which place was also a manufacturing point for war munitions on a small scale, also had a large cotton factory: The enemy were moving on two roads, converging into Fayetteville, one road opposed by Rhett's Brigade of South Carolinians (General Rhett having been captured a few days before). General McLaws sent for me about daylight and instructed me to take one or two members of the company and ride across the country to the road occupied by Rhett's Brigade, stating that Rhett's pickets had been run in the night before, then after watching the road for some time, if I found no enemy passing, to ride up the road until we met or heard of them. We rode up the road to the eleventh milepost, when we discovered some women up in a field near a house, watching the road and decided to go and interrogate them on whether they had seen any enemy passing. I told Jim Freeman, one of the party, to stay in the road and carefully watch the direction from whence we were expecting the enemy and Joe Hungerford and I would go up and talk with these women, suggesting to Jim if the enemy came in sight and he had time to come to us, to do so, but if he had not, to fire his pistol and run in toward town or go back the way we had come and report to General McLaws and on his firing his pistol we would make our way across from where we were. After reaching the women they told us they had been watching for an hour or more and had seen no passing, but had heard, the night before, that the enemy were advancing on that road. After getting this information they insisted on our waiting a little while, that they were cooking breakfast and wanted us to share it with them, which we decided to do, remaining on our horses. Very soon Jim Freeman came up to us and reported that he saw a Yankee vidette picket about a half a mile ahead of where he stood. We concluded, as we had time, that we would finish our breakfast and go down and run him in, which we proceeded to do. When reaching the place in the road where Jim saw this Yankee, he could not be found. I then suggested that he was not a picket, but had strayed away from his command for some purpose and would no doubt be found at some house. We soon discovered a house a few hundred yards ahead, but a little swamp between us and the house prevented us from going directly to it and after proceeding a couple of hundred yards down the road, we found a dirt road coming into the plank road, but at the mouth of this road, owing to a turn in it, we were unable to see the house. I then suggested to the boys that they wait there and I would go up to the house and see if this Yankee was there.

After proceeding some little distance, the road turned and brought me in full view of the house, with this Yankee at the gate, his gun on his shoulder, just starting in. Having on my Yankee overcoat, I slipped my pistol out of its holster, intending to ride up and make him lay down his gun, when he discovered me and smiled, mistaking me for one of their own men. Just as I got ready to throw my pistol down on him the boys on the plank road started in a fast lope down the way we had come, which was notice to me that the enemy were on to them. I had but little time to decide. I knew if I shot this Yankee it would attract those on the plank road and if I wheeled to run away from him he would perhaps shoot me, but I decided to take my chance on the latter and broke for the plank road. Just as I entered the plank road I noticed a column of infantry within about one hundred and fifty yards. I wheeled to the right very suddenly, which threw the cape of my overcoat over my head, put spurs to my horse, made him do his best, expecting every moment to be shot off the horse, but they never fired a shot, simply calling, "Halt, halt!" The blue overcoat no doubt saved my life, as they evidently thought I was one of their own men. When the boys heard me coming, they stopped and after we got together we struck across the country the way we had come and reported to General McLaws, which soon started our little army on a hasty march into Fayetteville, where we found Rhett's Brigade, who had moved in during the night, and had sent notice by a courier, which notice never reached General Hardee. Our army then passed through Fayetteville very rapidly, whatever stores there were in the place, of any value to our army, had been removed, and the bridge across the river was all ready to be burned in an instant.

After the army had safely passed over, as also our cavalry, I stopped at a store near the market-house to try to sell a ten dollar gold piece, belonging to one of my comrades, for Confederate money. This was perhaps the last gold piece we had in the command and the last of two hundred dollars in gold my comrade had sent to him from Texas. I found in this store a few yards of butternut jeans and forty or fifty pairs of knit socks, all the goods the fellow had and with his little safe half full of stacks of Confederate money. I asked him a hundred and fifty for one for the gold piece, when he offered me seventy-five for one and while dickering on this trade, we heard the guns fire up the street, when he counted me out fifteen hundred dollars, very quickly for my gold piece. I just had time to spring on to my horse and cross the bridge, which very soon after, was burned, with the enemy moving into Fayetteville.

The army then moved down the river to Averysboro, where they built an earth breastworks from a swamp, through which had passed a hurricane down to the Cape Fear River and in front of this, another, perhaps a half mile from the main works—a short line of works, which was occupied by Rhett's Brigade, with a battery of artillery. While our company with General McLaws and staff, were awaiting developments near where the roadway ran through the earthworks, General Hardee dashed up and called to General McLaws to send two of your Texas people down the line on our left and ascertain if the enemy are flanking in force, when I, in company with Lieutenant Bennett, dashed down the line until we struck the swamp, then turned into the swamp among fallen trees and brush until we became separated, when I was finally fired on by the enemy's skirmish line, which forced me to run back through this fallen timber. But having a clear-footed horse, I succeeded in getting through to the end of the woods, and there started to run back, away from the fire of the infantry, when a Colonel Fizer commanding the brigade immediately behind the works, called me back and gave me a message to General Hardee, which I was forced to carry up the line, exposed to the fire of the main line of the enemy, which struck our works obliquely. I delivered my message to General Hardee just as Rhett's Brigade was moving inside of the works from their advanced position, protected by the gallant defense of a regiment of Georgians he had thrown forward outside of the main works. When the main line of the enemy poured a hot fire onto that part of the works where we were halted, we dashed into the woods somewhat out of range. Here a ball struck Captain Lamar's fine mare on the back and she commenced laming. Lamar thought that she would fall with him and begged me to take him up behind me, which I refused to do, unless his mare actually fell. He still insisted on my taking him behind, when I proposed to swap, to which he readily assented, but the mare never gave out and I brought her into camp safely that night.

This animal, one of the finest in the army, was a present to Captain Lamar from a friend of his in Savannah and was said to have cost a thousand dollars in gold. After eating our supper that night General McLaws sent for me to come up to his camp fire, when he asked me to exchange back with Lamar, saying that Lamar prized the mare very highly, as she was a present to him. I told him most certainly I would do so, that I did not expect to keep her, but tender her back to him, which, of course, was very gratifying to all concerned.

CHAPTER XXI

My Service With Captain Shannon.

It was our custom, when on these scouts inside of the enemy's lines, to rest for a part of the night out of sight and hearing of the road, turning in when away from any settlement or house, so we would not be seen and spend the balance of the night in sleep in perfect safety, without having a guard. After spending that night in the woods, we returned to the road and found a large number of fresh horse tracks leading towards Little River. We construed these to mean that a Federal scout had passed during the night, which we decided to catch up with; charge their rear and stampede them. In about two or three miles from there our road rose up on a little bluff against a fence, then turned down the fence to the west into a lane, past a house. In the corner of the field was a barn lot, with several barns, where we found about thirty or forty Federals saddling their horses. We immediately withdrew unobserved, under the bluff, to consult, and I suggested to the boys to go around this field, in the woods, strike the road below, wait in ambush until these fellows passed, then charge their rear, as intended. Virge Phelps refused to listen and insisted on charging them right there and then, which I conceived to be a very foolish thing to do, but finally had to yield. As we rose the bluff the second time, we discovered one of Shannon's men coming over the fence, out of the field, which we knew meant that Shannon was camped there with a lot of prisoners.

Captain Shannon was instructed by General Hood at Atlanta to select twenty-five or thirty men out of the regiment and operate inside of Sherman's lines all the time, getting information, and punishing marauders wherever found engaged in their nefarious business of robbing and burning homes.

Shannon's selection of the men he had with him soon won for him and his scout a reputation with our army, and especially with the enemy, second to no scout ever sent out by any army. Mosby's exploits in Virginia have been considered most wonderful achievements for any small body of men. The operations of Shannon's scouts have never been written, but where they were known, surpassed anything ever heard of.

Immediately after recognizing this man, coming over from the field, we hunted up Captain Shannon and reported to him our work of the day before, when he stated he was going to send these prisoners to headquarters and suggested that I make my report to General McLaws by the lieutenant in charge and that we go back with him, as he expected to go over the same ground that we had passed over the day before. This we were very willing and anxious to do, having never been in any engagement with him.

Shannon made it a rule that wherever he struck the enemy he would charge them at once and when he found they were too strong for him he would run out and leave them, sometimes drawn up in line of battle, shelling the woods after he was gone. As soon as ready, Shannon moved out with our little party in the rear, they having better horses than ours, as they managed by some means, to keep in fresh horses all the time.

One of the first places we stopped to inquire proved to belong to a very intelligent old Rebel lady, who reported that an officer and a private and a negro soldier had just left her house, the negro driving her buggy, carrying off a lot of fine dress goods and silverware and valuables in the buggy and the others having threatened to hang her if she failed to tell where her money was, forcing her to give up about a hundred dollars in gold and several thousand dollars in Confederate bonds. She told Captain Shannon, "If you will just hurry up, you will catch up with them," which we did, in about two miles from there. The first one of the party caught up with was the negro soldier driving the horse and buggy, when a member of the advance guard rode up by the side of him and shot him out of the buggy. It seemed as though the ball of his big pistol sent his body about five feet on the roadside, which made the scout smile, looking back at us.

At a house about a quarter of a mile ahead of us, we found two horses hitched, which turned out to belong to the lieutenant and the private, who had taken the old lady's money. Shannon called back, "Don't but two of you stop here." A couple of Shannon's men threw their bridle reins over the fence and rushed into the house, when immediately afterwards we heard pistols rattle in that house. We then continued on this road to where it enters the main county road, running parallel with the Goldsboro & Weldon Railroad. Just before reaching the main county road Captain Shannon halted us, when he went forward, looked up and down the road, came back, commanded, "Form fours and charge!" I don't think I ever saw men going into a charge like Shannon's men, all breaking ranks, trying to get to the front, not knowing whether they were charging a small body of thirty or fifty men or a whole brigade until they got into the main county road, which disclosed about sixty or seventy mounted infantry with their guns swung on their backs, at the mouth of the lane, drinking and talking. The head of Shannon's column entered the body of the Yankees, shooting their way in among them. All offered to surrender, throwing up their hands with only one gun fired by them and that by a man about to enter a swamp below the field, firing back at us over his shoulder. These cowardly devils were not soldiers, only in name, they were a band of highwaymen and plunderers in the uniform of the United States and the most of them loaded down with plunder of every description.

We next proceeded on the main road towards Pikesville, taking a batch of prisoners along with us, guarded by only two or three of Shannon's scouts. We found these plunderers at every house on the way to Pikesville, a distance of five or six miles, and also in the town. Pikesville was a town of about fifty or seventy-five inhabitants, a blacksmith shop, store and postoffice, railroad station and a few residences. On entering the town our party became very much scattered, as we found Federals in nearly every house. A party of about six or eight on horseback tried to escape, when I, with two or three of Shannon's boys, started after them, capturing the whole bunch.

Returning to town I noticed the house where we stopped the day before and had such a tirade of abuse from the woman, of which Shannon's boys with me, knew nothing. I suggested to them to let us go by that house and get a drink of water. The prisoners begged for water also. Riding up to the house, the door opened and my good lady of the day before put in her appearance, when I said to her, "Now, run and get your friends some drinking water; they are very thirsty." "No," she said, "I wouldn't give them a drink of water to save their lives. Come in, sir, and see what they did in my house." I told her that I did not care to see it, but to run and get some water for her friends, when she again started to abuse the prisoners. I told her she must stop that, they were our prisoners and could not be abused by her.

After getting together the prisoners taken in this town and leaving about a half dozen men to guard them, somewhere near a hundred, we started out on a short scout on the road we had run over after the parties trying to make their escape. When about a mile and a half from town in a straight lane, having very high rail fences on both sides, we met about eighty or a hundred more, evidently on their way to town. The head of their column halted, viewing one of their dead bodies lying in the road, one of the men that was killed by our little party running after them, trying to make their escape.

I forgot to mention when starting out on this last scout that I told Shannon our party wanted to move in the advance guard, as we had hardly got a shot, his men always keeping ahead of us and we did not want to go back to the regiment and say we had been with Shannon's scouts unable to do any effective service. Captain Shannon replied, "All right; go ahead and report to Bill Smith," who was a first lieutenant and always commanded the advance guard. When within about two hundred yards of this column, viewing the body, I asked Smith, as he was moving us quite rapidly, "What are you going to do; are you going to charge these fellows?" He said, "Come on; come on." I looked back and saw Shannon coming up in a lope with about fifteen or eighteen men, then noticed the Federal column getting restless and probably four or five of them break, when I said to Smith, "Now is our time," and we drove ahead, scattering the whole business, capturing a number of prisoners, besides a number left in the road.

We next collected all our prisoners in the town and found that perhaps not more than seventy per cent could speak the English language and we were told that these foreigners had just been imported from Europe, rushed through Castle Garden, right to the army. They were told by the recruiting agents in Europe that they would receive large bounties, good pay and good treatment and be entitled to everything they captured, which latter of course, proved the greatest inducement of all.

We camped with Shannon that night near the town, and parted with him the next morning, they moving in the direction of Goldsboro, while we started back to our army, which we never saw again until the night of the day of the surrender, which was several weeks after.

CHAPTER XXII

We Receive Notice of Johnston's Surrender—I Decline to be Paroled and Resolve to Make My Way Out.

After leaving Bentonville our army continued its retreat, the main part of the army finally moving in the direction of Greensboro, where it surrendered. Our little party continued to operate on Sherman's flank, when we heard that there was a large amount of meat collected by the Federal cavalry at a little place called Marlboro, and we decided to get a wagonload of this meat and carry it with us to our army. For this purpose we impressed a wagon and team and loaded up with hams, which proved a great encumbrance to us and about the third day we left all with a poor widow woman, with her promise to hide out the hams in the woods and try to save them from capture. We finally reached our regimental camp the night of the surrender of Johnston's army. Our regiment at first notice of the surrender, decided to make their way out and not take parole, but General Wheeler came down and made them a talk, stating the terms of the surrender to be that the cavalry would be permitted to retain their horses and sidearms and go home unmolested, if they could show a parole; but if not they would be treated and shot as Guerillas. Under this condition General Wheeler advised them to surrender, which they decided to do.

After feeding my horse and eating a little supper, I tried to make up a party to make our way out without taking a parole, believing that the army would be sent to prison, and, having determined never to see the inside of another prison, I prepared to go out and succeeded in inducing about thirty of the regiment to go out with me. We rode all night, and next morning came to a place where we found Colonel Harrison on crutches, standing in the door. I dismounted and went in to tell him that the army had surrendered and when about half way to him in the yard, he motioned to me with his hand, saying, "Back to your command; back to your command." I told him that we were on our way to Texas, the army had surrendered and the Rangers had decided to surrender with the army and take a parole, which brought tears to his eyes. He repeated, "The army has surrendered and the Rangers going to surrender with the army? You did right, sir, in coming out; the Rangers shall not surrender with the army; I am going to send them word to come out." He then bade us good-bye and we proceeded on our way.

That night we got to the town of Lexington, where we decided to stop for the night, camping at the edge of the town. I went into town to have some bread cooked for the party and it commenced to rain. Finally I succeeded in finding a place where a lady agreed to cook the bread for us all. The gentleman insisted on my staying at his house until his wife could cook the bread, which would take her all night, and as a further inducement, said if I would stay he would go with me the next morning and show me where about thirty barrels of Catawba wine was hid out, from which we could fill our canteens. The next morning, going down to where I had left the boys in camp, loaded down with bread, I found they had gone and left me. They had evidently become alarmed during the night and, not knowing where I could be found, they decided I would be able to make my way out all right. I then struck out, taking as much of the bread as I could conveniently carry, but did not take time to get any of the wine. I took the main Charlotte road, when in about two or three miles, the road forked, one seemed about as much traveled as the other. About six miles from there, towards Charlotte, I came to a house where I found Major Jarmon of our regiment, badly wounded, with several of our men taking care of him. These men told me that our party who had left me, had divided at the forks of the road, part of them taking the right hand, intending to go through Middle Tennessee and East Tennessee, the others going on to Charlotte, there to cross the river and go over into South Carolina. I then decided to go back to the forks of the road, take the right hand and try to catch up with the party going to Tennessee.

After following this road about two or three miles, I came to a branch, where I stopped to water my horse and immediately discovered about eight or ten old men and young boys riding horses, unshod, and with citizens' saddles. They had a few squirrel rifles and no other weapons, and were also watering their horses in the branch near me. They asked me what command I belonged to. I told them I belonged to the Texas Rangers and my company was just ahead, when I asked them what command they belonged to. They said they belonged to General Lee's cavalry, which I knew was not true, but that they were bushwhackers and I decided to get away from them as soon as possible. I started across the branch and at a little turn of the road I struck a trot, when two of them loped up behind me, separating, one on each side of me, one of them demanding to buy my saddle. I told him it was not for sale. The other wanted to buy one of my pistols. I told them they couldn't have anything I had; "I know what you are after and if you know what is good for you, you had better drop back and let me alone." They stopped and, I thought, started back to their party. I soon got to another turn of the road out of their sight, and struck a lope and ran about a mile and a half. I concluded perhaps they would come no further. I discovered a woman plowing in the field, at the far end of which was a log house on the edge of the woods, and just at the corner of the fence I noticed some fresh horse tracks turned off the road, which I concluded perhaps was our party who had gone to the house to get something to eat. I waited in the fence corner for the woman to return to the end of the row and asked if she had seen any men riding down the line of fence to the house, when she claimed she did not and while talking with her here this gang of bushwhackers came dashing up and surrounded me in the fence corner. I pulled out one of my pistols and told them the first man that raised a gun I'd kill "and I'll get a number of you before you get me, for I am an expert shot and never miss," when one of them said, "Come on, boys; let's leave the d—— fool." I told them," Yes, you'd better leave." Unfortunately for me, they turned right up the road, the way I wanted to go and when they concluded I had quit watching them, they turned into the woods, no doubt expecting me to continue on the road and they would then ambush me.

I first concluded that I must catch up with our party, as I was exceedingly anxious to go with them into Tennessee and it was not safe for me to go by myself, therefore decided I would ride along leisurely until I got up to the point where they turned out of the road, then, with my pistol raised, I would put spurs to my horse and run the gauntlet, which on further reflection, I concluded that I had better not attempt, as they would be bound to hit my horse in running by. I therefore turned back the way I had come. When within about two or three miles of the main forks of the road, I struck a well-beaten path, running in the direction of the Charlotte road, which I decided to take and getting back into the Charlotte road, I would ride on to Charlotte. After riding in this path about a mile and a half, I came to a large log house, to reach the front gate of which I had to pass through a barn lot that had a large gate, fastened by a log chain wrapped around the bottom of the gate and the gate post. When I got down off my horse to unwind this chain, I heard some one speak and when I looked up I found an old gentleman on the other side of the lot with a shotgun leveled on me. I told him not to shoot, "I am a friend and want some directions." He said, "Now, that animal isn't fit for you to ride and would be of no use to you, but you can't take her." I told him, "My friend, I don't want your horse, I have as good a horse as I want. I only want some directions," and after talking with him a little, satisfied him that I was not after his horse, when he invited me in. I then told him about being on my way home to Texas and how I had been separated from the party I was going with and wanted to get to the Charlotte road the nearest way I could get there. He then begged me to spend the balance of the day and stay all night with him. After finding that he was a good Southern man, I decided to do so, satisfied I would never catch up with our party that had taken the Charlotte road and I needed rest very badly, as also my horse.

The old gentleman told me that that whole country was overrun by a band of marauders that had been pillaging and robbing their homes and they had had a meeting of the people in the neighborhood and decided whenever a house was attacked they would blow a horn and all rush to the place of attack, there to shoot down every man they found that had no business there. It is hardly necessary to say that he wished they would attack his house the night I was there, because I had four pistols and was regarded by him as pretty good reinforcement, but nothing of the sort happened. I spent a very restful and pleasant night, with a good supper and breakfast, and next day started out, by a near road, to strike the Charlotte pike, which I did some several miles ahead of where I left Major Jarman, the day before, badly wounded.

When I finally reached Charlotte, I stopped to make some inquiry of an infantry guard stationed at a big stable, who told me that the guards in town had orders to arrest every man from Johnston's army without a parole and advised me to pass around the main part of the town, into the road I was going on to. He furthermore told me that our whole Confederate Government was then in Charlotte; President Davis, with General Breckenridge, then Secretary of War; Judge Reagan, Postmaster General, and all the rest, and they had just heard the news of Lincoln's assassination, which seemed to have cast a gloom over the entire party.

I now proceeded on my way, around the town, back into the main road leading out to Bady's Ferry and when within four or five miles of the ferry, I met a citizen who had just crossed there and reported that Colonel Clarence Prentice, with about two hundred Kentuckians, had just crossed there and had been captured by a heavy force of Federal cavalry and by them paroled and permitted to go on his way home. Then further conferring with this citizen about where I could best cross the Catawba River, he told me of a batteau at a mill about twelve miles below Charlotte, when I decided to ride down there and cross in this batteau, which I did, putting my saddle and everything in the batteau, paddling across and swimming my mare, which landed me in a wheat field, in the State of South Carolina.

After getting straightened out again for the road I got directions to Anderson Courthouse, which I reached in due time and found Colonel Harrison, with a large party of Rangers, resting and having a good time. Harrison, if the reader will remember, was badly wounded and was just recovering, using crutches, when a party of Rangers came along after we had left, secured an ambulance and crossed the Catawba River with two batteaux, one on each side, thus bringing him out to Anderson Courthouse, which was his old home and where he had relatives.

After resting another day we again struck out for the Mississippi River, passing through South Carolina, into Georgia, then into Alabama. Before reaching the State of Alabama, we heard that the Mississippi River was out of its banks and about thirty miles wide, which forced us to scatter out and lay up at different points, until the river ran down so that we could cross. I had promised a messmate, Joe Hungerford, whose home was at Uniontown, Alabama, that I would spend some time with him.

Riding along one day in Alabama, some miles from Marion, I was taken with a severe headache, which forced me to stop and lay up, try to get some rest and sleep. When I woke in the night I was prevailed on by an old gentleman at the house, to spend the balance of the night, which threw me considerably behind the party of men I was with.

When our party left Greenville Courthouse we decided if we struck any horses or mules, belonging to the United States Government, we would take them along with us, for the purpose of probably raising money to pay our expenses home and if we found any small parties of the enemy, we would attack them and on their surrender, would parole them, taking their arms and horses.

On riding into the town of Marion, I saw a guard in front of a livery stable, rode up to him, when he accosted me, "Hello, Texas; have you come after mules, too?" I told him, "Yes, where are they?" He said, "This stable is full of the finest kind of mules;" he happened to be an Arkansas man and told me that my party, who went through the day before, went out with a lot of mules, each leading two. I told him, "All right, open the door and I will go in and get a couple." He said, "No, you know I want you to have them, but they are in charge of Major Curry, who has a strong guard here and is waiting to turn them over to the Yankees, who are expected in here by train every minute and you had better not attempt to take any mules by yourself, as Curry, with his guards, would surely arrest you and turn you over to the Yankees." Then I concluded best to drop the matter and proceeded to get directions, from a citizen, to Uniontown.

Stopping on the road, about five miles from Marion, to get dinner, I found at the house four Confederate soldiers—one young man on crutches, who had been wounded in the Virginia Army, the son of the owner of the place; one of the Eleventh Texas Cavalry and two Arkansas men. At the dinner table the old gentleman told me about Major Curry, a Confederate Quartermaster, who had impressed about two hundred fine mules in that section for account of the Confederate Government and had these mules in a large livery stable in Marion, protected by a guard, to turn them over to the Federals. These mules had not been branded and the owners had plead with Major Curry to return them to them, but Curry refused, claiming it would get him into trouble with the Federals, as they would certainly get the information. The old gentleman told me that the feeling against Curry was very bitter and that he was regarded as a very mean man, persisting in his determination to turn over the mules, on account of his antipathy to his old neighbors and friendliness to the Federals, thereby courting their favors.

Presently one of the Arkansas men proposed that we go back and take a couple of mules apiece, by force, to which we all consented. Our crippled man, not having a gun, his father told him of a rich neighbor some two miles from there who had quite a number of mules taken by Curry and was very bitter against him on that account, that he had a very fine shotgun and would no doubt loan it to him for the purpose of a raid on that stable. Stopping at this house on our way into Marion, this young crippled man secured the shotgun, when we moved on. Just before we entered town I stopped the party and told them that I was satisfied we were very liable to have trouble with Major Curry and there was no use in starting into it without going through with it. "Now, if there is a man among you that don't want to go in, let him say so now." They all said they were willing to go and wanted me to take command of the party. I told them, "All right, now, if you are asked any questions, who I am, tell them I am Lieutenant Jones, Company C, Eleventh Texas."

We now started in and found a big lattice door to the stable open, and as soon as we came in sight the guard rushed to the door to close it, when I dashed up with my pistol on and told him to leave that door open. I then told our crippled young man, with the shotgun, to hold that door open, to stay there and to shoot the first man that attempted to close it when the balance of our men went in to get the mules. There were two shed rooms, connected with the main room; the large room had stalls on each side. Not finding any good mules in the large room, I went to the far end and turned into one of the shed rooms, the balance of the men scattering around, hunting good mules. While engaged untying a mule in the shed room, I heard a man call to some of our men, "Who are you, and what are you doing here?" They told him they had come after mules. "Who commands this party?" "Lieutenant Jones of the Eleventh Texas." "Where is Lieutenant Jones?" They told him I was in that shed room. In the meantime, a number of men in citizen's clothes, had entered the main room. Major Curry came around into the shed room, where I had untied a mule and asked me if I was Lieutenant Jones, in command. He said, "I am Major Curry of the Confederate States Army, in charge of these mules, with orders to turn them over to the United States Army and if you don't take your party out of here and leave these mules, I will have to arrest you and turn you over to the Federal authorities." I told him that we would be very much disappointed if he didn't attempt our arrest, that we had come on purpose to get the mules and him, too, when he approached very near me and said in a low tone of voice, "You know this stable is full of Yankee spies now, come in advance of the army to find out what they can, and for their benefit I have to make a show of resistance." He said, "You go ahead and take what mules you want. You Texans are entitled to them; you are a long ways from home."

We then completed our selection and led out two mules apiece, with two for our lame friend at the door, passing by a number of strangers, looking on, in the main room. Major Curry followed me outside, when I told him, "Now, if it will be of any benefit to you, Major, I am willing to give you a written statement that I appeared here with an armed force and took possession of so many mules," which he said he would appreciate very much, it might prove of benefit to him with the Yankees, and invited me up into his office with him, around on the square, where I drew up this statement and signed the name of R. F. Jones, Company C, Eleventh Texas Regiment. We then departed with our mules, back to the young lame man's home, where we separated, perhaps never to meet again.

After obtaining directions for Uniontown, on my way through Green County, Alabama, I stopped at the little town of Newbern, where I met a Doctor James Webb, who insisted on my stopping with him. He had a beautiful home; his family being away on a long visit to some other section of the State, he felt quite lonely and wanted company. I decided to accept his invitation, when he made me feel at home and my visit there for nearly two months, waiting for the Mississippi River to run down, proved very pleasant indeed, besides forming many new and pleasant acquaintances.

After spending nearly two months at this place, we had information, which we considered reliable, that the Trans-Mississippi Department had surrendered. I therefore concluded best to abandon my ride to Texas, leave my horse and arms with Doctor Webb and proceed to New Orleans, from there by steamer to Galveston. Doctor Webb succeeded in finding an only twenty-dollar gold piece, which he advanced me to pay the expense of my trip.

Armed with a parole, copied from one in the possession of an Appomattox prisoner, I proceeded to Uniontown, where I took rail for Selma and entered the Provost Marshal's office, threw down my parole and demanded transportation to Texas, which was granted me as far as New Orleans.

Arriving at New Orleans I found that the Trans-Mississippi Department had not yet surrendered, but the agents of General Kirby Smith, who was in command of the Trans-Mississippi Department (Doctor

Ashbel Smith and Mr. Ballinger of Galveston), were then negotiating with General Canby, its surrender. Here I found a large part of Hood's brigade, as also General Hood and members of his staff from Texas and General Thomas Harrison of our brigade, with some few members of the Eighth Texas, also many members of Granbury's and Rector's brigades, awaiting the close of negotiations and transportation to Texas, when finally, in about a week or ten days, the surrender of the Trans-Mississippi Department was completed and a large transport, in charge of a Federal captain, was ordered to take us to Galveston.

On arrival at the entrance of Galveston Bay we met a sloop of war going out, when our captain in charge signaled to it to return to Galveston and anchor off a certain wharf, where he expected to land our men, which he did. On arrival at this wharf, after tying up the boat, a stage was run out, when a lone gentleman standing on the wharf, claiming to be Mayor Leonard of the city, called to the Federal captain not to allow a single man to come off that boat until the trains were ready to take us into the interior. This brought forth a spirited rebuke by our Federal captain, telling him that the men were going to land and stay in the city until they could be taken out by the railroad and if they mistreated any of the men while there, he would order the gunboat to lay his town in ashes.

In explanation of the Mayor's action, it seems that when the army disbanded in the interior, that a lot of bad men entered Galveston and conducted themselves badly, when the City Council met and passed an order that no more soldiers would be permitted in the city. The Mayor, of course, had no idea that a large number of the men aboard were citizens of Galveston nor as to the character of the men aboard, hence his mistake.

In connection with this I recall the departure of the Bayou City Guards in 1861 for Virginia, who afterwards constituted a part of the Fifth Texas Regiment, Hood's brigade, and reflected such credit on the Confederate arms in Virginia. I happened to be present in Houston when this company, marching through the streets of Houston to the railroad depot, were escorted by a cavalry company and a large concourse of citizens—on their departure for Harrisburg, there to be mustered into the service of the Confederate States for the war.

After boarding the train a few speeches were made and a few words spoken by Captain John G. Walker, commanding the cavalry company, which I well remember, as follows:

"If you fight bravely we will honor you; if you return safely we will welcome you; if you die in battle I swear to Heaven we will avenge you."

Taking this in connection with our reception at Galveston, which of course, was a mistake, by accident, we can well afford to pass it.

As soon as the trains were made up for the interior, after spending a day and night in Galveston where we were treated royally by its citizens, we proceeded to our different homes and I soon landed in Hempstead among a sad, dejected and ruined people, resolved to do the best they could under the circumstances and submit gracefully to the powers that were.

It would, I consider, be entirely fitting for me to close this part of my life's history by publishing what I may call General Joseph Wheeler's farewell address to his cavalry corps (General Wheeler issued the following order to his entire command):

"Headquarters Cavalry Corps,

"April 28, 1865.

"Gallant Comrades: You have fought your fight. Your task is done. During a four years' struggle for liberty you have exhibited courage, fortitude and devotion. You are the victors of more than 200 sternly contested fields. You have participated in more than a thousand conflicts of arms. You are heroes! Veterans! Patriots! The bones of your comrades mark battlefields upon the soil of Kentucky, Virginia, North Carolina, South Carolina, Georgia, Alabama and Mississippi. You have done all that human exertion could accomplish. In bidding you adieu, I desire to tender my thanks for your gallantry in battle, your fortitude under suffering and your devotion at all times to the holy cause you have done so much to maintain. I desire also to express my gratitude for the kind feelings you have seen fit to extend toward myself, and to invoke upon you the blessing of our Heavenly Father, to whom we must always look in the hour of distress. Brethren in the cause of freedom, comrades in arms, I bid you farewell.

"JOSEPH WHEELER,

"Major General.

"Official:

"WM. E. WAITES,

"Assistant Adjutant General."

The Reconstruction Period

PREFACE

For the unpleasant facts recorded in this, I am not responsible, but only the powers that were then. I would much prefer to forget as I have forgiven, and not reopen old wounds, but a sacred duty I owe my family forces me to submit the unvarnished truth and use expressions, though harsh, to properly represent conditions as they existed, to protect my lifetime fair name and character, which I must leave my family untarnished, and also to redeem my promise to them and my many interested friends, who were personally acquainted with me during the years of this terrible experience.

Do not fail to bear in mind that this is written altogether from memory, nearly fifty years after it occurred, hence dates are omitted.

In order to give the reader a full appreciation of my remarkable preservation and escape from being murdered by the powers that ruled at the time, I treat the subject as I do. Drifting into this trouble was certainly not of my own choice, but altogether owing to conditions and surroundings. I was simply the instrument in God's hands to relieve a law abiding and submissive community of a terrible calamity about to be enacted by a lawless band of marauders in the uniform of the United States, protected by their officers and permitted by the, then, General Government, and my life was spared by the interposition of a Divine Providence. It was this firm conviction that gave me strength and hope that all would be well and enabled me to pass through this terrible ordeal.

There was no law to protect or appeal to, only the whim of a vindictive military satrap, whose order was supreme and who regarded the best citizens of the country fit subjects for his vengeance and persecution.

Our State Government, organized under the terms of our surrender, composed of the best and most solid element of the State, working in conjunction with the returned Confederate soldiers to rehabilitate our ruined homes, was ruthlessly set aside by the infamous order of General Sheridan, as an impediment to reconstruction.

To longer submit to such conditions and subject our families to dangers worse than death, made men desperate and called forth every spark of manhood in man, particularly in one who had followed Sherman's march through Georgia and the Carolinas and made him liable to resent outrages when brought directly to his own home in the most effective way, regardless of consequences.

As a result of our action, having removed the bandit leader from among them, our community was no longer subjected to their deviltry. They were completely overawed and behaved themselves forever after, thereby avoiding much bloodshed. Had they burned Hempstead that night, which no doubt they would have done, an outraged citizenship would have gathered and visited vengeance on these devils incarnate and no promise of General Sheridan, as in the case of Brenham, could have stayed them, then what would have been the result?

I had the sympathy of the best citizens of the country, offers of men and money, which were always declined in the interest of peace.

To better explain the cause for the conditions existing with these garrisons: When the Federal Government sent their recruiting agents abroad, they accepted some of the worst element in Europe, as well as in this country, promising them large bounties, good wages and treatment, and all they could capture, hence a certain element in the army started in for plunder only, and with no other object. Some garrisons in the State had a band of plunderers with a desperate leader, as was the case at Brenham when it was burned and again at Hempstead at this time.

At the conclusion of the war the best element in the Federal Army, the brave and gallant men who won the fight, did not re-enlist, but returned to their homes to engage in peaceful pursuits and could never have been induced to assist in degrading their own race and color by elevating the negro over us, which was the avowed intention of the fanatical element of the North who were responsible for the war.

That gallant soldier and conscientious gentleman, General W. S. Hancock, in command of New Orleans, refused to do their bidding and was immediately superseded by General Sheridan, who proved a fit tool in their hands.

CHAPTER XXIII

Upon My Return From the Army I Find My Business Affairs in Bad Shape.

I returned from Johnston's army, surrendered in North Carolina in the summer of 1865, to my home town, Hempstead, Texas, where I found my brother, six years younger than myself, who had also just returned from the army, and a younger sister, who had been boarding at a friend's house during my absence in the army. We were orphan children.

On my return I found the business of Faddis & Graber, which I left in charge of R. P. Faddis, the senior partner, totally vanished. I had not even a change of clothing, of which I had left a trunk full. Brother had given them to needy Confederate soldiers.

After resting and recuperating for some months, a guest at the homes of different friends, awaiting an opportunity for business, I was persuaded by an old friend, Mr. Leander Cannon, to make my home at his house at Courtney, Grimes County, until I could secure something to do. Mr. Cannon before the war had the largest general mercantile business in the interior of the State, while I kept his books for him at Hempstead before I entered into business on my own account with Faddis, Mr. Cannon having sold out in the meantime.

After the return of the Confederate soldiers from the army, the first year, they were engaged in peaceable pursuits, trying to rebuild their lost fortunes and also to recuperate their health, which, in many instances, had been sacrificed in the army.

While so engaged, the Federal Government organized its Freedman's Bureau, establishing its agencies in all the populous negro districts in the State, supported by the army. As heretofore stated, among these garrisons were a lot of desperate and bad men, bent on rapine and plunder, and they had the sanction of their officers, notably in the case of the town of Brenham, which they sacked and burned.

This aroused the resentment and desperation of the best people of Texas and very soon a thousand or more of the best citizens of the State collected and determined to wipe out this garrison. General Sheridan, in command of Texas and Louisiana, with headquarters at New Orleans, telegraphed Governor Throckmorton to proceed there at once and beg the people to desist and not to take any action until he could send a commission to investigate and secure the guilty parties for punishment.

Governor Throckmorton succeeded in dispersing this avenging host, and General Sheridan, instead of sending a commission, reinforced the garrison and arrested some of the best citizens of the country.

The Hempstead garrison also had a band of marauders, headed by a desperate character, who occasionally attacked citizens at night and robbed them. This was the condition at Hempstead.

In the meantime I started a small general merchandise business at Courtney, with the assistance of my friend Cannon. While boarding at Cannon's house I occupied a room with a Mr. White and son, from Tarrant County, who were there, ostensibly, to trade a flouring mill he had in Tarrant County for one of Cannon's Brazos bottom plantations. I soon concluded that Mr. White had no flouring mill to trade and was imposing upon Mr. Cannon for his and his son's board and also to recuperate his horses.

I also met at Mr. Cannon's ex-Governor Morehead of Kentucky, who was then a refugee from the General Government. While rooming with Mr. White and his son, we had frequent discussions about the battles in Virginia, he claiming that he had served in that army, and his son on General Johnston's staff. I noticed that Mr. Cannon showed these gentlemen a great deal of attention and frequently these three were seen in the woods, sitting on a log, talking. I was puzzled to know why it was that Mr. Cannon could be so easily imposed on by this man White.

Some months or more after they had left, and I had moved to the hotel down in town, I met Mr. Cannon on the street and he said to me, "I have just heard from Mr. White." "Well, has he sold his flouring mill?" I asked. Cannon said, "No, you knew he had no flouring mill. You knew that it was General Wigfall and his son, Holsey." I told him no, that I was unaware who he was, having only met General Wigfall one time at Raleigh, North Carolina, at a hotel, when he wore a heavy black beard, and at Courtney he was clean shaven. Cannon told me, when he heard from them, they were in Havana and would take a steamer the next day for Great Britain. I never knew what became of ex-Governor Morehead after he left Cannon's, but do not think that he was ever arrested.

While at Courtney, I was called on by an old comrade, Ben Polk, in company with a friend of his by the name of T. J. Thorn, who were looking for a large plantation to lease. This they failed to find. Both had their old family set of negroes to work for them. Ben Polk went over on the Trinity, where he rented and cultivated a plantation, and Captain Thorn rented the Stevenson's Ferry plantation, about six miles from the town of Hempstead, where he pitched a large crop of cotton and corn.

Several months after I happened to meet with Thorn at Hempstead, when he made a proposition to me to join in the cultivation of this crop, as he felt financially unable to carry it through.

After investigating his proposition, which was most liberal, and considering the further fact that the location presented a better opportunity for business than Courtney, I decided to accept and moved down there with my stock of merchandise, boarding my family in a friend's home in Hempstead, as the house on the plantation was in bad repair. Captain Thorn also boarded his wife and two children with his father-in-law in Hempstead.

It was our custom to spend Sundays with our families in town, sometimes going in on Saturday night, returning Monday morning, and occasionally going in on Sunday morning.

CHAPTER XXIV

THE AFFAIR AT HEMPSTEAD.

One Sunday morning Thorn and I rode into town, and met on the road going towards the river, eleven Federal soldiers. We thought nothing of it as they had never before crossed the river. Captain Thorn stopped at the place where his wife was boarding and I started across the square to where my little family were stopping. I noticed a group of our solid citizens armed, talking excitedly, and rode up and asked them the news, when they told me that a band of soldiers had raided the town the night before, committing a number of depredations and had threatened to burn Hempstead that night.

A committee of citizens, headed by the Mayor, Mr. Whitworth, had visited the camp that morning and complained to the commanding officer, Captain Lancaster, of the conduct of his men the night before and told him of their threat to burn Hempstead that night. They asked permission to organize a patrol to keep their town from being burned. He cursed them in answer and told them that he wanted every one of them to hunt their holes that night at eight o'clock and that he would have a patrol out to see that they did it.

Knowing the temper of the people, as I did, I suggested to them not to do anything rash, telling them that whatever was done without the authority of the powers that were would only bring greater trouble, and that we would be powerless to secure redress. I pleaded with them and cautioned them to submit, rather than to make matters worse, as in the case of Brenham.

I then proceeded to my wife's place of residence and spent the balance of the day until about four o'clock in the evening. All during that day we heard wild rumors of the threats of the soldiers of what they were going to do that night and I decided it was best to take my wife and baby to the plantation and keep them out of trouble. About a mile from town I met one of our negro men, with his wife. His wife's clothes were badly torn. He told me that eleven soldiers had been out to the place, robbed the house of several guns belonging to the negroes and one very fine gun belonging to Captain Thorn. They had tried to break into my storeroom, but had failed to get in. They had then gone to Buckhorn, about four or five miles west of us, where there was a store and postoffice, and he thought on their return, they would break into my store. I asked him where he was going. He said he was going into camp to report them. I told him not to do so, that they would nearly beat him to death for making such a report, but to go and see his Marse Tom and tell him what they had done and to tell him that I had gone on out and to come out immediately and to bring out a good lot of pistol ammunition. We both had pistols but no ammunition for them, never having any use for them, though it was the custom with most people to carry six-shooters.

My first impulse was to watch their return from Buckhorn and, on their approach, to go into the storeroom, well prepared with loaded guns, and resist any attempt on their part to break into the store.

I drove on out to the place, very much alarmed; fearing that I would meet these devils on their return to town, but fortunately, they had not returned that far. After crossing the river at the ferry, I drove through the open fields, where I could see clear up to the house, about a mile, and when I reached the house the negroes reported that they had already left there, for town, on the river road, through a piece of bottom.

I had promised my wife that I would do nothing in the matter and intended to make good this promise, but when the negroes told me of the soldiers' doings in the negro quarters and at the house, I lost all control of myself, ushered my wife into the house, told her that I had to go down to the barn to see the mules fed, by way of an excuse to get away from her, went into the storeroom, got an only pistol, partly loaded, rushed to the barn without a saddle, jumped on my horse's back and set out in pursuit of them.

Fortunately they had already crossed the river when I got to the ferry. There is no question but what I would have dashed in among them with only three shots in my pistol and would not now live to tell the tale.

At the ferry I met a young man by the name of Stevenson, a son of the owner of the place, and a young man by the name of Hartsfield, who had been acting as our overseer. Stevenson was armed and so was Hartsfield. I got some ammunition from the ferryman for my pistol, which I completed loading. When about ready to cross the river, Captain Thorn hailed for the boat, crossed and secured another pistol from the ferryman. Thorn was very much stirred up. In meeting them the leader of this gang had made him get off of his horse, get down on his knees and told him to say his prayers, but finally let him off. We then started in pursuit and when within about a mile of their camp we caught up with them. When they heard us coming they broke, their leader and several companions taking to trees, from which they fired upon us. In the mix-up they got the worst of the affair. Two were left dead on the field, while we miraculously escaped without a scratch.

Our first decision was to report the result to the commanding officer, but being admonished by the manner in which he had treated our citizens that morning, and also the history in the case of Brenham, we finally concluded we had better keep out of their clutches and not risk our lives in their hands.

A military satrap was the law of the land; there were no courts to appeal to, only the tender mercies of General Sheridan.

We immediately returned to the river. After crossing, I asked the party to hold the ferry until I could get my wife and baby to a friend's house, about two miles distant. Hartsfield and Stevenson both refused and left, but Thorn, taking my pistol, in addition to the one he had, sat down by a tree and told me to take my time, that he would hold that ferryboat against the whole garrison.

I went to the house, took my wife and baby to a Mr. Waller Cochran's, where they spent the night, and then I went back to relieve Captain Thorn. We then went to another friend's house, where we were joined by our overseer, Hartsfield, and there spent the night. I instructed Mr. John D. Cochran, an old messmate, to go over to his brother's place the next morning, get my wife and baby and either take them to Courtney to her sister's home or bring them to Navasota, where we expected to meet them the next evening.

In crossing the ferry the next morning there were in the boat with them twelve men in command of a lieutenant, heavily armed, who had been out to the place, searching for us. My wife heard them make their threats that if they caught up with Thorn or Graber that they had orders to shoot them down without benefit of a court martial.

After spending that night at a friend's house, we three started for Navasota, on the west side of the river, Stevenson having left us at the ferry the day before. I have never seen him since. We crossed the river at Old Washington and arrived at Navasota in the evening, where I met my wife, who was taken to a Mr. Felder's house.

Our arrival at Navasota created great excitement. We were visited by many of the best citizens of the town, some of whom begged us to stay. They just wanted a chance at them, when they came after us, but I told them no, that our case was bad enough and that it would only result in involving our friends without accomplishing anything, which I was determined not to do. I therefore arranged to leave next morning for Waxahachie, where I was well acquainted, having spent two years of my boyhood there.

After a day's reflection we just began to realize our condition. Outlawed by the powers that were, everything that we had in the world lost, confiscated, dependent altogether on what financial aid and assistance we might accept; and, although we had abundant aid offered us, it only made us more desperate. We felt that our fate was sealed, though we had not a moment's thought of regret; we felt that we had done right, that we could not have done otherwise and were simply the victims of conditions existing.

I parted with my wife next morning, never expecting to see her again, telling her whenever she heard of my being in their hands, it would be my dead body; I would never surrender.

We now started on our trip to Waxahachie, without incident, stopping at houses at night, without disclosing our identity, giving fictitious names. When we reached Spring Hill we found a Mr. George H. Porter of Houston, an old army acquaintance of Thorn's, who was out collecting for T. W. House of Houston. We also found a Federal quartermaster from Waco, out buying horses for the troops stationed at that point. Now, my friend, Thorn, had got to drinking very hard, getting more desperate every day and conceived the idea to hold up this quartermaster and make him give us his money. I spurned the idea, telling Thorn that he could not do it while I was there. I was not willing to turn highway robber, which it would have amounted to. Here was the turning point in our lives, especially in the case of Thorn, who didn't seem to have any compunctions in the matter, though, in the eyes of many, he would have been fully justified. The Government, through their soldiers, had robbed us of everything we had and was seeking to take our lives without the benefit of a court martial, and, under the circumstances, Thorn's idea might have been justified.

My friend Thorn readily yielded when I called his attention to the disgrace such an act would bring on our families, to say nothing of having entered into such practices, which would have carried us further into an infamous career. To me, the fact that we had to depend on misrepresentation and lies to save our lives as long as we could, with a faint hope of ultimately living out of it, was bad enough. Lying was revolting to my very nature. I always detested a liar, as much so as I did a thief, but in this case, I leave it to the reader whether we were justified or not.

On parting with Mr. Porter, the next day, he pulled out a large purse of twenty dollar gold pieces and offered it to Thorn; told him to take it all, but I pushed back his hand and told Thorn that he must not take a dollar of it, as it was money collected by Porter, belonging to T. W. House. Porter insisted on him taking some of it; saying that he could replace it from his salary account, but I said no, I had good friends at Waxahachie, who would furnish me whatever money we actually needed. George A. Porter is still living in Houston and has built up one of the largest commission businesses in the place.

We now proceeded to Waxahachie without further incident and put up at the Rogers House. E.W. Rogers being an old friend of mine he did his best to make us feel at home. Here, as stated, I was known by many of the old citizens and we passed under our own names. About a week passed, during which time we watched the daily papers and read every report from South Texas, expecting daily pursuit. One day, while in a store across the street from the Rogers House, old man Rogers came in, somewhat excited, and told us a man had just got off the stage at the hotel and registered as "Brown, from Hempstead." He thought, from his talk, he was a Federal and advised us to go over and investigate. We immediately started across, and noticed the man in the door. When within about fifteen feet of him, he recognized me, saying, "Hello, Mr. Graber; are you here? We thought you were in Mexico by this time." I told him, "No, we are going to Mexico, but not the way you thought we were." By this time Thorn had got inside of the door and said to Brown, "Let me see you a minute," and led him into our room. As soon as inside, Thorn jerked out his pistol, saying, "Get down on your knees and say your prayers; d—— you, I 'm going to kill you." I quickly pushed his pistol aside, told him to hold on and let us hear what he had to say; "if he is here on business, after us, you can take him."

The fellow told a straight tale about his business there, saying that he came to see an aunt of his, who lived about fifteen miles from Waxahachie, a woman who was known to me. I told him to get up, that he was all right and not on business for us. He said that he never would tell of seeing us there if we did not want him to do so. He said that he was a Missourian and had been in the Federal Army; was wounded at the battle of Elkhorn, in his left wrist, a bad scar of which he showed us, and said this brought him to his senses; he quit fighting us and went into the sutler's business, to make what money he could out of them, and came to Hempstead with the troops in that capacity, though when I became known to him there, he was a mail clerk in the post office, though I did not recall his face. He told us, furthermore, that he was quite intimate with Capt. Lancaster and had heard Lancaster say that he told these fellows if they didn't quit their deviltry somebody would kill them, but Brown said Lancaster told him that he had his orders, received from General Griffin at Galveston, who was then in command of Texas, and Griffin had orders from General Sheridan to make an example of us and have us shot down wherever we were found, without the benefit of a court martial. I told Brown, when he got back, to tell Captain Lancaster where he had met us and also his treatment at our hands and since he, Lancaster, had orders to show us no quarter, which we didn't ask or expect at his hands, and if we should ever meet up with him I would make it a special point to get him, like we did the chief desperado at Hempstead.

Realizing that my friend Thorn had become too desperate for me to control, especially while drinking, I determined to cut loose from him, which I felt justified in doing, as he was then comparatively out of danger, and I suggested to him to start to California, where his mother was living. She was wealthy and able to take care of him and his family if he could succeed in bringing them out. This he decided to do. I then borrowed some money and had a business friend to rig him out in some good clothes and charge to me. I gave him a very fine gold watch and chain I had and started him for California, by way of Kansas City and the Union Pacific Railroad. I parted with him about two miles north of Waxahachie, he continuing in that direction and I turning east, out of sight of the town, suspecting that we might be watched, as to the direction we were both going. I forgot to mention that I exchanged horses with my friend Rogers' son, for one of the best saddle horses in the country, and on this horse, well armed, having four six-shooters (two in holsters on my saddle and two on my belt), I felt I could ride all around and through that garrison in Hempstead, or any pursuing party. I then struck out for Navasota, with the determination to bring my wife and baby out, fearing they would arrest her and hold her as hostage.

Riding along the main road in Freestone County, about noon, with a severe headache, I discovered a white house on the prairie, about a mile to the right of the road and noticing a negro ahead of me, crossing the road going towards the house, I hurried and caught up with him. I asked him who lived at that house. He answered "Marse Dick Oliver," who proved to be an old army friend of mine. I rode up to the house and found my friend Dick at home, and he introduced me to his family under my real name. They insisted on me spending the balance of the day and night with them. Dick said he would send for several of our old comrades, who lived in that neighborhood, to come and see me, which he did. One of them, Bulger Peeples, remained all night with me.

The next morning Dick made him go to a neighbor's and get what money he had, which proved to be fifty dollars in silver, which he insisted on my taking before we parted. I hesitated, but finally accepted it. I now proceeded on down to Navasota, where I arrived in the morning, early, and went to the store of an acquaintance, a Mr. Guy. I remained in his back room all day long, while he sent to Courtney for my wife and baby to come up and meet me at Mr. Felder's that night. We there spent the whole night with Mr. Felder and his family, planning what was best to do. I learned that they had been watching Dr. Hall's place at Courtney, my wife's sister's home, closely, ever since I left, hoping to catch me there on a visit. It was decided that it would be impossible to take them out with me, as they would, no doubt, exert extra efforts by scattering troops around immediately, when they found that she had left home. We finally decided that my only chance for escape would be to go to Mexico. Mr. Felder had a brother living in Tuxpan, Mexico, to whom he gave me a letter of introduction and assured me that I would be safe with him if I ever succeeded in reaching there. I also arranged with my wife to correspond with her by means of an acid, which can be used as ink, but is invisible until held up to heat, which brings it out black. I would then get some friend to write to Dr. Hall, my brother-in-law, on some business subject. Only a few lines would be written and when he received our communications he would understand it and hand the letter to my wife, who would bring out the acid writing on the remaining blank of the sheet. In this letter I would tell her where Dr. Hall could direct his letter and by that means we kept in communication.

About daylight next morning, during a severe thunder and rain storm, one of the darkest nights I was ever out in, Mr. Felder took me through his field to the Piedmont Springs road, which I followed by the lightning, as best I could, swimming one slough, but got safely across the Navasota River and soon arrived at a house where I decided to stop and have my clothes dried, take a nap and get some breakfast.

I called at the house and found the gentleman very pleasant. I told him I was in trouble and wanted to stop and get some breakfast and have my clothes dried. He very cordially invited me in, loaned me a change of his clothes, while his wife dried my clothing and prepared some breakfast for me, during which time I took a nap. I then left the house, refreshed, and started on to Centerville, Leon County.

CHAPTER XXV

I NARROWLY ESCAPE CAPTURE.

Before parting with Thorn at Waxahachie, he told me if ever I happened to be in the upper part of Grimes County, to hunt for a man by the name of Camp, who was an old California friend of his father, having gone there with him in 1848. "You only need to tell him who you are, that you are associated with me in this trouble and he will do all he can for you." I had nearly forgotten Thorn's mentioning this, when I rode up to a house late in the evening, that seemed to me perhaps a stage stand. I decided to stop and stay all night there, calling at the gate. An old gentleman came out, to whom I told my business, and he told me, "Certainly you can stay; I am keeping a public house;" furthermore saying, "You walk right in, take a seat on the porch, supper will be ready directly; I will take your horse down to the barn and feed him." His barn was some three hundred yards down the lane and across the road. I walked in, took a seat on the porch and very soon was called in to supper. I found at the table his wife and daughter and a gentleman traveler, who, in conversation with the ladies, stated that he had passed two companies of troops from Hempstead, coming on, and saying that they were nearly due there. I made out a hasty supper, immediately went down to the barn and told Mr. Camp I must have my horse right quick; told him who I was, by way of explanation why it was urgent for me to get my horse at once. He, of course, was surprised, and told me anything under the sun he could do for me, not to hesitate to demand it; said that he would go to the house and talk with this man and ascertain whether these troops were infantry or cavalry; furthermore, if they were infantry they were on their way to Centerville, where they had been expected for some time, to garrison that town. He says, "If they are infantry, they are evidently not after you and don't know you are here; then you have got to stay all night with me and rest; you will be perfectly safe. I will put you in a room where there will be no danger to my family, in case anything should happen. I have a good shotgun that I will know how to use in your defense."

I told Mr. Camp that I had promised my wife on parting with her, that I wouldn't recognize the best friend I met anywhere, let no one know who I was and made him promise not to tell this man nor his family. He soon came back to the barn, while I was watching the road that these troops were on, and reported they were infantry, on their way to Centerville and made me leave my horse and go back to the house with him. These troops camped within about a quarter of a mile, at the mouth of his lane, and came to his house for milk, butter and chickens, while I was in bed asleep.

He gave me an early breakfast next morning and I started on with this gentleman, who Camp assured me was a particular friend of Tom Thorn's and would fight for me, if he knew who I was. I told him that I did not intend to make myself known to him. We rode on together for about six miles, when we struck a creek, out of its banks. He suggested to me that he knew a foot log not far above there, where we could cross with our saddles and riggings; he would drive in his mare and she would cross and my horse would follow her, which he did. As soon as his mare got on the other side, she went flying up the road, with my horse following. He said he was satisfied that some friend of his would stop her somewhere on the road and we would hurry on afoot and try to get her, also my horse, and I had nothing to do but accept the situation. I spent nearly two anxious hours, watching the road in the direction in which the troops were coming, when he finally came up, leading my horse. We then saddled up and proceeded on our way and upon reaching the forks of the road, one leading to Centerville, the other to Leona, we parted; I taking the Leona road, which was called the old San Antonio road to Shreveport. I continued on this road, day and night, until I reached Marshall, where I found an old prison friend by the name of Fisher, who lived about a mile from the town and he insisted on my going out to his house to remain until I could take boat at Shreveport for New Orleans.

I spent several days with him, going up town, making my headquarters at the office of Ochiltree & Shaw. I was acquainted with Judge Ochiltree, whose son, Bill, was a public auctioneer. I turned him over my horse and saddle to sell at auction. While he was riding around the streets, crying the horse for sale to the highest bidder, he stopped in front of the office, called me to the door, said he was offered one hundred forty-eight and one-half dollars and that he had met a Federal lieutenant, who was stuck on the horse and he was going to make him pay two hundred dollars for him before he quit. I told him not to take another bid from him, as I did not want any Federal to ride that horse, so he had to sell him at one hundred forty-eight and one-half dollars.

I was now ready to move and, on investigation, found that two boats would leave Shreveport for New Orleans on Wednesday evening and on that day I went down to Shreveport to take passage on one of these boats. On arrival at Shreveport the stewards of these boats came aboard of the train and announced that the boats had failed to receive sufficient cotton to justify starting on the trip and had postponed sailing until the next Friday and if there were any passengers aboard, for New Orleans, they could go aboard of the boats at once and save hotel bills for several days, which I decided to do.

After registering on the "Bart-Able," which was the finest boat on the river, I took a seat on the guards, the front of the passenger deck, and awaited for what would next turn up. Very soon a party of four men came aboard, whom I took to be gamblers. I was soon recognized by one of the party, who proved to be Ike Hutchison, who started out in the army with us, but was a professional gambler, a class of people I never had much use for. During the short time he was with us in our company, I treated him somewhat indifferently, which might have resulted seriously at this time. As soon as recognized by him, he came forward, grasped my hand, was very glad to see me and started to introduce me to his companions, when I drew him near me and whispered in his ear, "Jones—" He caught on, and introduced me to his companions as "Mr. Jones." We then entered into a general conversation, took a drink together at the bar, when we both made it convenient to draw away from the crowd, out of hearing, when he asked, "What's the matter, Henry?" I told him of my troubles, that I had the whole Federal Army hunting me to take my life, and that I was going down to New Orleans to try to get some sailboat for Mexico. He seemed surprised at my statement and told me that he was in the Government Secret Service, drew back his coat and showed me his badge, but said earnestly that I need not be apprehensive on that account; that he wouldn't betray me. I told him, "Ike, my life is in your hands and I depend on your promise, but if you do betray me, some of my friends will get you." He next told me that Lieutenant Black, an ex-member of our regiment, was at the Southwestern Printing Office, a commercial editor of the paper, and that I ought to go up and see him. He said he knew Black would be glad to see me. With this information I parted with him and went up and found my friend Black who, of course, was greatly surprised at my statement of my condition. When I expressed my fears about Hutchison betraying me, he said he did not believe that Ike would do that, but, studying a few moments, he said, "Now, if Ike does betray you and you are arrested, bring them up here; I have more influence than Ike. While I would not do such a thing for any other purpose, and would rather have my right hand cut off, but to save your life, I am willing to swear that Hutchison is mistaken and that you are 'Mr. Jones.' This will give us time enough to get a couple of good horses, which we will mount and go off together."

Considering this proposition, realizing the enormity of the step he was about to take to save my life, from a lucrative and valuable position, commanding the esteem and confidence of the entire business community at Shreveport, to join me in becoming an outlaw, I consider he was one of the grandest and noblest characters that I have ever known and, at this writing, I regret to have to report that he has long since passed over the river, having died in Houston in the late seventies, a victim of consumption, and I was deprived of the pleasure of ever seeing him afterwards.

At the supper table that night I found only a little group of passengers aboard; two young ladies, one about twelve and the other about eighteen years old, a gentleman, whom I took to be their brother, wearing a mustache like my own, just about my age and size, and the captain of the boat, who sat between us, at the head of the table.

From their conversation I learned that these young ladies' mother was aboard and was sick. After supper I went forward, took a seat on the guards and had a smoke.

The next morning I found only the two young ladies at the table for breakfast. Having planned to try to get access to the ladies' end of the cabin during the trip, thereby avoiding the men aboard, I decided to form the acquaintance of these two young ladies and their brother and for this purpose entered into conversation with them, inquiring about the condition of their mother. While engaged in conversation, eating breakfast and sitting with my back to the front part of the cabin, I heard stateroom doors slamming behind me and, in looking around to ascertain the cause, found a policeman opening every door and looking in under the berths. Looking still further around I found six more policemen in the front end of the cabin, standing talking. This first man mentioned, continued his search in the staterooms, one after the other, until he passed us about two doors, then looked around and stared at me. I asked him, "Do you wish anything, sir?" He says, "Yes, sir; I am looking for a man about your size and appearance." "Well, take a seat, sir!" I replied, "I will talk with you as soon as I finish breakfast." He did not take a seat, but went back forward and joined the other policemen.

On the spur of the moment, I, of course, concluded that they were after me and, having resolved never to surrender, I started to run into my stateroom close by, get out my two pistols and start to shooting, but on a further reflection, was puzzled to know if they were after me. I could not understand why civil officers should be sent after me in place of soldiers, of which there were a good many in Shreveport. Then, I remembered the young man at the table the night before, and thought that they perhaps were after him and if through a mistake I should kill some of these civil officers, who no doubt had families and may have been Confederate soldiers, I would feel badly. I reconsidered by resolution and went forward to talk out of it, if they were after me, and with the assistance of my friend, Black, I believed I would have no trouble in doing so.

I walked up to this officer, who had spoken to me and said, "Now, I am ready to talk to you, sir." He answered, "I beg your pardon; you are not the man we are after, but he is aboard here and we have just learned where he can be found." I said: "All right, I am going up to the Southwestern Printing Office to see a friend and, if you do decide that I am the man you are hunting, you will find me at that place for the next hour."

I then went up and spent an hour with my friend Black. When returning to the boat I met the police officer on the stairs, coming down, and he said to me, "We have found our man; he was in that woman's stateroom, under her berth." I asked him why he was arrested. He said he did not know, only there was a requisition from the Governor of Georgia for him. It seems the sheriff's office had been abolished by the military, the sheriff removed from office as an impediment to reconstruction, and this was the reason this business was turned over to the city police department.

When I reached the cabin guards, I found the young ladies crying and asked them what was the matter. They told me that Colonel So-and-So, an old acquaintance of theirs, had just been arrested, but they did not know for what cause. It seems that these ladies and their mother lived in Louisiana, not far from New Orleans, and had been on a visit to Henderson, Texas, and were just returning home. It is hardly necessary to say that I kept shy of these folks the balance of the trip.

The next day I met up with an old gentleman by the name of Wilkerson from Columbia County, Georgia, who had been to Tyler, Texas, for the purpose of getting his son, who had been acting deputy sheriff, and had got in some trouble. I found the old gentleman a true Southern man, expressing his unreserved sympathy for the fallen South and denouncing in bitter terms the crime of reconstruction, as carried on. Needing some one to talk to and confide in, I had no hesitancy in making a confidant of him, which immediately enlisted his sympathy and kind interest and, without hesitation, he extended me an urgent invitation to go with him and make his house my home, saying that the armies had never touched his section of the State; they had got his negroes, but he had plenty of everything left and as long as he had a morsel left he would divide it with me. He further said whenever it was safe to send for my family, to do so, and we could stay at his home where we would be most welcome by all of his own family, besides himself, his wife, daughter and two sons, until I got out of my trouble.

Before reaching Marshall I had decided not to go to Mexico and place myself out of mail communication with my wife, but to go to Memphis, Tennessee, to see General Forrest, with whom I was well acquainted, having served under him in the early part of his career. I wanted to ask him to secure some kind of business for me, then to smuggle my family there and remain until the military were withdrawn.

On a further consideration of Mr. Wilkerson's generous offer, especially the feature of being isolated away from any town and public travel, I decided I had better accept, which I had no hesitancy in doing and on our arrival at New Orleans, we took a boat for Mobile, thence by rail to Atlanta and his station in Columbia County, somewhere between Atlanta and Augusta.

My reception at the Wilkerson home by the rest of his family, especially his wife and daughter, after learning of my troubles, was most cordial and unreserved and certainly they tried to make me feel at home and forget my trouble during my stay of six weeks. It was here that I received my first letter from home. After six weeks, doing nothing, having nothing to occupy my mind, I decided that I ought to do something more than kill valuable time and try and get into business somewhere, where I might make a new start in life. For this purpose I requested Mr. Wilkerson to give me a letter of introduction to his commission merchant in Augusta, Georgia, where I must try and get into business. The whole family tried to persuade me to not take such a great risk. I, nevertheless, parted with them with expressions of my high appreciation of their kind interest in my behalf and proceeded to Augusta, armed with Mr. Wilkerson's letter of introduction to the commission merchant, whose name I have forgotten.

On arrival at Augusta I put up at the best hotel and, I forgot to mention, having assumed the name of James E. Smith while at Mr. Wilkerson's, I registered under this name. Having to pay five dollars per day for board and room, I decided that I must get a cheaper place, some good boarding house if possible. Presenting my letter of introduction to Mr. Wilkerson's commission merchant, they stated they were not making a living for themselves, which was the condition of most of the business houses in Augusta, as some of the rich people in the country were sending in and drawing rations. These gentlemen then referred me to the only good boarding house they knew of which was reasonable in their rates. It was kept by Mrs. Oakman on Green Street, where I called and was informed by the lady that she could board me, but had only one place for me to sleep and that was in a room with two double beds in it, one of which had only one man sleeping in it, a printer and ex-Confederate soldier from Macon; if I was willing to sleep with him, she could take me and to which I agreed.

At the supper table that night I was shown a seat by a one-legged Federal captain, who was the Provost-Marshal of the place. When I entered my room that night I was introduced by my bedfellow to a Mr. Rice of

Syracuse, New York, and a telegraph official, whose name I have forgotten, both occupying the other bed.

I found that Mr. Rice had been sent there by Henry A. Wilson of Massachusetts, the ex-Vice President of the United States, and Kelley of Pennsylvania, who were touring the South inciting the negroes to riot and murder of the whites, which will be remembered by the Mobile riot, which surpassed perhaps all the other places they visited.

Rice had instructions to buy out the Augusta Chronicle and Constitution, perhaps the most influential Democratic paper in Georgia and run it in the interest of the Radical Party, the object being to create a strong sentiment among the negroes and stimulate their hatred toward their old masters and the white race generally, and also to keep the scalawag white element of the country well in line with their fanatical scheme of making a finish of the South.

While stopping here I claimed to be an ex-Confederate soldier from Tennessee, seeking employment. I had frequent discussions with Rice about the causes of the war and especially its cruel conduct by the Lincoln Government, which he approved unhesitatingly, saying that we deserved no better and he had come down here for the purpose of getting a slice of what was left. He said that he expected to make a cool hundred thousand and go back home and live on it for the balance of his days, in peace and plenty. On one occasion in our discussions, he seemed to get mad and said if he had his way about it, he would hang the last d—— one of us and commence by hanging Jeff Davis. He had hardly finished the sentence when I had a chair over his head and if it had not been caught by the telegraph official, I would likely have knocked him senseless.

On another occasion, when he was organizing his publishing force, he offered me the position of mailing clerk at a salary of $75.00 per month, which I turned down contemptuously, telling him that whenever I got ready to go to the dogs, I would affiliate with his sort. He said he thought he ought to have one good Rebel in his office. Now, I do not recall whether he succeeded in buying out the Chronicle and Constitution, or brought on new material for his paper.

After spending a few days in Augusta, I found that one of my old commanders, General Lafayette McLaws, was then acting clerk of the Superior Court, with his office at the court house. I scouted for General McLaws from Savannah, Georgia, to Bentonville, North Carolina, and immediately called upon him. I found him wearing his old Confederate gray, with buttons and trimmings shorn off, and in conversation, referred to his love of the old uniform, still preferring it, but he said it was not a matter of choice, but a matter of necessity. He had a large dependent family and his fee, or salary, hardly furnished him sufficient means for a decent support; besides, he expected to be ousted most any day, as the Radical sheriff, whose name I have forgotten, and Foster Blodgett, the mayor of the city, a renegade ex-Confederate major of artillery, would no doubt, succeed in their efforts to oust him. It is hardly necessary to say that during my stay here of several months, I made him daily visits and had a most pleasant, but sad, intercourse with him. He seemed to be at a loss as to his future; said he was educated a soldier, which he had always been and never tried to make a living as a civilian, in fact, didn't know anything else. He had an urgent invitation from General Pope, he said, who was in command of Georgia, with headquarters at Atlanta, and who was an old classmate of his at West Point, to make him a visit, but was almost afraid to accept, fearing unjust criticism by leading men of the State of Georgia, who would suspect that the object of this visit was to get office and join the Radical band. This he never expected to do, though the State of Georgia had treated him badly and especially his rich acquaintances, at one time friends, and he seemed to feel he was an outcast with no prospect of ever re-entering the army, therefore, not knowing what to do.

He declined the visit to General Pope, with due and proper thanks, but, after a few years, during General Grant's administration, was appointed marshal of the Southern District of Georgia and subsequently, by some other administration, postmaster of the city of Savannah, Georgia, in which position, he died. I had several nice letters from him while postmaster at Savannah; one just before his death.

I never cultivated or had much to say to our one-legged captain, the Provost-Marshal of the place, and in a few days, induced Mrs. Oakman to give me a seat at another table, thereby keeping my distance. No one at Augusta, Georgia, ever knew my secret but General McLaws, nor ever suspected anything wrong.

After spending nearly two months in Augusta, with no prospect of any business of any character, and having received notice from my wife that it was thought that they had got on my track, I concluded best to leave there for Lebanon, Tennessee, where I formed some pleasant acquaintances during the war, notably Captain James Britton, commanding a company from that town, called the Cedar Snags, which formed a part of the Fourth Tennessee Regiment. Captain Britton advised me to stay there until it became too dangerous, as quite a number of people knew me and I had to retain my own name in order to keep down discussion of my case among these people that knew me, thereby making it too public if I had assumed another name.

At Lebanon I found the family of General Anderson, whose son, Dewitt, became an intimate friend of mine, while in the army. He insisted on my spending a couple of weeks at his father's ranch, about five miles out on the Nashville pike, which I decided to do. In the meantime, I was introduced by Captain Britton to Judge Green, the Dean of the great Law School at Lebanon, also to ex-Governor Campbell, and the Motley brothers, bankers, over whose bank I roomed with Captain Britton and boarded at Mr. Toliver's, his brother-in-law. The above mentioned gentlemen, except Mr. Toliver and General Anderson, were influential, strong Union men during the war, but on account of the fanatical reconstruction policy, had just turned Rebels. I confided my trouble to ex-Governor Campbell and Judge Green and was assured by Governor Campbell that if I ever had the misfortune to be captured and my life was spared before my case could reach Washington, he would personally proceed to Washington, being an intimate friend of President Johnson's, and intercede to have my life spared.

I finally went down to the Anderson ranch to fish and hunt squirrels, in company with Dewitt, and found the old gentleman in charge, he preferring the ranch to his home in Lebanon. Returning from a hunt one day, alone, I found a horse at the gate and was met by Dewitt before reaching the gate, anxious to explain the object of the visitor's presence and especially his character.

Dewitt stated that he was a captain, whose name I have forgotten, who commanded a company in Stokes' Regiment, a notorious renegade; Captain Blackburn, commanding another company, was frequently on scouts with this gentleman and his company. During the war a Lieutenant Davis of the Terry Rangers, with eight of his men, were surrounded in a house by Captain Blackburn, with his company and this man's company. They demanded Davis's surrender, which Davis refused and kept them from the house all night, until their ammunition, gave out. Davis was badly wounded, in the nature of a broken ankle, unable to stand up, when he agreed to surrender, Blackburn promising that their lives should be spared and they should retain their horses, provided they would leave Tennessee at once, which Davis agreed to do and advised his men to move out and turn over their arms. After being disarmed, Blackburn had them led out into the woods and shot down in cold blood; he, himself, dragging Davis out to the gate post, cursing him and emptying the contents of his pistol into his head. Now this man, the guest of General Anderson, was present with his company, and Dewitt was anxious to apprise me of his great friendship to his father, during the war. When the Federals entered Lebanon the first time, General Anderson had some very fine horses and about eight thousand dollars in gold, with which he fled to the mountains near

Middleton and made this man's house his home, being old friends and acquaintances. While staying there a short time, this man came to him one day and told him that he felt that he could not stay at home longer, that he was a Union man in principle and, on account of it, was ostracised by some of the neighboring families and said he had decided to go and join Stokes' cavalry, but his joining the Federal Army should make no difference with General Anderson, that he wanted him to continue making his house his home, assuring him that he would be as safe, although he had joined the Federal Army, to stay there, as though he had joined the Confederate Army. Knowing the man as he did, General Anderson had no hesitancy in accepting his generous offer, but remained there for several months with his fine horses and eight thousand dollars in gold, and this man never betrayed him. This was the man, then, that was a visitor at General Anderson's, with his horse at the gate, of whose character Dewitt was anxious to have me acquainted, satisfied if he learned that I belonged to the Texas Rangers, he would refer to the Davis murder.

I entered the house and was introduced to him by General Anderson as Mr. Graber, formerly of the Texas Rangers. At the table this gentleman brought up the case of Lieutenant Davis and his man, and denounced it as a brutal murder, saying that he did his best to keep Blackburn from executing them, begged and plead for their lives, but to no purpose; he was second in command and could do nothing.

It seems strange that I should have met with a man who was present at the murder of Davis and his companions, which happened when I was a prisoner at Fort Delaware. Had any of Blackburn's men been caught by any members of our command, they would certainly have been given a like treatment.

After spending a week with General Anderson and his son, Dewitt, at their ranch, I returned to town and had a conference with my several friends, deciding it would be prudent to leave there and go to Hickman, Kentucky, where Captain Britton had a cousin, a prominent attorney of the place, by the name of James Lauderdale, to whom he gave me a letter of introduction and told me not to hesitate to make a confidant of him and he would, no doubt, have influence to get me into some kind of business. Hickman, and a section of country tributary, were considered somewhat prosperous, at that time, and Hickman was doing a fair business. Being right on the Mississippi River it was a shipping point for considerable territory.

On my arrival, I presented my letter of introduction, in the name of J. D. Roberts. He received me very kindly and made me make his house my home until I could get into business. Here I found only his wife and his old father, who were exceedingly kind to me. He soon told me of a young lawyer, who used to be a member of our regiment, by the name of Theo O. Goalder, who resided there and practiced law. I immediately called on him at his office and asked him to assist Major Lauderdale to get me into some kind of business position. He said he had a young friend by the name of John Murphy, who was clerking for a Mr. Bailey in a grocery store. He said that Murphy was getting $50.00 per month and didn't need the position, as he was well fixed, and was satisfied that he could induce him to resign in my favor and he could, no doubt, make it satisfactory with Mr. Bailey. We called upon Mr. Murphy, to whom I was introduced as Mr. Roberts, and also to Mr. Bailey, and after stating to him and Mr. Bailey that I had been a Confederate soldier and was out of business, seeking work, said I would very much appreciate the position, which was readily tendered me, through Goalder's influence. I immediately went to work at this place, on a salary of $50.00 per month, and board, which was furnished me at the Bailey home, and a room in the store.

CHAPTER XXVI

I SAVE THE LIFE OF AN ENEMY

After probably six weeks or nearly two months, getting acquainted with nearly all the county officials and leading citizens of the town, I found it a most charming community, and with few exceptions, Southern in sentiment. One day Goalder came to me, stating that there was a position open in a large dry goods establishment, the firm of Amberg & Company, two Jew brothers. The oldest one seemed to be quite a gentleman, but the younger, a black Radical, so stated by Goalder. We immediately went and applied for the position and when asked the question if I knew anything about dry goods, was able to state that I knew more about that business than I did about groceries and was satisfied that I could meet their every demand, referring them to Major Lauderdale. Goalder was present and made his own statement, vouching for my integrity and ability. They immediately employed me at a salary of $100.00 per month and I soon ingratiated myself in their favor by close attention and ability to do business, proving, as they expressed themselves to Lauderdale, the best man they ever had.

After working two or three weeks, getting well acquainted with their customers, especially those in the town, Mr. Roberts became the talk of the town, especially the lady customers, and was favored with many invitations to dinners and entertainments, which were always declined by me, as I was unable to feel at home and enjoy other company. I spent my time, principally, in my room, talking with Goalder and others, whose acquaintance I had formed and when they left, re-reading letters from home, of which I had a considerable batch and which I always carried in the inside pocket of my coat.

It seems my reserve and refusal to attend functions created a little suspicion, particularly so in the mind of young Amberg. One day, after about three weeks' service, while I was at work straightening out some drawers containing silk goods, I had pulled off my coat, the day being warm, and laid it on a stack of domestic on the outside of the counter. Young Amberg slipped to my coat, took out my letters, the discovery of which I made when I went to the coat. Here was a dilemma. I decided the best thing to do was not to say anything about it, appear as though I did not know the letters were missing and allow him to take his time to read them. I went over to the warehouse to do some work, stayed about an hour, which gave him ample time to read the letters, then returned for my coat and found the letters replaced. After closing that night, I was called into the office and found both of the Ambergs present. They told me that business had got somewhat dull, they were paying me a large salary, and they must save this expense and requested me to quit, saying they would cheerfully pay me a month's salary, if I quit at once. I told them it was all right. When they paid me my salary we parted.

Here now my cherished hope to prepare a home for my family and begin life anew again, had vanished and, in a moment of desperation, I decided to go back to Texas and bring my family out from among them.

During my absence my wife, soon after I parted with her, had made a visit to Centerville, Leon County, to a Dr. McLendon and his family, who were old Alabama friends, and while there they made up a music class for her and she continued to live there. With the object of immediately returning to Texas, I went around in Hickman and bade adieu to all of my kind friends and acquaintances, a few of whom were acquainted with my condition and tried to persuade me against incurring such great risks but, as stated, I felt desperate and had decided unless I could get my family out from among them and be with them, I did not care to live any longer.

I took passage on the first boat for New Orleans and paid my fare to the mouth of Red River, where I expected to meet a boat for Shreveport.

On arrival at Memphis, Tennessee, the boat laid over for several hours, delivering freight, during which time I hunted up General Forrest, who was then in the commission business. The General soon recognized me and after telling him my trouble, requested him to look out for a situation for me, under an assumed name, while I went to Texas after my family, which he cheerfully agreed to do.

While awaiting the Red River boat, a lieutenant who was the Bureau Agent of a nearby parish arrived, also awaiting a Mississippi boat for New Orleans. A few hours afterward an upper boat arrived to deliver some freight for Red River. The lieutenant, being very fond of ardent spirits, and there being no bar on the wharfboat, immediately went over to the Mississippi boat where he imbibed a few drinks. After delivering the freight the boat rang a bell to depart and the lieutenant ran down to the lower deck to get back to our wharfboat. The Mississippi boat already having cast off its bow line, was moving slowly apart from the wharfboat when the lieutenant attempted to step across, and, losing his headway, he became balanced between the two boats—with the boats moving apart. Discovering his predicament, I jumped over to where he stood and offered him my hand and pulled him over, thereby, no doubt, saving his life. If he had lost his footing he would have dropped in and pulled me in with him and both would have drowned as there is a strong underflow at this point and nothing which falls in ever comes to the surface. I did this under the impulse of the moment, at the risk of my own life, and saved the life of a man who, had he known who I was, no doubt would have been instrumental in having me captured.

On arrival at the mouth of the Red River, where with some other passengers, we had to await a Shreveport boat from New Orleans, I met a Mr. Black from Leon County, who had been over to Alabama after his brother's family, moving them to Texas and was expecting a couple of mule teams at Grand Ecore, to haul them to Leon County. I confided my secret to Black, who knew all about our case and insisted on my going with him on his wagons, which I decided to do. At Grand Ecore we met his wagons, which were so heavily laden with household goods and the family of his brother, three or four little children, that I preferred to walk behind the wagon, holding on to the same, to keep up with them.

We traveled the old San Antonio road in order to find good crossings at the different rivers and when we reached Alto, Cherokee County, I took stage for Rusk, where I had an old army friend, Judge Sam A. Wilson, the only man I knew in the place.

On arrival at Rusk, meeting with my friend, Wilson, who was much surprised to see me and particularly to learn of my troubles, I requested him to get me the best horse that he could find about the place, one that would do to ride in among the enemy. After studying a while he said that he did not know of a good saddle horse in the place, but thought that we could be accommodated at the livery stable, where I was furnished what turned out to be an old plug. I parted with my friend Wilson, he never expecting to see me again, and started for Centerville, Leon County, assuming the name of R. F. Jones.

Arriving within four or five miles of Centerville about noon, I decided to stop at a house and go into the town at night. For this purpose, I called for dinner and told the landlord I was looking around for a location in Texas, that I was from North Carolina and from what I had seen of Texas, was favorably impressed with it. After dinner, discussing several localities I had passed through, he asked how I liked his place. I told him I thought he had a good place. He then offered to sell to me and also a tanyard he had on sale; although I had never seen a tanyard, I looked it all over carefully and his entire place, leaving the impression with him that I meant business and consumed the balance of the evening in that way. After supper I told him I believed that I would go on to Centerville and stay all night and that I might be back again and try to drive a bargain for his place, unless I found something that suited me better. By way of excuse, my leaving so late, I told him I had heard of a particular friend, who had lately moved to Centerville, with whom I wanted to spend the night.

I now started for Centerville, where I arrived about nine o'clock at night. The night was very dark and I stopped to inquire where Dr. McLendon lived, expecting to find my wife at his house. At Dr. McLendon's home I was informed that he was at a doctor's office up in town, and directions given where I could find him. I concluded best to see him first before asking for my wife at the house.

On entering the doctor's room I found four gentlemen talking, but did not know Dr. McLendon, having never seen him before, nor had he ever seen me. I asked for Dr. McLendon; he spoke and said he was the man. I then told him that I was camped on a certain creek, some several miles from town, and had a very sick child, that I wanted him to go and see at once. He said all right and started out of the room with me. When we got to the gate he said, "You will have to go with me up to the house, for my horse." I told him all right and walked by the side of him, leading my horse by the bridle. He soon asked me, "What seems to be the matter with your child, sir?" I answered, "Nothing, I hope, Doctor. I haven't seen my child in ten months and have come after it and my wife; tell me where I can find them. My name is Graber." He jumped like he was shot and said, "For God's sake get on that horse and leave here quick. You are certainly not up with the excitement." "Well," said I, "if there is any extraordinary excitement here, I am not." He said, "Your family are not in town tonight; they are about seventeen miles from here, on a visit to her sister, who is at Dr. Baldwin's. They are visiting there, refugees from yellow fever." He says, "Let's get out in the brush where nobody will see us and we will talk matters over." We then walked to the edge of the town and sat down on the ground in the brush, out of hearing, when he detailed the situation, saying that Tom Thorn, my partner, had been ranging around there for two or three weeks, annoying Capt. Bradford, in command of the garrison, which was camped near town. Tom had registered at the hotel, "T. J. Thorn and friend," taking a meal there. Then, one night at roll call, he and his friend had fired into the camp and finally he had sent Captain Bradford a challenge, that he would fight him and any ten of his men at any time and place he might designate and signed the challenge "Thos. J. Thorn and friend."

Captain Bradford naturally concluded that this "friend" was Graber and knowing his and his family's friendship for my wife, concluded that Dr. McLendon knew Graber's whereabouts and showed him a big roll of money that morning, claiming it was four thousand dollars, saying, "Dr. McLendon, here is a reward offered for Thorn and Graber. You know where Graber is; here is your money." Dr. McLendon was a practicing surgeon for these troops, as they had no regular army surgeon. I told Dr. McLendon I had come after my wife and baby and intended to take them out or die in the attempt, even if the whole Federal army of Texas was there to guard them. He furthermore stated that Captain Bradford had issued an order to the sheriff of the county to arrest Thorn and Graber by the next Monday morning, or be removed from office as an impediment to reconstruction.

I now had Dr. McLendon to give me directions to reach the place where my wife was visiting, which he did, however saying that it would be impossible for me to find the way there, on account of the darkness of the night. Nevertheless I started out and soon got lost, and when I finally gave up the effort, I found myself only three-quarters of a mile from town. I was tired, suffering with a great headache and called at a house, where I was permitted to stay for the night and, after breakfast next morning, getting fresh directions to Dr. Baldwin's house, where my wife's sister was stopping, I immediately proceeded there.

After discussing the situation with my friends, as well as my wife, we decided best to have them get up a hack and a confidential driver, by the next morning, which they succeeded in doing and we started on the main road, leading into the San Antonio road, following that every day, stopping at houses at night and finally reached Rusk, Cherokee County, without an accident or any trouble. Judge Wilson was again surprised at my success in bringing my family out, as he never had expected to see me again. I then told him, "Now, for a good stopping place," and after considering all families in the town, where we might get board and none having any extra room, said, "The only place I know of, that has room is at my old daddy-in-law's, Judge M. D. Priest, who is the meanest old Radical in the State of Texas, but he has a most excellent family, who will do all they can for your wife and child and make you feel at home. We will make a confidant of him and he will never betray you." I said, "Judge, you know what you are doing; anything you say will be satisfactory to me." We then proceeded to Judge Priest's house, where I was introduced in the name of Jones and was kindly received and made to feel at home. Really we could not have found a more desirable place. We had excellent rooms and good board, just on the outskirts of the town. Rusk, at that time, was a very small place, about three or four hundred inhabitants, but it was the county seat of Cherokee County. We sent back our driver with his hack and team and he never betrayed us.

Civil Record

CHAPTER XXVII

I GET BACK INTO THE BUSINESS WORLD.

During the first month of our stay there, I visited the business part of town occasionally and made a few purchases at the house of Boyd, Frazer & Parks, a firm composed of John A. Boyd, who thought he was a merchant; Dr. Frazer, a practicing physician, who tried to be the bookkeeper, and M. M. Parks, who was a farmer, living out in the country, who furnished the money for the business. Boyd knew nothing about keeping or showing off his stock. In appearance it was one of the most conglomerated mixtures of merchandise I ever saw, but they were very popular men, particularly with the farmers in the country, and did a large business, considering their limited territory.

I soon got tired of lying around, doing nothing, but I felt that Rusk was about the safest place I could find anywhere, as the entire community, in sentiment, were true to the Lost Cause, with only one doubtful character, which was Judge M. D. Priest and he was really not a bad man at heart. When we confided my secret to him, telling him my life was in his hands, he appreciated fully the confidence reposed and declared that he never would betray us, which promise he fully kept and of which he afterwards expressed himself as being very proud.

Happening in to Boyd, Frazer & Parks one day, disgusted with the appearance of his stock of goods as kept, although it was none of my business, I concluded this would be a good place to get acquainted, on my knowledge of the business. I proposed to Mr. Boyd, who was the active member, running the business, that with his permission I would rearrange and straighten out his stock, without charge, as I had to remain over for a few weeks, had nothing to do and thought I could improve the appearance of things considerably. He readily consented, so I pulled off my coat and went to work, which proved a great treat to me. In a few days I had made such a change in the appearance of the stock, that customers seemed surprised and asked, "John A., have you been getting in a new stock of goods?" About the third evening, the partners got together, had a consultation and I was asked if I was able to keep books. I told them that I had kept books for a very large business in Southern Texas before the war, when they made me a proposition to go to work for them, keep their books and attend the sales department on a salary of $75.00 per month, which I accepted and soon felt here was the place to keep hid out from the powers that were, as there was no military nearer than Tyler, Jefferson and

Shreveport and no one knew of my secret, except Judge Wilson and Judge Priest, whose families were not made acquainted with it.

After considerable time, spent pleasantly at the home of Judge Priest, we decided to move into town for better convenience on account of its being nearer my business. We rented an humble home and went to housekeeping. I soon had an extensive acquaintance through the county, but always in the name of Jones, yet gradually imparting my secret to the most reliable friends I made in the town, notably the Bonner brothers, Judge R. H. Guinn, Judge James E. Dillard and others. After nearly a year in the service of Boyd, Frazer & Parks, I met an old gentleman by the name of T. L. Philleo, who had done an extensive business in general merchandise before the war. Mr. Philleo had a fine storehouse on the north side of the square, empty, except as to some castings, and had owing him perhaps as much as fifty thousand dollars in notes and accounts, acquired before the war. He was unable to collect much of it and conceived the idea that to make a success of this collecting, he ought to go into business again, which he was unable to do, on account of his age. I having established a reputation of being the best merchant in the town, Philleo made a proposition to me to go into copartnership with him. While he had no money he had a most excellent credit in New Orleans and suggested that I could go down there and buy for his account such stock as I needed to enable us to enter into competition with the balance of the town. Canvassing the subject thoroughly, I decided that I could make more money with my half interest in the profits of the concern, than to work on salary. He was willing and anxious to give me the full management and control of the business. Considering my condition then, I decided best to accept, which I did, and soon proceeded to New Orleans, armed with a letter in the name of R. F. Jones, to Speak & Buckner, his old commission merchants, and other leading houses in the different lines of merchandise that we had to buy.

Arriving at New Orleans, I put up at the Southern Hotel, then the headquarters of nearly all Texas merchants, within one block of the custom house, where General Sheridan had his headquarters, and went to work, buying a general stock of merchandise for account of T. L. Philleo & Company; "R. F. Jones being the company," so Capt. Buckner stated in introducing me. Speak & Buckner also accepted several thousand dollars on cash purchases, such as groceries and staple hardware, nails, etc., for which he asked us to send him cotton in the fall. I now returned home with my purchases and began to feel that I had a new life before me and some prospect of making a good living.

I arranged my stock very attractively, for which the house was well suited, though I had some trouble inducing farmers to come over on my side of the square. It was the only business house over there, the center of business being located on the east and south side. By close application and hard work I gradually succeeded in building up a fair business.

After some months, I found the unpleasant condition of Mr. Philleo's state of mind, worrying over his old matters and trying to collect, which seemed a complete failure, seemed to bear heavily on his mind and I noticed it was giving way under the pressure. He had a most excellent family, wife and two daughters, who had been raised in wealth and affluence and were somewhat extravagantly inclined, and the thought of perhaps losing all of his outstanding accounts and old age creeping on him very fast, made him very despondent and unhappy. He would go to the store every night after supper, open his safe, take out all of his notes and accounts, scatter them around on his table and a double bed, used by a young man clerk in the store, who reported his actions to me, and would study and look at them, occupying hours, sometimes until one o'clock at night, then replace them in the safe. Many of the makers of the notes and accounts had been killed or died during the war and their estates were not able to pay anything. I was satisfied if this condition continued his mind would finally break down and it kept me in a state of uneasiness. I, therefore concluded that I would wind up this first year's business and quit, which I finally did, after settling up all bills and the entire business, satisfactorily to all concerned. The year's business showed us each a net profit of about eighteen hundred dollars; outside of this I had demonstrated the fact that I was able to do a nice, clean business, safely.

Just as I feared, poor Mr. Philleo, some two or three years after, committed suicide in the back room of his store, at night, with his notes and papers laying all around him, stabbing himself with his pocketknife through the heart.

Mr. Philleo was one of the most kind-hearted, benevolent and charitable of men, and was known as such all over the country and he left many friends, but his family was poorly provided for.

After winding up the business of T. L. Philleo & Company, I was offered a position with R. B. Martin, an old merchant of the place, who at one time had done a large business. His stock had been run down for the want of means to keep it up, the result of poor management. Martin had a wealthy brother at Shreveport, of the firm of Gregg & Martin, cotton commission merchants. They had agreed to back him for ten thousand dollars, so he represented to me, with which he expected to buy a fifteen thousand dollar new stock in New Orleans. Martin agreed to pay me a hundred dollars a month to begin with and increase my salary as business justified it. I then proceeded to New Orleans, to buy this stock of goods, stopping over at Shreveport to obtain letters from Gregg & Martin, authorizing me to draw on them for ten thousand dollars.

Mr. Dave Martin denied having promised his brother this acceptance, but told me to go on to New Orleans, that Bob's credit was good and he could buy all the goods he wanted, without their acceptance. I then proceeded to New Orleans. Calling on his old houses, I found he was owing a great deal of money and having promised through traveling men, who had called on him, that he would furnish Gregg & Martin's acceptance for ten thousand dollars and then not being able to do so, his credit was so greatly impaired that they refused to sell him any more goods. I then wired Dave Martin again for authority to draw, reporting that Bob was unable to buy goods without his backing. I laid over, awaiting an answer, several days, and in the meantime, called on Speak & Buckner, who were glad to see me. I told them of the failure of my trip, unless I heard favorably from Gregg & Martin.

In the course of conversation, Captain Buckner said, "Jones, you've got no business working on salary; why don't you go into business for yourself?" I said, "Captain Buckner, that is simply out of the question. I have neither name nor money." He said, "Go and ascertain how much money you will need to buy such stock as you would be willing to start with." Already acquainted with the custom on terms, I stated that with five thousand dollars in cash I could buy a fifteen-thousand-dollar stock of goods, on four and six months. Captain Buckner said, "Go ahead, and get to work buying and draw on us for five thousand dollars on the same arrangement that I had with T. L. Philleo & Company." That was to send him cotton next fall. I said, "Captain Buckner, you don't know who you are talking to, as I have told you I have neither name nor money and you cannot afford to take this risk." He says, "You go and do what I tell you; I know all about you and don't want to know anything more." This gave me to understand that he was acquainted with my trouble and that I was under an assumed name and not having any other prospects of business in Rusk (which I could not afford to leave on account of the great security this place offered), I decided to accept and told Buckner that I would do business in the name of S. A. Wilson & Company, S. A. Wilson, being a lawyer and a great friend of mine. He was well known and a man of great influence. Buckner said to arrange that to suit myself. He was already slightly acquainted with Wilson and well posted on his character as a man. I immediately went to work, buying goods for a stock of general merchandise, which consumed about a week, and when ready to close up matters, Captain Buckner suggested that instead of drawing drafts on them, he give me the money to pay cash, in order to lead the merchants to think that I was paying my own money, thereby establishing a better credit. This was done.

Winding up my affairs in New Orleans, I took the first boat for Shreveport, with my stock of goods aboard, and arrived in Rusk in due time, followed by the stock. When I communicated my actions to Judge Wilson, he seemed greatly surprised, but stated it was perfectly satisfactory. I was at liberty to use him he said, whenever it was necessary. The best storehouse in the place, though isolated from the center of business, was vacant, and I rented this at a nominal figure. When the goods arrived I soon had it the most attractive place in the town.

Bob Martin, of course, was disappointed and made me the scapegoat of his disappointment, blaming me for not buying his stock of goods. I gradually built up a desirable business; went to New Orleans twice a year and bought goods under the very shadow of Sheridan's headquarters.

When, after several years, the infamous reconstruction era was terminated, the military withdrawn and civil government restored, though in the hands of negroes and Radicals, I decided to assume my identity and proceeded to New Orleans to settle up my bills.

After doing so, I would tell the managers, from this time on, the firm is no longer S. A. Wilson & Company, but simply H. W. Graber. "Why, Mr. Jones, have you sold out?" "No, sir; I have not sold out, but simply correcting a fictitious name." "Well, who is H. W. Graber?" "This is the man," which of course created surprise and when asked for explanation, would tell them that I had been forced to hide out for nearly four years, to keep General Sheridan from having me shot down, which he had ordered his Texas garrisons to do, without the benefit of a court martial, therefore I was forced to resort to hiding my identity. I then suggested, as these people were all Northern houses, that, "You don't want to sell me any more goods?" when they said, "Mr. Graber, go ahead and buy all the goods you want; your credit is not the least impaired; a man that can pass through such an ordeal, as you have done, unscathed, is entitled to more credit than he needs."

While, of course, this created a sensation in New Orleans business circles, the most astonished man of them all was Captain R. T. Buckner, who, it seems, didn't know as much as he thought he did, when he handed me his money.

Soon after my arrival at Rusk, I was made a Mason and also joined the Odd Fellows Lodge. I joined these institutions in my own name, satisfied that my secret would be safe with the membership. During a great revival of the union of all churches, wife and I joined the Presbyterian Church and I was ordained a deacon in the church, in due time.

CHAPTER XXVIII

I ASSIST IN ESTABLISHING THE MASONIC INSTITUTE.

In conjunction with some members of the Masonic Lodge, we conceived the idea of creating a Masonic Institute, a school of high grade, which was very much needed. I was appointed chairman of the building committee. I went to work actively, in conjunction with the committee, and raised means by private subscription, which enabled us to go to work, building at once. When trustees were elected I was made a member of the Board of Trustees and on the organization of the faculty, we elected a Scotchman, one Professor John Joss, believing that he would prove a good disciplinarian. He had a great reputation as a teacher. There were some bad boys in the community and in the language of Judge Guinn, who was a member of the board, "We needed somebody to use the rod to straighten out these bad characters." In this, however, we were mistaken; Professor Joss did not use the rod, but only kindness, commanding the respect of the entire school, including these bad boys, on account of his great knowledge and manner of imparting instruction. He was a most popular teacher, beloved by all who came in contact with him, and he built up a large and popular school, which turned out such men as Governor Hogg and Governor Campbell and no less than a dozen eminent lawyers and physicians known all over the State. I regret to have to report that, in the course of four or five years, on account of delicate health, Joss was forced to give up the school and move to Galveston, where he died.

The town of Rusk, being left out by the International & Great Northern Railroad, caused us to haul freight fifteen miles, over mountains and bad roads. I began to plan railroad connection for the town and conceived the idea of building a tap road, though unfamiliar with railroad business and especially the cost of a road.

In accordance with my plans, I called a meeting of the business men, submitting the same, which was to build a narrow gauge road from Jacksonville to Rusk, getting a charter with a State land donation of sixteen sections to the mile, which policy had been adopted by the State to encourage the building of railroads. In accordance therewith, we instructed Judge James E. Dillard, who was our Senator from that district, then attending the Legislature in session, to procure the necessary legislation and had him draw up a charter for the Rusk tap road. The bill covering the same he immediately introduced. I told my Rusk friends that with the aid of sixteen sections to the mile, and a further bonus of twenty-five thousand dollars in cash, which we believed could be raised in the town, we could induce Ward, Dewey & Company, lessees of the penitentiary, to accept these assets and build the road, as they had several thousand convicts to feed and had no use for them.

While these matters were pending and the International Railroad had been extended to Rockdale, I concluded to visit Rockdale, prospecting for a new business location.

On this trip to Rockdale, I met Ira M. Evans, the Secretary of the International Railroad Company, and submitted my plan of building a tap road, suggesting that perhaps his company might be induced to take hold of it, for the subsidy of the State land donation and the twenty-five thousand dollars in cash. He laughed at the idea, saying that they could not afford to run the road for its earnings, if we were able to build a first-class connection. He said our community would not be able to raise one-tenth of its cost and soon convinced me that it would be cheaper to move the whole town of Rusk to Jacksonville, than it would be to build a first-class road. I then submitted that, if we were unable to build a railroad, why not build a tramway, which would be within the bounds of our means and a vast improvement on the wagon road. He readily fell into my scheme, suggested that it was feasible, even with wooden rails, and that we had plenty of pine timber, the heart of which could be bought cheap and would make good, durable rails, amply strong, provided we would place ties eighteen or twenty inches apart.

I now asked him, he being a practical railroad man, to submit a specification on the grade, ties and rails, which he was pleased to do, and suggested that we change the charter we had had introduced, to that of the Rusk Tramway.

Immediately on my return to Rusk, I called a meeting of the business men and leading citizens and submitted the plan for the Rusk Tramway, having no difficulty in convincing them that we were unable to build a railroad. A committee, appointed by the meeting, was instructed to communicate to Senator Dillard our desire to change the charter to that of the Rusk Tramway, which he did, and included a clause granting eight sections to the mile.

After having established my business and a good credit in commercial circles, I decided that in mercantile pursuits I was too much circumscribed on account of existing conditions.

The bottom lands in Cherokee County were then the only productive lands for cotton and, as the uplands were light and largely worn out, and as I had a good knowledge of the prairie country around Waxahachie, where I had spent several years of my boyhood, I decided that this would be a better section of the State to build up in, and arranged my matters to make this move within the next twelve months.

When the charter for the tramway was returned, they proceeded to organize and elected a Rev. Davis, a very influential and good business man of the community, president of the company, after my having refused the same, on the ground that I did not feel permanently located, expecting to make a move to Waxahachie as soon as possible. Rev. Davis proved a valuable man for the position and immediately went to work canvassing the territory tributary to Rusk, for the sale of stock, which he succeeded in doing, to a limited extent and, by my advice, they commenced negotiations with Ward, Dewey & Company, lessees of the penitentiary, for the construction of the road. As heretofore stated, these people had a large force of convicts which they had to feed, and no work for them. The country subscriptions, which Rev. Davis secured, were paid in provisions and forage by the farmers, which enabled the company to feed the convicts while at work. After a time, I arranged to move to Waxahachie and soon after I left Rusk. Ward, Dewey & Company went to work on the construction of the road and before its completion it was decided to use a little four-ton Porter-Allen locomotive, in place of mules.

I forgot to mention, after submitting my plan for a railroad, Judge Dillard came home on a visit to his sick wife and while spending a few days at Rusk, had a meeting of the business men, which numbered only seven or eight, in Captain Barron's office. He submitted that the Legislature had decided to branch the penitentiary in Eastern Texas in the iron region, which was supposed to be near Jefferson, at Kellyville; a Mr. Kelly having demonstrated the existence of good iron ore in that section, manufacturing plows, andirons, chimney backs, etc., the same as Mr. Philleo had done in Cherokee County, but Dillard said, "Now, if you all want the penitentiary located here, I believe I can secure it for you."

One after another of these gentlemen got up and stated their serious objections, saying they had one of the best and most moral communities in the State of Texas and would not give up their school prospect for the penitentiary. I suggested to them, saying, "You know I am making my arrangements to leave here, because I do not see any prospect for future growth of the place, but, gentlemen, now is your time; you have been talking unlimited iron in the ground, of the highest quality, but it will have to be demonstrated to private capital that it is here in unlimited amount and high quality before you can ever hope to induce private capital to expend the amount necessary for such demonstration. There is no question in my mind that this iron, if you are correct in your claims as to its quality and amount, will prove the greatest resource of wealth, far greater than your farming interests. Locate the penitentiary here; the State will be forced to develop it and immediately build you a railroad connection to Jacksonville." After a full and fair investigation by this meeting they became enthusiastic and instructed Dillard to go for it.

To secure the location of Rusk for the penitentiary, it was necessary to canvass its advantages with the Legislature and especially take charge of a committee appointed by the Legislature to select a location, which required a great deal of time and ability, and, with the assistance and influence of friends of Dillard, who was one of the most popular men in the State Senate, they finally succeeded in landing the decision of the Legislature to build their branch penitentiary at Rusk.

On the withdrawal of the Federal troops and the dissolution of the Freedmen's Bureau, E. J. Davis was appointed Temporary Governor of Texas, until an election could be had for his successor. The election was held in due time, resulting in a Radical Republican Legislature, composed of some of the meanest men in the State and a few negroes, with E. J. Davis elected his own successor and the solid white element of the State disfranchised. They took charge and commenced an era of plunder. I do not believe there were more than a half dozen good men, including Judge Dillard and Professor J. R. Cole, members of this Legislature, but these did everything they could with the risk of being assassinated, to stem the drift of plunder.

Davis soon organized a State Militia and a State Police Force, stationing them in populous negro districts, formerly occupied by United States troops and Freedmen's Bureau, all under the leadership of Adjutant-General Davidson, who was as unscrupulous a character on graft as any man ever in public office. He arrested leading citizens in different sections of the State, without charges being preferred against them, as they had not committed any unlawful acts, and demanded large sums of money as ransoms. One case was notable—that of a wealthy farmer near Hillsboro, a Mr. Gathwright, whom he made pay ten thousand dollars for his release.

We had stationed at Rusk a lieutenant-sheriff, with his police, who was a great friend of Judge Priest and whose daughter he courted and finally married.

A Captain McAnally, who commanded a Confederate Scout in Texas during the war and had proven a gallant soldier in the army, was appointed by Davis, captain of police, and his acceptance urged by his friends, thinking it would be for the best interests to have him command a company of police, than any of the Radical gang. He was finally induced to accept the appointment. His home was at Brenham. He was instructed by the Governor to proceed to Huntsville and await the orders of the District

Court, presided over by the infamous Judge Burnett. While court was in session, three young men were arrested by McAnally for whipping a few insolent negroes who had insulted some young ladies on the street returning home from a shopping tour. These young men were taken before Judge Burnett, with arms concealed about their person. The judge called McAnally up to his bench and whispered his order to him, "Take these men to the penitentiary, but be careful, I suspect they are armed, and hold up the execution of this order until I can get to my hotel." Soon after the judge left his bench for the hotel, McAnally demanded of these young men to throw up their hands, when they immediately drew their six-shooters and commenced shooting at him and his gang of police, shooting their way out of the courthouse, wounding McAnally in the arm and he dropped between some benches, pretending he was dead. This was, no doubt, what saved him. Judge Burnett had not quite reached his hotel when he heard the guns fire, broke into a run and crawled under the hotel. These young men, after shooting their way out, mounted horses and started north for the Indian Territory, by way of Rusk and Paris, with McAnally and his police in close pursuit.

Arriving at Rusk he commanded Lieutenant Sheriff and party to join him in this pursuit, which they did. On parting, on this trip, with his sweetheart, Miss Lou Priest, Sheriff told her where he was going with McAnally and on their return, they were going to arrest Mr. Graber. The whole Priest family being good friends of ours and Miss Lou's sister, the wife of my friend, Judge Wilson, she immediately went over to Judge Wilson's and imparted this information about my contemplated arrest. Judge Wilson came over to town and had a meeting of a few of the leading lawyers of the place, notably the Bonners, Judge R. H. Guinn and Judge J. E. Dillard, who after canvassing the matter, decided that the object of my arrest was altogether political. They were expecting to make great capital out of it for the necessity of continuing their Radical regime. Satisfied that they might manufacture evidence to convict me in a Radical court, these friends advised that I had better go into exile again, thereby probably saving my life. I told them to tell me what to do in order to stay, for I had done all the running I ever expected to do. I was satisfied this police had no legal authority for my arrest, as I had never violated any civil law and I could not afford, in justice to my family, my friends and my creditors, to again have my business wrecked.

When these friends found that I was determined not to be arrested by this infamous police and in order to be doubly sure, they advised me to go down to Austin County and investigate the records and know positively that this police had no authority for my arrest.

On leaving for this trip, armed with a letter from Colonel T. R. Bonner to Judge J. D. Giddings, whom they suggested I call on for advice in the matter, and leaving a message for Lieutenant Sheriff, that I had gone on a trip for a week or ten days and promptly on my return I would report to him, I left for Austin County.

Passing through Anderson, I conferred with Hannibal Boone, who suggested there was no necessity for my going to Austin County, where he was living at the time I had trouble with the soldiers. He said that there could be no case against me, as I had violated no civil law and my dealings were altogether with the military. Stopping at Brenham, in my conference with Judge Giddings, he became very much exercised on the threatened arrest of myself and said, "Mr. Graber, go back home; resist their arrest in the most effective manner. It is time we were calling a halt on this infamous police system; resist them, and the whole State of Texas will be at your back." I said, "Judge Giddings, I thank you for the advice; it is exactly my feeling and determination not to submit, peacefully, to this arrest."

Being so close to the town of Bellville, I decided to finish my trip, went there and called on Hunt & Holland, leading attorneys, who repeated Judge Giddings' advice. I now returned home and immediately sent word to Lieutenant Sheriff that I could be seen at my place of business at any time he wanted me.

I returned at night and next morning proceeded up to my store, sent word to Mr. R. B. Reagan, a brother of Judge John H. Reagan, a man of iron nerve, the sheriff of the county, to come up to the store at once. On reaching there I told him that Lieutenant Sheriff, with his police, had threatened to arrest me, that I had just returned from Austin County and had investigated, finding that they had no authority or warrant for my arrest and I claimed his protection. He said, "Mr. Graber, load up your shotguns in your stock, set them behind your door and when they come to effect your arrest, open on them and I and John and George, will be about." John Reagan was his deputy and a George Taylor, another deputy, all men as fearless and resolute as any set of men ever together, with nerve to fight a hundred police. In about an hour I noticed Lieutenant Sheriff coming up the south side of the square, by himself, apparently unarmed. I met him in my door, when he said, "Mr. Graber, Miss Lou Priest told me that you had some very nice gentlemen's hats." I told him I had; he told me he wanted to look at some. I got down a box of hats from the top shelf and allowed him to select his hat out of the box, the size he needed, treating him indifferently. He got out his number, put it on his head and stepped up to a glass suspended on the shelf, passing between the counters. Looking at the hat in the glass he said, "I believe this becomes me pretty well; what is it worth?" I told him, "Five dollars." When he turned around to walk from behind the counter, he espied the shotguns behind the door. I noticed it seemed to affect him a little but he soon recovered, paid me the money and left the store, saying, "A fine day today," and this finally settled my trouble. He evidently came there with the intention of spying out the situation before attempting my arrest. When he left the house he noticed Sheriff Reagan with his deputies near.

This ended my trouble. I felt I had conquered a peace which would be a lasting one, as far as the military and our Radical Government were concerned. This changed condition gave me a free hand to engage in further enterprises and to rebuild my own fortune, as well as to work toward the benefit of the community in which I made my home.

CHAPTER XXIX

I REMOVE TO WAXAHACHIE AND GO INTO BUSINESS THERE.

As heretofore stated, I had spent several years of my boyhood in Waxahachie, during the fifties, and became attached to its people because of their great interest in me, on account of my being an orphan. I felt ever grateful. Furthermore I recognized the value of the rich lands of Ellis County and territory tributary thereto, and I decided to make Waxahachie my permanent home.

Arriving at Ennis, one of its shipping depots, I took stage for Waxahachie, where I rented a storehouse belonging to Judge McMillan, and employed his son, N. A., as bookkeeper and salesman in the house. The two-story building next to the Getzendaner & Ferris Bank, was the most modern store building in the town and young Mr. McMillan, one of the most popular and best posted men on the Ellis County farmer, I could find, having been in business with his father in this house for several years, moving there from Alabama.

To give the reader a fair idea of the condition existing, I found the old set of merchants, who were doing business there before the war, still adhering to old-time methods, selling goods on twelve months' time and charging about twenty-five per cent more for same than the towns of Ennis or Palmer, which were selling altogether for cash. These towns were doing a more lucrative business than Waxahachie. Not a house in Waxahachie would buy a bale of cotton for cash, thereby turning the cotton market over to the towns of Ennis and Palmer. The stage driver that carried me back to Ennis had money sent by a lady at Waxahachie, to buy a dozen spools of thread at Ennis, where spool thread was selling at 75 cents a dozen and Waxahachie charging a dollar a dozen.

This encouraged me in the belief that Waxahachie was a good place to start in again, as I expected to do business altogether for cash and buy cotton for cash, as cotton always controlled business.

Having bought goods almost exclusively in New Orleans, except a few purchases in St. Louis and Galveston, I found that Galveston was about as good market as the others and, on account of its nearness, adopted a plan of buying goods often, in smaller quantities and ordering them as they were needed, which always gave me a fresh stock of goods and proved very satisfactory.

While engaged in buying my first stock for Waxahachie, at the house of P. J. Willis & Brother at Galveston, I met a Mr. Joe Farley, who was one of the traveling credit men for the house, and was also a partner in the house of Clift & Farley of Waxahachie. He came to me, saying that he understood I was buying a stock for Waxahachie and wanted to tell me that I could not find a more undesirable place to begin a new business, as he had decided to reduce prices materially, to a point that would not leave any profit. I thanked him for the information and especially for his resolution to reduce prices, which I told him I intended to do, and would much prefer his saving me the unpleasant duty. Farley, however, never carried out his threat until after I had started my business and forced them to do so. I also forced them to buy cotton for cash, thereby making Waxahachie a cotton market.

On my return to Rusk, I immediately packed whatever stock of goods I had left and shipped to Waxahachie, then moved my family over there and went to housekeeping in a rented house. I next proceeded to Galveston, where I arranged with Mr. Willis to give me an open account of twelve or fifteen thousand dollars, on which I made remittances every week and continued to order goods almost every week, which always gave me fresh stock and proved very satisfactory to Willis, as well as myself, and very attractive to the public.

I now commenced the purchase of cotton for cash. I was a good judge of cotton classification, and being very careful in keeping posted on the course of the market, especially Galveston, and cotton being in transit only a short time, I was enabled to handle cotton without any great risk, besides I made shipments altogether to Cannon & Company. Mr. Cannon, as heretofore stated, was an old friend before the war, for whom I had kept books and worked in his sales department at Hempstead. In entering the cotton market and paying cash, the old mossback business element of the town sat around in front of their stores, smoking and whittling goods boxes, making all manner of predictions that that fellow wouldn't last long—I would soon get out of money and "bust."

I bought cotton from farmers over about Bristol, on the Trinity, on the other side of the Houston & Texas Central Railroad, paid them cash, and 75 cents a bale to haul it back to Ennis, then they would turn around and spend the money with me for goods and return home happy and contented.

About this time we had the Grangers, a strong farmers' organization, who had decided to concentrate their business at one house. They had a general meeting of the county organization at Waxahachie, and sent a committee, inviting me into this meeting, when I was requested to make them a proposition to handle all of their business on a basis of ten per cent profit. Not wishing to take advantage of my competitors, I persuaded them not to make such an arrangement, as it would not prove satisfactory, especially to their families, being restricted by contract on this basis to buy only at one house. Entering into a full detail of the objections, I persuaded them that it would not be to their interest to make such a contract and induced them to drop it.

While I could have made a great deal of money out of this proposition, I preferred to take no advantage of my business neighbors, thereby incurring petty jealousies and enmity, having in view the building of a tap railroad to connect with the Houston & Texas Central, and it was of the greatest importance for me to retain the friendship and the confidence of the old business element, who were the only men in the county of any great financial ability.

CHAPTER XXX

THE TAP RAILROAD.

Concerning the "Tap" Railroad just referred to, I cannot better explain the trials and difficulties of that time than by reprinting an article which I wrote, some years ago, at the request of one of the Waxahachie papers, which was anxious to clear up the seeming mystery which enshrouded the building of the "Tap."

Dallas, Texas, Sept. 4th, 1912.

Editor Ellis County Herald,

Waxahachie, Texas.

My Dear Sir—Your valued favor of the 26th ult., requesting a history of the Waxahachie Tap Railroad is at hand.

Complying with your courteous request, permit me to assure you and my old friends that it is not my purpose in this to ventilate old grievances at the hands of people who were the greatest beneficiaries of the building of the road, but simply to state facts and to keep the record straight. Carefully considering conditions existing at that time, my board of directors were not so much to blame for their want of confidence in the feasibility and possibility of the enterprise, as this feeling was shared largely by some of the best business men of Houston and Galveston, but were to blame for allowing one or two of their members to control their action in opposing me. I incurred the enmity of these directors through people's expression of approval of my efforts to accomplish what seemed to them an impossible undertaking.

Entering into this labor of love, without promise of fee or reward, with my board of directors (composed of the principal business men of the town) depreciating my business character by expressions well calculated to bring about ruin, which they accomplished in about two years, it required about all the moral courage in my composition to determine not to recognize such word as "failure."

Have said this much in defense of this article, which may prove hurtful to the feelings of friends and descendants of the men who have claimed the credit of building the road, but I cannot do otherwise than adhere strictly to facts and truths, as all fair-minded men who were then citizens of Ellis County, still living, will bear me witness. I have never had a public expression of thanks for the enormous sacrifice to me then of ruining my splendid prospect in business to save your town from isolation and ruin.

The object in going into these details is only to emphasize the claim of friends at that time that I was the only man connected with it who did any work, and if the "board" would quit meddling with it, I would soon have the road built. These expressions I tried my best to hold down, knowing well it would increase their opposition to me. Another object: There are few people now in your city who know that I ever had anything to do with it, but I consider it due my children to inscribe in my own history one of the proudest acts of my business career, representing two years of the best labor of my life.

Please do not fail to note that I had to depend on memory altogether for this article, hence its disconnected character, and am entirely unable to supply dates, which, however, is immaterial. I moved to Waxahachie in 1873.

To give your readers a fair conception of existing conditions at Waxahachie and Ellis County, I found on my first visit to your town by stage from Ennis that your merchants were still adhering to old-time business methods; selling goods on time, at large profits, thereby losing the most desirable business; Ennis selling goods on an average of twenty per cent less for cash, buying the farmer's produce, principally cotton, and paying cash therefor. Waxahachie did not buy a bale of cotton for cash, but only on account. The result was that Ennis, though but a few years old, soon outgrew Waxahachie, and aspired to be the county seat, which caused a bitter feeling between the two communities. Knowing the magnificent territory contiguous to Waxahachie, I decided that with proper efforts your town could be made one of the best in the State, and arranged to locate there. Had I supposed that to locate there, it was necessary to ask the permission of the old business men, and then conduct business as they directed, I would certainly have gone elsewhere, but of this I was ignorant, and after starting in, determined to exercise my own judgment. I sold goods for cash, at reasonable profit; bought cotton for cash, all that was offered, paying Dallas prices; bought cotton from east of Ennis and Palmer, then paid the farmer seventy-five cents per bale to haul it back to the railroad for shipment. Many of these farmers, after I paid them the cash for cotton, would turn around and spend every dollar of it with me for goods. I bought cotton from Hill, Johnson and Bosque Counties, and did not lose any money on it, although my old competitors predicted that I would soon have to quit. When disappointed in this, a few of the progressive ones, Messrs. Pickett, Trippett and McLain, joined in with me, and we soon established in Waxahachie a good cotton market.

I now began planning for railroad connection, and when I had my plans sufficiently matured, I submitted them to a meeting of the business men, who expressed grave doubt about the possibility of the undertaking, and I only induced them to enter into it by suggesting that an effort, even though a failure, would have the result of throwing Ennis on the defensive and induce them to drop their county seat agitation. They then told me to go ahead and get my plans fully matured, which I submitted at a subsequent meeting, and which were as follows: To get a charter for a Waxahachie tap road with a State land grant of sixteen sections to the mile and have the town issue bonds to the limit of the law, which proved to be $75,000, then augment this amount with farmers' stock subscription of $25,000 more; to sell these bonds at par to the business men of Waxahachie and commission merchants of Galveston and New York who were doing business with Waxahachie—thus giving us $100,000 cash and the State land grant to build the road with. I stated this could only be done by the adoption of second-hand iron, which I believed could be had, and which would answer the purpose. To buy new iron would cost several times the amount of our cash asset, as it was then quoted at $85.00 a ton at the mills. There was serious doubt about the Legislature passing a bond bill at the time as they had up the repudiation of international bond bill granted under a fraudulent charter, and the International Railroad Company had Galusha Grow of Pennsylvania and John H. Burnett of Galveston at Austin, trying to bulldoze Governor Coke and his Legislature into the issuance of their bonds; hence both the Governor and Legislature were committed against the issue of bonds of the State in aid of railroads. But I believed that Judge J. W. Ferris, who was then one of the most eminent lawyers in the State, and who, through his International bond decision while acting as special Supreme Judge in the case had endeared himself to the Governor and Legislature, as well as the entire people of the State, would be able to overcome this objection, as we were only asking permission to tax our own town. It was then determined to send Judge Ferris to Austin for the purpose of obtaining a charter and bond bill. The committee appointed to make the request of the judge met his positive refusal, but he stated at the same time that if it was attempted to build the road, he would back the enterprise with his money. I was now urged and finally persuaded to go to Austin and endeavor to obtain the necessary legislation. I called a meeting of the taxpayers of Waxahachie, and explained to them that it was of the utmost importance to get up a petition to the Governor and Legislature, asking permission to tax themselves, and I succeeded in obtaining every taxpayer's name to the petition. I then had the county clerk examine the tax rolls and certify that he found every taxpayer's name to the same. I then proceeded to Austin, armed with this petition, a letter from Judge Ferris to Governor Coke, and from Dr. Aldredge to friends in the Senate. On my arrival at Austin, I met John H. Burnett and Galusha Grow at the hotel, who proposed to me, if I would assist them, they would assist me, which I declined, telling them that I was opposed to the issuance of their bonds, thus at the outset defining my position with the Legislature. The next morning I sought and obtained an audience with Governor Coke, presented my letter from Judge Ferris and petition from the taxpayers, and after reading this, the Governor said, "Mr. Graber, I will promise you this, if the Legislature passes your bills I will sign them. The question involved in the International bill is the taxing of the whole State to benefit the section through which the road runs, but in your request the good people of Waxahachie are only asking to tax themselves to save their town." I thanked the Governor for his kind assurance and asked permission to make the statement to the members of the Legislature, which he readily gave. Though I had never before looked inside a legislative hall I soon felt perfectly at home and had the privilege of the House and Senate. In my canvass of the House and Senate I found little opposition to the bond bill after reading our petition, but considerable objection to the further donation of land in aid of railroads, which, however, I was able to overcome by satisfying them we would never be able to build our road without it. As many of the influential members were old army friends to whom I became indebted for valuable assistance, I was able to return home in three weeks, both bills having been signed by Governor Coke a few weeks later. It would not be inappropriate here to mention a little incident to show a proper appreciation of my services at that time. I had wired my wife that I would be home on Saturday, but detained en route, I failed to make it, which saved me considerable embarrassment, as the stage was met a short distance from town by the mayor, city council and concourse of citizens, with a brass band, intending to give me an enthusiastic reception. On the next Saturday a mass meeting was held for the purpose of organizing under our charter, and electing officers. At this meeting I explained to them that I had taken the liberty of stating to members of the Legislature that Judge Ferris would be the president of the company, and asked his election, telling them that it was all-important the enterprise should be headed by the most influential man in the community. Judge Ferris being present, stated he could not under any circumstances consider the acceptance of the position as he did not have the time to give it the attention necessary to make it a success, and placed my name in nomination, which created great enthusiasm, and it was attempted to be carried through without further consideration. I tried to check this movement, by telling them I had as little time to spare from my business as Judge Ferris, had already given them three weeks of most valuable time away from my business and was unable to do anything more than act on the board of directors, if they saw fit to use me in that capacity; but the meeting would not have it that way, and plainly told me if I wanted the road built, I would have to serve, and promised to sustain me with all the means and power at their command. Under this assurance I was finally persuaded to accept, and, after completing the organization with Judge Ferris as vice-president, the meeting adjourned subject to the call of the president.

I forgot to explain that through the issuance of the bonds, it was agreed that the town should be issued stock to the amount, thus every taxpayer became a stockholder and was entitled to vote in the organization. While at Austin, in company with some members of the Legislature, I called on General Braxton Bragg, who had just come to Texas with a party of civil engineers, with the intention of making this his home—he was anxious to get a first job and promised me he would undertake the location of our road at his actual cost (estimated not to exceed 500 dollars). As soon as organized I took up a correspondence with him, and entered into a contract to run three preliminary lines and cross section the line adopted, furnish plans and specifications of a first-class road. He surveyed one line to Ennis, one to Palmer and one to the nearest point on the H. & T. C., which was adopted. We next advertised for bids for the whole work complete, contractor furnishing the road complete, ready for operation, except equipment, and another for the grading only. We had a bid on each, one from John McCarthy of Kansas City, who was returning from Galveston, where he had in a bid for a large contract with the Gulf, Colorado & Santa Fe and had lost out. He carefully examined our assets, which were one hundred and eighty-five sections (estimated) of land certificates to be issued by the State (the line being 11 45-100 miles long), $75,000 of Waxahachie bonds and about $13,000 of farmers' stock subscriptions which I had secured by hard labor, and in which I had valuable assistance from Judge Anson Rainey, who was then a young lawyer in Judge Ferris' office. Mr. McCarthy, satisfied with our assets, submitted a proposition to deliver us the road complete as per General Bragg's specification, except to substitute fifty-six pounds of good second-hand iron approved by General Bragg, which was considered sufficient for our purpose, in consideration for our entire assets, and complete the same in two years. We also had a proposal from Roach Brothers & Tierney for the grade only at thirteen cents per yard. As John McCarthy's bid was the best for us we awarded him the contract, and immediately notified him by wire at Kansas City, to which we received a reply from his wife, by letter, saying Mr. McCarthy was not at home, but we would hear from him as soon as he returned. In the meantime I wired General Bragg at Galveston, who was the chief engineer of the G., C. & S. F. for a report on Mr. McCarthy, but had his answer, "Drop him." This in connection with an indefinite letter finally received from McCarthy, made me conclude it best to let him alone. In the meantime, I had induced Mr. Roach to hold his bid open (which was 13 cents per yard, one-third cash, one-third in bonds and one-third in provisions and forage he expected to use to feed his teams and men) until we heard definitely from John McCarthy and in case of his failure to make us a good bond, and furnish us ample evidence of his ability and good intentions, we would give him the contract for the grade, as in his bid. After our decision to drop Mr. John McCarthy, we entered into a contract with Roach Brothers & Tierney for the grade, to go to work at once—as he had his outfit at Fort Worth already. He was on the ground sooner than expected, and gave us only a few days to prepare for a formal beginning of the work. We wanted to celebrate the event with a great barbecue. On account of the short time for notifying the farmers, the board of directors opposed my plans of having the celebration, but I determined to have it anyway, and sent out invitations to all interested in the building of the Waxahachie Tap, to join us in celebrating the commencement of the work. I solicited a few of our best farmers to donate the meats, which they did cheerfully in the greatest abundance. The day set apart for the celebration, the farmers began to arrive in the early morning in large numbers—not only our own Ellis County people, but a large number from Hill and adjoining counties, and by one o'clock the crowd was variously estimated at from 1500 to 2000 men, women and children. Such a large enthusiastic gathering had never been known in this part of the State. The board of directors had in the meantime concluded to join in with us, and, although they had told me they would have nothing to do with it, had ordered carriages, and I was invited to a seat with Mr. John C. Gibson, who informed me they had not prepared any program, which I had asked them to do in the morning. I asked Mr. Gibson his age, and found he was the oldest man on the board. When everything was ready, I was handed a spade by Mr. Roach, who stated that it devolved on me to turn the first dirt. I climbed on top of a wagon bed with the spade and addressed the crowd in a few words which I remember about as follows:

> "Fellow Citizens: We are proud to see so many of you here, manifesting, by your presence, an interest in our work; an interest on your part it has been charged did not exist, particularly with our farmers, who recognize that they are as much interested in the building of this road as our town. The doubting Thomases will directly witness actual beginning of the work by our contractor, Mr. Roach, who has one of the best-equipped grading outfits in the country and will push his work to an early completion. Upon such occasions it is customary for the president of the company to turn the first dirt, an honor which on this occasion I turn over to Colonel John C. Gibson, the oldest member of the board of directors." I then turned the spade over to Mr. Gibson, who eagerly accepted the honor and performed the duty. Mr. Roach having his teams ready, then proceeded with the work. Permit me to say here, that it proved a grand sight to everybody

present, the most of whom had never seen anything like it, to see about fifty splendid teams with their scrapers turning up the ground, and the moral effect at that time cannot be overestimated, as the effort of Waxahachie's building of a railroad had been ridiculed by people interested in our failure, particularly the people of Ennis. I omitted to mention, I visited Ennis before we definitely determined on a location, and to a meeting of their business men, submitted a proposition to adopt their line for a subsidy of twenty thousand dollars, which created considerable ridicule, but I told them they might laugh as much as they pleased, the road would be built and some day would become a main line by an extension east and west, and though the point of junction might never become a rival town, it would always prove a standing menace to their town, and prevent capital from locating with them. How well my judgment was founded is proven by the result. On the completion of the road to Fort Worth, this road has furnished more tonnage than the main line from Garrett to Denison, which no doubt proved a great surprise to the H. & T. C. management, who had expressed themselves unwilling to operate it for its earnings—hence I had to conclude a traffic arrangement with them to enable us to operate it. Then, again, when the Central undertook its extension from Garrett east, Ennis sent a committee to Houston to try to secure this connection, and failed, although it was rumored they were instructed to offer a bonus of one hundred thousand dollars. I also forgot to mention that before the adoption of the Garrett line, I secured a donation of one hundred acres of land from Mr. Garrett, divided into town lots—this in spite of the strenuous opposition of his agent, Mr. Neal. Mr. Garrett at that time resided somewhere in East Texas. After the commencement of the work it soon became evident that I must get to work and sell bonds outside of Waxahachie; we were needing cash to meet payments to Mr. Roach—although I had an understanding with our business men, that they would take as much as ten thousand dollars, at par, they were slow to come up with their money—I therefore made a trip to Galveston for the purpose of selling $20,000 of our town bonds. I called on Mr. R. S. Willis, who was then the president of the Gulf, Colorado & Santa Fe Road. Mr. Willis was a good friend of mine and I was buying my goods of him largely. He said, "Mr. Graber, let me advise you to drop that scheme, it is visionary, you can never build the road. Attend to your own business. If you were to succeed, you would never receive thanks for it. I'll not subscribe one cent." I said, "Mr. Willis, I appreciate your advice, and esteem your judgment highly, but must decline to be governed by it. We are going to build that road."

I next called on Ball, Hutchins & Company, and Mr. Seeley asked, "Have you been to see Mr. Willis?" I told him I had and had his refusal. He then asked to be excused. Walking down the street, I met Mr. W. L. Moody, in front of his place of business. He expressed himself as glad to see me, and said, "I see in the News you are down here for the purpose of placing $20,000 of your Waxahachie bonds; step into the office. Colonel Jameson will put us down for a thousand dollars." He furthermore said, "When you get your $20,000 placed here, I think I can place the balance for you in New York." I thanked him, took their $1000 subscription, and dropped into Leon H. Blum's. Met Leon coming out. He said, "Go back in the office, tell brother Sylvan to put down a thousand dollars for us." I next called on several other commission houses, who assured me they would subscribe, but could not just then. It soon became evident to my mind they wanted their customers personally to ask them. I therefore concluded to return home, and induce my board of directors, who were all shipping cotton to different houses to assist me in the matter, by going down with me, but could not induce them to go. This want of interest on the part of the board at that critical period was indeed discouraging. They well knew that the taking of $10,000 by Waxahachie and $20,000 more by our commercial city at par, would establish the solid character of the bonds in New York, but they were unwilling to spare the time and incur the expense. Could there have been anything more discouraging? It seemed as though they were determined that I should not succeed, and did not want the road built, which was talked frequently by people in Waxahachie as elsewhere. They seemed afraid of inviting competition in their business, and preferred to continue as they had. Meeting with Major Douglas of Tyler one day in Galveston, he said to me, "Graber, why don't you go ahead and build your little road?" I gave an evasive answer. He said, "I know what is the matter—you have seven old mossbacks pulling back." He said, "My board of directors told me to go ahead and build the road, and I am doing it. I have not had a meeting of my board since I commenced." Major Douglas was then building the Tyler Tap Road and was president of that company.

I now began looking around to secure iron, ties and bridge work. I soon had the latter promised by our carpenters for stock—there were only a few small culverts and bridges. On one of my trips to Houston I met Mr. H. M. Hoxie, general superintendent of the International & Great Northern Railroad, with whom I was well acquainted, who was changing the iron on the Galveston road to a heavier lot. He made me a proposition to furnish us sufficient iron for our road, taken up from the Galveston road, which was fifty-six pound and in good condition, subject to our inspection, for $20,000 f. o. b. cars at Houston, which proposition I accepted subject to the approval of my board. I had a contract with the Houston & Texas Central Railroad to haul iron, ties and bridge timber, for stock in our road. In about a month's time I had a wire from Mr. Hoxie, "Come down, inspect and receive the iron. Answer." I immediately had a meeting of the board and asked their consent to close the deal, but they wanted time to consider. "Wait and see what the crop is going to do; where is your money?" etc. I told them I was satisfied I could induce Hoxie to accept bonds. But they insisted on waiting. I begged and plead with them not to lose this splendid chance of securing iron, which they certainly would by waiting, telling them it might be lost to us in three days. There were other tap roads building—the towns of Henderson, Georgetown and Tyler were all busy, but my pleadings were in vain.

I now felt that I must give up, I could do nothing more. They were determined that I should not complete the road; in fact, it seemed they did not want it at all, and I immediately tendered my resignation, which was promptly accepted, and John C. Gibson elected to succeed me. As soon as it became known that I had resigned, the people demanded of the board to send me down to close the deal for the iron, and soon the secretary came with a request for me to close the deal and a tender of the money to pay my expenses. I told him I was ready to waive all personal feeling in the matter and now go down in a private capacity, close the deal and have my successor sign the contract, as my only ambition was to see the road completed, even by a set of men that deserved no consideration at my hands, but that I must wire Hoxie first and know if iron was still on hand. I wired Mr. Hoxie at Houston and received no answer. I repeated the wire the next day and had his answer, "Too late, iron sold." This proved a surprise and disappointment to all concerned and for a time it seemed as though Waxahachie was doomed. I had turned over to my successor and his board, the grade, a splendid piece of work completed and paid for; sixty-five thousand dollars in Waxahachie bonds; a farmers' stock subscription of about eight thousand dollars; about one hundred and eighty-five sections of State land certificates to be issued on the completion of the road, and every alternate lot in the town of Garrett out of the subdivision of one hundred acres.

The board now went to sleep over the situation; they had no one to suggest or try to do anything towards the completion of the road, which, for nearly three years was a dead enterprise—and left the board with an investment in bonds of about $6000, which would prove worthless unless the road was completed under the terms and provisions of the charter, which were: the completion and operation of the road within five years. They now got desperate, and induced Mr. Royal A. Ferris to go to New York and offer the charter and its franchises, and all of the assets of the company to any responsible party that would complete it, even with old iron, and run a train in before the expiration of the time in the charter. Mr. Ferris succeeded in inducing a Mr. Riordan to accept the proposition. He went to work and completed the road, and after a few months' operation, demonstrating to the Central people its value, sold out to Mr. Waldo for account of some individual stockholder of the H. & T. C. what Waldo termed a pretty good bank of dirt with two streaks of rust for $85,000. In the hands of the Central it was soon refurnished with new iron and completely overhauled, making it a first-class road, and soon extended to Fort Worth.

This terminated the history of the Waxahachie Tap Road in the loss of all interest the town had in it through the farcical conduct of its leading business men, acting as its board of directors.

When a meeting was held just before the election on the bond proposition, I told the people, as long as I could control it, if they would vote the bonds, the road should never pass into other hands, only with their consent, and should pay its value. It was my intention to hold on to the State land donation until it would become valuable and already had the promise of a few surveyors to locate the same free of cost, save actual expenses. I believed then the land within our day and time could be sold for from $5 to $10 per acre, which would amply reimburse the town for its issuance of the bonds, and they would own the road besides. The result was, we had a unanimous vote on the bond. To fairly illustrate the character of the men I was connected with in this enterprise, some few years after the Santa Fe was completed west of Waxahachie, we had a proposition from the management to build a branch of their road into Waxahachie for a bonus of

$10,000. A meeting to consider the proposition was held; and these men who were still in control, expressed themselves as opposed to meeting the Santa Fe proposition, saying, If they propose to build in here for $10,000 they will do so anyway. Realizing that they were about to lose another valuable opportunity, I told them that I came to subscribe my money and not to talk, knowing well any suggestion I might make would fall flat, but felt that they were about to make a serious mistake in turning down this proposition; there were movements being made on the railroad checkerboard constantly and something might occur that would force the Santa Fe Company to withdraw their proposition in less than thirty days, and rather than have this happen I was willing to subscribe $1000. One of the old members of the board of railroad directory smiled at my suggestion, and made a motion to adjourn sine die, which was carried and thus Waxahachie was again cheated out of another golden opportunity; as in less than thirty days this company had to withdraw its proposition on account of a trouble with the Gould lines. When about three months after Mr. N. A. McMillan was sent to Galveston to have them renew or make another proposition, Mr. R. S. Willis told him they could not consider such a thing; that they had all they could do to look after their main line; but frankly told him, "You people missed your opportunity. Had you accepted our proposition when we made it, we would have built into your town."

I have thus given an important part of Waxahachie history, which I trust will prove instructive in its future. There are great opportunities presented every now and then, which should be taken advantage of and properly cared for by the progressive citizens of a community and should be ably seconded by a public spirit. This is due from every man who is a beneficiary of the growth of his home city.

It should be borne in mind that in the period when we first submitted the railroad proposition, Texas had hardly felt the great benefits of railroads and it was difficult to induce small communities to take hold of such enterprises; besides there was no money with which to build them.

It is easier now to build a long line of road, provided it is practicable and the inducement sufficient, than at that period of time to build a little tap road.

In conclusion, I must be pardoned for a seeming egotism in claiming to be the originator and having done the principal work in this enterprise, but I cannot do otherwise and state facts. Whilst it is true that others completed the road, it was comparatively an easy task to do this by giving it away. The only recognition I have ever had for my efforts in behalf of your town was an occasional expression from prominent citizens whom I met in years after: "Well, Mr. Graber, if you had not come to Waxahachie when you did, our town would have been an old rat hole."—Dr. Conner. "Mr. Graber, they treated you badly."—Captain Patrick. And other like expressions, but permit me to say I feel compensated in the fact that I was probably instrumental in starting your town on its upward march, and therefore feel that I have been of benefit to others, and have not lived in vain.

Thanking you for this courtesy, I am with great respect,

Yours very truly,

H. W. GRABER.

CHAPTER XXXI

BUSINESS TROUBLES.

The second year of my labors in building the Waxahachie Tap Road required all of my time, and, in consequence, a neglect of my business. This, coupled with the fact that many good farmers seemed to shun my business, fearing I would tackle them for a railroad stock subscription and the further fact that jealous competitors, joined by a man representing P. J. Willis & Brother of Galveston, a house I was dealing with most extensively and with whom I had a credit and a running account of about twelve or fifteen thousand dollars, and the representations of these competitors that I was investing heavily in the tap road, which was not a fact, caused me to become embarrassed in business. I paid my account with P. J. Willis & Brother in order to get rid of this jealous competitor, and this amounted to a withdrawal of fifteen thousand dollars of my capital.

In November of that year I owed nearly twenty-three thousand dollars, which I reduced to ninety-four hundred dollars by the first of March following.

At this time I was caught with a remnant winter stock and, in order to keep up my business and to arrange for a spring and summer stock of goods with no money to buy, I decided best to proceed to St. Louis and submit a statement of my condition to my creditors. This statement showed an indebtedness, as stated, of about ninety-four hundred dollars, and assets, about fifteen or sixteen thousand. These assets consisted largely of East Texas accounts, a balance of my old Rusk business, a winter stock of goods and a few acres of land in East Texas that could not be sold for more than a dollar an acre. At that time, everything I had in business was unavailable.

The object of my St. Louis trip was to get an extension of my indebtedness until the next winter. The largest part of my indebtedness was with L. Cannon & Company of Galveston, cotton commission merchants, who were satisfied with any arrangement I made for an extension. The next largest creditor was Samuel C. Davis & Company, St. Louis, whom I owed a balance on open account of about eight or nine hundred dollars. After submitting them my statement, the manager, whose name I have forgotten, told me that I was not entitled to an extension and they were not in favor of granting it unless the balance all agreed, but if they all granted an extension, that they were willing to do so, but would not sell me any more goods. They explained to me that upon a review of my assets, I would not be able to pay more than thirty or thirty-five cents on the dollar, and if I succeeded in compromising on that basis, they were willing to sell me again, on their regular terms, any reasonable amount and would consider my credit unimpaired. I told the gentlemen that I would never compromise, as it was considered disgraceful in Texas.

I next went to see the house of Hamilton & Brown, who were then in their infancy in their business, but were considered one of the rising shoe houses in St. Louis.

On presenting my statement their judgment was the same as Samuel C. Davis & Company: that I was not entitled to an extension and to continue in business, having to ask further credit, my only course would be to compromise, say thirty cents on the dollar. I owed these people little less than two hundred dollars, a small balance of a considerable account. I told them I would never compromise, when one of the gentlemen said, "You are working with a millstone around your neck and we want to put you on your feet. If you don't compromise before you leave St. Louis, we will send your account to an attorney at Waxahachie, with instructions to sue." I said, "If you do, I will make an assignment and quit business, and in doing so you can take the coat off my back—you will never find me behind a valuable Texas homestead." In connection with this I will state that after a two weeks' stay in St. Louis, trying to persuade these people to meet my proposition, I heard from my friend Cannon in Galveston, who offered to let me have money to settle with the St. Louis creditors on the basis of thirty-five cents. I finally gave it up and on my return home found the Hamilton & Brown account in the hands of Judge Rainey for collection with order to bring suit, and I immediately made an assignment in the Bankruptcy Court at Tyler, thereby protecting all of my creditors.

When the United States Marshal came and took possession of my assets he persuaded me, for the protection of my family, to retain two hundred acres of land in Cherokee County, which at the time could not have been sold for more than a dollar an acre, for which I had paid two dollars and seventy-five cents an acre. This land I traded for a few town lots in Waxahachie, on one of which I built an humble little home the next year and out of the balance realized about three hundred dollars.

It is hardly necessary to say that my business failure proved very discouraging at the time and caused the breaking down of my general health. My jealous competitors in business continued to refer to it, claiming that it was injuring the prospect of the building of the road, the presidency of which I finally concluded to resign.

Considering that several of these men were the richest of any men in the community and that I had sacrificed my all to build up their interest in connection with the town, I felt that it was one of the most unjust and worst cases of persecution without cause a man ever had to submit to, but I determined to outgrow it and ignore these foolish people's work against me.

Recurring to my visit in St. Louis where, as stated, I spent a couple of weeks: I stopped at a private boarding house, where I formed the acquaintance of a business gentleman, who, with his wife, had a room next to mine and in a few days invited me to visit their cotton exchange, which invitation I accepted. I, of course, had not told him of my financial embarrassment, but had made him acquainted with my railroad enterprise.

At the cotton exchange I was shown a great deal of attention by some of the members present and especially Mr. J. W. Paramore, the president. When about ready to depart Mr. Paramore extended me an invitation to join him in a visit to his compresses, saying that he had a horse and buggy at the door, waiting. I accepted his invitation.. On our drive out to the compresses, he gave me his history in connection with the business, saying that he came to St. Louis from Nashville, Tennessee, with seventy thousand dollars in cash and decided that St. Louis ought to be made a cotton market. For this purpose he met some of the leading business men and suggested the building of a large compress and asked them to take stock, which they considered a huge joke and readily turned down his proposition. He then concluded to undertake the building of a compress by himself, which he did, meeting with great success the first season. These same men whom he tried to induce to take stock with him, came to him and begged for stock, with the proposition to enlarge the plant, which he did and had made it a great success the second year. The enlarged plant enabled him to pay a handsome dividend. After showing me around his compresses and expressing himself much interested in Texas cotton shipments, I finally suggested to him the idea of getting up an excursion of a number of his business friends who were interested to know about Texas conditions and resources, to visit Waxahachie, where I was anxious to show him our little railroad enterprise and especially our rich land in this black land district.

Meeting with him again upon another occasion I again urged him by all means to get up this excursion, satisfied that he and his friends would find it interesting and profitable, and having no doubt but they would succeed in opening business relations. I found he was much interested and he became somewhat enthusiastic on the proposed visit, promising me that he would certainly do so.

Some three or four months after, I saw an account in the Galveston News of where J. W. Paramore, a business man of St. Louis, with a number of other business men, had arrived at Tyler, Texas, on an excursion to investigate Texas resources and conditions, with a view of establishing business relations and will here state, knowing the business community of Tyler, its brains and capital, I immediately concluded that their proposed Waxahachie visit was doomed, which proved to be a fact.

Tyler had just completed a short line narrow-gauge railway to connect with the Texas & Pacific at Big Sandy and soon induced Mr. Paramore and associates to buy this road and extend it, an independent line, to St. Louis, which, after a few years, they accomplished, creating the St. Louis Narrow Gauge, and after a few more years, changed it into a standard gauge, which is now the Cotton Belt.

I trust the reader will not consider me egotistical, but I have always taken a great pride in the belief that I was perhaps instrumental in having one of the great lines of railroad built from our State to St. Louis. Had I not suggested this excursion to Texas by these St. Louis people, which was altogether a new idea with Paramore and his friends, the St. Louis Narrow Gauge might never have been built. It was only through just such men as Paramore that great enterprises are started in their infancy and carried to a successful realization.

CHAPTER XXXII

I Start Anew.

Immediately after my failure in the general mercantile business, I went to Dallas to try to make some commission deal to sell farm machinery, and called on Mitchell & Scruggs, who had just opened business with one of the best lines of machinery in Dallas and had the State agencies on these lines. I succeeded in making a contract with them to handle these goods in Ellis, Navarro, Hill and Johnson Counties on a basis of five and ten per cent. I knew nothing about machinery and had to post myself, reading catalogues and asking questions of Mitchell & Scruggs and the factories they represented.

Having no money I bought a few groceries on time, until I could make something and had the tender of a horse and buggy from a Mr. Johnson, the pastor of our Presbyterian Church. I drove over these counties, very often without a road, especially in Hill County, visiting people who were reported in need of cotton gin machinery, harvesters and threshers, never making a dollar for nearly five months. I finally made my first sale of an Ames engine, on which I had a commission of eight per cent. For the next three months succeeding I sold a number of engines and boilers, several threshers, a number of harvesters, etc., winding up the first season with a net profit of about fifteen hundred dollars. After paying my debts I had left about five hundred dollars to invest in a home. I planned a cottage, which Meredith & Patterson agreed to build for me for a thousand dollars, accept in part payment five hundred dollars and the balance of five hundred dollars, payable next fall with five per cent per month interest.

The next season's business I wound up with a profit of twenty-eight hundred dollars and the next season with thirty-five hundred dollars profit and the next season with something over ten thousand dollars profit. This put me on my feet but I needed engineering skill and was unable to secure it, as it was scarce in Texas at the time.

Having formed the acquaintance of Colonel John G. Hunter (through his visit to me, in the interest of the Ames Iron Works, whose engines and boilers I was handling), I persuaded Mr. Leonard Ames the first time he called on me in conjunction with Colonel Hunter, to let me have Hunter, he was just the man I needed. He finally consented, provided it was agreeable to Hunter. I made a proposition to Hunter to give him a half interest in the profits of the business, which he accepted and after a copartnership of two years, we both decided that our territory was too small; our business too much circumscribed to justify the services of both, when I advised him to go to Dallas, both realizing that it would be the future commercial center of Texas. He decided to do this and immediately moved to Dallas, where his ability found better compensation and I told him that I would follow as soon as I could wind up my business here, realizing that Waxahachie would never amount to much until the old mossback element died out and the young men would get into the saddle, which prediction I believe has been realized.

Before leaving Waxahachie I tried to get up the money for a cotton compress, for which I was authorized by a friend at Jefferson, Texas, who had a compress at that point, to subscribe for him ten thousand dollars of about thirty-five thousand dollars needed for a good Morse ninety-inch cylinder press. I headed the subscriptions with this man's ten thousand dollars and added mine for one thousand more, then called on a number of business men, financially able, besides the two banks, who all agreed to take stock provided a certain somebody else would take stock. It finally resolved itself into the consent of one, John G. Williams, who was always arbitrary and dictatorial. When I asked him to subscribe a thousand or fifteen hundred dollars, telling him that it was important for us to take immediate action, as Ennis was also trying to get up a compress company and there was not sufficient business for both, he insisted on postponing it, saying that he would let me know when he got ready.

Already disgusted with such dilatory conduct, I told him I wanted him to understand that I was not begging him nor others, like I used to do when trying to build the railroad, that I had other business to attend to and I wanted him to say right then and there what he was going to do. He told me to take the compress and go to the devil with it. I said to him, taking the subscription list, "Here goes," and tore it up, leaving him in disgust.

The town of Ennis commenced building their compress in less than three days, but the conduct of these old mossbacks, in this case, finally proved the straw that broke the camel's back. I immediately resolved to get out of there as soon as possible and move to Dallas, which I have never had cause to regret.

After moving to Dallas I succeeded in making better contracts with the factories whose goods I had been handling through Mitchell & Scruggs, and had a number of contracts, which they had held, turned over to me direct, thereby enlarging the profits of my business from fifty to one hundred per cent and soon established one of the largest and best businesses in my line in Dallas, except that of R. V. Tompkins, who had large capital and more extensive factory arrangements than mine. Having large capital he was able to employ a large corps of traveling salesmen, besides he, himself, having a practical, thorough knowledge of machinery.

CHAPTER XXXIII

THE METHODIST SCHOOL AT WAXAHACHIE.

I forgot to mention, soon after entering the commission machinery business, I met a friend by the name of Meeks who was the owner of the Marvin College property at Waxahachie, established and built up by the Methodist Church of Texas, and governed by a Board of Trustees who had permitted the school to go down, after having been in operation for perhaps two or three years. They borrowed ten thousand dollars in gold from my friend, Meeks, giving him a first mortgage on the property, which mortgage he had to close by public sale and had to take the property for the debt, though the trustees claimed that the property cost the church about a hundred thousand dollars. The same old mossback element that persecuted me in my railroad and other business, too, were largely responsible for the failure of Marvin College and boasted that it should never succeed again. Mr. Meeks asked me to undertake the sale of it, which of course could be used only for school purposes, as it was unfit for anything else. Having received his promise that he would give me full control of the sale of it, I agreed to take hold of it for a commission of ten per cent.

I immediately went to work, got out an attractive circular letter, giving advantages of Waxahachie for an educational point. I soon had responses, or inquiries from the North and East, and a strong one from a Presbyterian school man at Lexington, Kentucky, who decided to take hold of it as soon as he could dispose of his property in Lexington.

Finding that I was about to sell the property to a Presbyterian who did not expect to make it a denominational school, the trustees of the Methodist Church, composed of Captain V. G. Veal, Fred Cox and Doctor Walkup, got busy among their Methodist friends and secured authority to take the property over again for ten thousand dollars in gold, Meeks waiving the interest, and paid me a thousand dollars cash and three thousand dollars in one, two and three years, with a mortgage on the property. In selling them the property on these liberal terms, I had it distinctly understood that if they failed to come up with their second payment I would close them out at once, which I was forced to do.

I soon got into correspondence with General L. M. Lewis, an educator of high order, then connected with a college in Little Rock, though he had already been connected with the A. & M. College at Bryan, where the faculty had a rupture, which resulted in the resignation of the whole board. I induced General Lewis to visit Waxahachie, where I introduced him to the Rev. Chas. E. Brown of the Methodist Church, who was one of the most popular preachers there and he, in turn, got him acquainted with Fred Cox and Doctor Walkup. These four gentlemen formed a copartnership and again bought the property and in less than two years built up a large school with many transient boarders. While on a deal with General Lewis, I frankly told him that he would have a difficult task to build up a school in that town on account of the sworn opposition of the mossback element and that he would have to depend upon transient patronage altogether for the success of his school when they began, having no doubt that Waxahachie's patronage would gradually follow.

As I predicted, soon after starting the school and having the children of Mr. John G. Williams, who tried to be the boss of the town, Williams demanded of General Lewis that he make a change in certain rules and General Lewis told him that if the rules didn't suit him he had better take his children home, which he did and the faculty were not sorry for it.

The second year of the school, having paid their indebtedness to Meeks, a demand for an addition became imperative, so they borrowed money and put up a large one, as also a separate boarding house. After two years more, the free school system of Texas obtained, thereby cutting down their patronage to a point that did not justify them to continue and were finally induced to sell out to the city for a public free school, which they had to do, at a considerable loss and thus crippled them financially.

CHAPTER XXXIV

MY LATER BUSINESS EXPERIENCES.

The Rev. Charles E. Brown had the business management of this college from the beginning to the end and displayed business capacity and indomitable persistence that impressed me with the idea that he would make a good business man. He came to me, asking for employment, saying that he wanted to enter commerce, that he had a number of children to educate and the pulpit did not support his family as he wished. He wanted to give his children as good an education as anybody else's children, and for this reason he wanted to go to work in business, offering to work for me for fifty dollars per month, in the sales department, until he was worth more.

Being sadly in need of assistance, I told Brown that I believed he had the ability to make good in the machinery business and if he proved the man that I was needing, I would give him a third interest in the profits of the business.

After a short time I found that I was not mistaken in the man and voluntarily raised his compensation to one-half interest of the profits in the business. Our business prospered and grew to a point that it was necessary for us to move to Dallas, which we did, where our business continued to grow and was considered, after a couple of years, the leading machinery house in the city, except that of R. V. Tompkins.

Owing to some misapprehension on Brown's part, (brought about by a statement of his oldest boy, whom he had employed in the business against my advice), differences arose which we were unable to reconcile and it was deemed best, under the circumstances, that we separate.

Having made him a liberal offer of ten thousand dollars for his interest in the business, besides the cancellation of his account, which amounted to six or seven thousand dollars and had his refusal to sell out, I then decided to sell out to him, provided he could induce a certain W. J. Clark, who was reputed worth a hundred thousand dollars, to join him in the purchase, which he succeeded in doing. I then sold out to Clark & Brown for a nominal sum, without taking a dollar out of the business until all debts were paid, taking their note for the purchase price. They paid all debts when due and then paid me.

On the dissolution of our firm and my sale to Clark & Brown, I notified all creditors that Clark & Brown were obligated to pay one hundred cents on the dollar promptly when due and if they failed to receive their money on that basis, to notify me promptly, as I was in position to make them do so. Never receiving any notice from any creditor that their matters were unsettled, I had every reason to believe Brown & Clark's statement that they had settled all indebtedness.

After a rest of several months I had a proposition made me by Mr. C. A. Keating, President of the Keating Implement & Machine Company, to take the management of their machinery department, succeeding in that position Colonel John G. Hunter and John Young, both excellent business men.

I expected to take stock in the Keating Implement & Machinery Company, but finally decided not to do so and simply worked on salary, commencing the first year with a salary of sixteen hundred and fifty dollars, when at the close of the season, Mr. Keating voluntarily paid me two thousand, then the next season raised my salary to twenty-five hundred. After my connection with the house for eleven years, the last three years of the time receiving thirty-six hundred dollars, I voluntarily resigned, under the protest of Mr. C. A. Keating. After I severed my connection with the house, they quit the machinery business, except threshers and some other goods that were not included in my department.

After severing my connection with the Keating Implement & Machine Company I went into business again, for my own account, on very limited capital and in a few years again built up a large machinery business, finally discontinuing cotton gin machinery, in which I was largely instrumental in inducing the Pratt Cotton Gin Company to enter the field with a complete system, which I assisted in developing.

On the formation of the Continental Gin Company, which took over the plants of four or five others, including my Pratt factory, I decided to drop gin machinery and confine my business to larger and high duty plants, in which I succeeded to my entire satisfaction. My success in this business was somewhat phenomenal. As heretofore stated, I was not an educated practical engineer, but in the organization of this new business I was careful to hunt up the record of every machine and its factory before its adoption, taking great care to get hold of the best and I don't think I ever made a mistake, as many of my customers repeated their orders, after having tried and used the machines.

Among the list of my machinery I would mention the American Diesel Engine, which was just being introduced in the United States and was largely owned by Mr. Adolphus Busch.

I was persuaded to take hold of the introduction of this engine through a promise of Colonel Meyer, who undertook its introduction in this country, with his headquarters in New York, and who had known me for fifteen or twenty years, in connection with his Heine boiler business, which I had been handling and continued to handle.

Relying on his promise that if I would undertake the introduction of the engine, that I should continue to handle it exclusively in the Southwestern territory, and believing that on account of its enormous economy it would ultimately supplant all steam machinery, I did not hesitate to put my whole efforts and influence into the work of its introduction.

After putting about five years of the best labor of my latter years into its establishment, and just at a time when I felt I was going to realize something handsome out of the business, my health gave way to an extent that forced me to quit business altogether, never having had a real vacation and rest in forty-three years.

In winding up the history of my business career I regret to have to record that throughout the whole of it I was always the victim of misplaced confidence, never realizing any of the men I had associated with me would ever do me a wrong, in which I was nearly always mistaken.

I am able to say that I had associated with me men whom I trained in several lines of business, in fact, assisted in starting them, and some of them have attained great success, a number of them now occupying high positions. One of the wealthiest manufacturers in Dallas is a man whom I took up on the street, hunting work. It was largely through a kind, friendly feeling, I took hold of him and taught him the cotton gin machinery business. He proved one of the best salesmen I had and, as stated, is now the president of the largest manufacturing cotton gin machinery in the South. Another one of my old clerks in the mercantile business, is today the president of a big trust company, commanding a salary of twenty-five thousand dollars a year. While I refer to this case with a good deal of pride, I am frank to say that he is in no way indebted to me especially for his rise in the world, but only to his natural ability as a business man and his own personal efforts and energy.

Among the many young men that I took into my business, first and last, and taught and trained them in business, I recall one case, especially, that of James Summers, who came to me, among a number of young men, then going to school at the Rusk Masonic Institute, and begged me to teach him business. Most of the young men, immediately after the close of the war, thought that the mercantile business would be about the easiest and most pleasant to engage in, hence these many applications, among whom I would mention ex-Governor James Hogg, who was then a boy of about eighteen or twenty, going to school. I recall my answer to him: "Now, Jim, if you want to be a slave all your life, get behind this counter and go to work, but if you will take my advice, go out on a farm, develop your muscles and make a man of yourself." He answered, "I expect to do that, Mr. Graber. I am going to make a man of myself," which he certainly did, but not in mercantile pursuits.

To give the reader a better appreciation of the character of James E. Summers: When he came and asked me to teach him business his father was the keeper of a saloon and a horse racer, and I had understood, had whipped Jim at one time to make him ride a horse race for him; besides the old man was very profane and his conduct as stated. Jim's nature and disposition revolted at it, though Jim had a noble Christian mother, whose disposition he, no doubt, inherited by nature, which, in connection with her teachings, made him the grand character that he proved to be.

Although I did not need any assistance at the time he asked for a position, which was about 1870, I decided to take hold of him and teach him all I knew about business, which proved a great pleasure to me, because he was always ready to receive instruction and profit by my advice. I soon made a bookkeeper out of him and I am prepared to say that I was rewarded for any salary I paid him and any time devoted to his instruction through his great success as a business man and his full appreciation of my efforts in his behalf, the knowledge of which I gained through several mutual friends, whom he told that he was indebted to Mr. Graber for what he was and everything he had.

After removing to Waxahachie, Jim married a daughter of a Doctor Francis, who could not bear the separation from her mother and family and, therefore, I advised him to go back to Rusk and get some of his farmer friends, of whom he had many, to advance him means to go into business for himself. This he did, and as soon as started, having the confidence and good will of all the people in Cherokee County, he soon did the leading business in the place and died about ten years ago, mourned by all that knew him, leaving an estate worth over one hundred and fifty thousand dollars, which was most extraordinary, considering the character of the town of Rusk and country surrounding it.

Having said this much in connection with my business career, I deem it unnecessary to enter into further details, as it would no doubt, prove irksome to the reader and I merely said as much to show that I always felt interested in worthy characters that I had associated with me in business, never caring much for a great accumulation of wealth, until it was too late.

Had I made the accumulation of money my main object, I no doubt could have been among the rich men of Dallas, the most of whom accumulated their fortunes in speculative channels. Had I engaged in speculative channels in real estate, I would certainly have made money and had the good judgment to quit before it was too late, wherein many of my friends and acquaintances failed.

My business always outgrew the amount of my capital and as a result I always owed the banks and other creditors and it was a fixed principle with me as long as I owed a dollar, that nothing I had really belonged to me and therefore I had no moral right to take money out of my business to put into speculative channels in real estate.

Before closing my business record in Dallas, I must pay a deserved tribute to L. Rector Cabell, who entered my service to study and learn machinery. I am able to say, although young and without business experience, he soon proved himself efficient in cotton gin machinery, and one of the most loyal and honest men in my employ, carefully guarding my business interests—just like his honored father, General W. L. Cabell, and devoted sister, Mrs. Kate Cabell Muse, in behalf of the U. C. V. organization. After leaving my service, Rector accepted a position with the engineering department in Havana, Cuba, where he has been engaged since, and is now receiving a handsome salary.

CHAPTER XXXV

THE CONFEDERATE VETERANS' HOME.

In connection with my personal history I will take the liberty of referring to my connection with the organization and work in behalf of the United Confederate Veterans' Association.

I realized that only by a combined effort of the old soldiers could we perpetuate our true history and especially take care of the indigent and needy old comrades, when sick and in distress. While associated with the Keating house, the Confederate Home at Austin was started by John B. Hood Camp of Austin and maintained by soliciting public contributions, as the State was prohibited by the Constitution to contribute anything towards its maintenance. Realizing the necessity of everybody interested doing all they were able to do and my own ability at the time being very limited, I conceived the plan of requesting donations by factories, whose machinery we were handling, of certain machines they were manufacturing as parts of a complete cotton gin outfit. In line with this I wrote a letter to each one of our factories, setting forth the condition of our Confederate Home and asking contributions of such parts as they manufactured, for a complete 3-60 saw gin outfit. These factories were all located in the North and East, but their response was prompt and cheerful. I had a sixty-horse power boiler, contributed by the Erie City Iron Works; a 3-60 saw gins and elevator by the Eagle Cotton Gin Company of Bridgewater, Mass.; a Thomas steam cylinder press by the Thomas Manufacturing Company of Little Rock, Ark., and Mr. Keating gave me a fifty-horse power Erie City Iron Works engine; a four-ton Chicago scale, by the Chicago Scale Company and a magnificent Schuttler wagon by the Peter Schuttler Wagon Company of Chicago, the whole worth about thirty-five hundred dollars.

I immediately notified Governor Ross of this handsome donation by Northern factories, giving him a full list of the donors, and he wrote a personal letter of thanks to each of the parties.

Cotton gin machinery, at this time, was rarely bought for cash, always sold on long time credit, which of course did not meet the urgent needs of the Confederate Home. In conferring with General Cabell and other prominent members of the Camp, we decided on a plan of having a drawing for this machinery, selling tickets at one dollar, believing we could raise a large amount of money in this way, as outside of a chance of drawing the machinery was the further inducement that the dollar paid for the ticket would afford relief to our needy Confederate Home. I then went to work actively, after first conferring with some of the best legal talent of the city, as to whether such a drawing was permissable by law. As it was by them held entirely within the law, taking the position that a drawing for charity was not a lottery, but a drawing for profit is a lottery, I had no hesitancy in permitting my name used in connection with it.

About this time we had an exciting contest for the Governorship of the State between Attorney General Hogg and Judge George Clark of Waco. On the policies of each, our comrades of the Camp were divided. While our Confederate Constitution prohibits the discussion of politics in the meetings of our Camp, still the members were not prohibited from expressing their views outside. The Clark element of the Camp insisted before we proceeded in this drawing to write Attorney General Hogg, asking his opinion on the legal status of such proceedings, hoping that he would rule adversely, thereby making himself very unpopular in the State. Knowing Hogg's disposition on such ruling and believing he would express a radical view on the same, I did my best to keep the matter from reaching his ears, but all to no purpose.

I forgot to mention I had gone on with the work of getting up tickets and an attractive circular with large cuts of each machine, and sent them broadcast all over the State. I sent a hundred tickets each to the sheriff and county clerk of each county, requesting them to act as sales agents for us, when we had numerous letters from different ones, saying that they could sell every ticket they had and to send more, thus we had a fair prospect of raising at least fifty thousand dollars.

The continued agitation by members of the Camp on the subject, asking Attorney General Hogg for his opinion, resulted in my being appointed a committee of one to write to him for his opinion in the matter, when he answered promptly in response that such proceedings would be illegal and he hoped that it would not be attempted. When I read his letter to the Camp the Clark men said they had always been satisfied that his ruling would be such and insisted on dropping the matter. Having cherished the hope that I would be instrumental in perhaps securing the magnificent sum of fifty thousand dollars for the benefit of the Confederate Home, which in connection with the opinion of several of the ablest lawyers in the State—such men as the Hon. Seth Sheppard and others, whose names I don't remember and whose opinions I regarded more highly than I did Hogg's, as their construction of the law in the matter, as before stated, seemed to me most reasonable and fair—I told the members of the Camp, "The drawing goes on. My name is on the ticket and if Attorney General Hogg wants to proceed in the matter, he is at liberty to proceed against me."

The Sunday following I wrote a personal letter to my old-time friend, Attorney General Hogg, setting forth the urgency of our action and finally told him, by my advice the Camp had decided to go on with the drawing and the object of my writing him was simply to say that we valued his opinion most highly and appreciated his good intentions towards the Confederate Home and his rulings were fully in accord with his duties, as he conceived them to be, and finally wound up the letter by saying, "the end justified the means," which expression proved fatal and got him stirred up about the matter to the extent, as I suspected, of notifying all sheriffs and county clerks that it would be dangerous for them to undertake the sale of the tickets and as a result, I regret to have to record that all the tickets were returned to me, except perhaps about a hundred.

In answer to my letter the Attorney General stated that if we persisted in having the drawing that he would use all the power of the State at his command to put it down and punish us.

The Clark men of the Camp soon circulated the result of our correspondence and proclaimed to the State that Attorney General Hogg was unfriendly to the Confederate Home and also to our Confederate organization, which of course he denied in several of his speeches.

Every Governor up until now, preceding his elevation to the office, had been an ex-Confederate soldier, but had never done anything to assist in the maintenance of the Confederate Home through any appropriation of the State's money.

As is well known, Governor Hogg was elected and soon after his installation into the office, he caused the appropriation of money collected from rental of a building that had been temporarily used as the Capitol, while the new Capitol Building was under construction and immediately after the assembling of the Legislature, urged the passage of a resolution, submitting a Constitutional Amendment to enable the State to take charge of the Confederate Home and also to give pensions to needy Confederates, not in the Home.

It is needless to say when this amendment was voted on by the people of the State it was carried by a large majority, thus enabling legislative appropriations for its maintenance in a suitable manner.

CHAPTER XXXVI

MY APPOINTMENTS IN THE U. C. V.

On the organization of the U. C. V. in 1892, I received the appointment by Lieutenant-General Cabell, who was elected Commander of the Trans-Mississippi Department, of Quartermaster-General of the Trans-Mississippi Department, with the rank of Brigadier-General. On receipt of my commission, issued by General John B. Gordon, one morning, while opening the package, Mr. C. A. Keating was looking on and on my being surprised at such promotion, never having had notice of General Cabell's appointment, Keating asked me what I was going to do about it? I told him that I was going to turn it down, that I did not think I deserved any such promotion, besides I feared it would take a great deal of my valuable time out of business, when he insisted on my accepting it, which I still refused. He made me promise to take the document home to my children, saying that they had more interest perhaps, in such an honor than I had and if they were willing to have me turn it down he would have nothing further to say. In connection with this, he asked a question, "Tell me of a Confederate soldier in this community that has done as much for the needy Confederates as you have and is more entitled to it than you are?"

I took the document home, as I had promised him, to show to my children and when I suggested to them that I intended to turn it down they would not hear to it, saying that they were as much interested in the matter and would appreciate it as a great honor conferred on them, as well as myself, when I finally had to yield in the matter and accepted the appointment, which I have never had cause to regret, though it was a heavy tax on my purse and time, which latter properly belonged to C. A. Keating, to say nothing of using his stenographer, etc., all of which he cheerfully contributed and is entitled to the credit.

Having served in this capacity for a number of years, I was finally elected to the command of the Fourth Brigade, composed of the principal Camps of North Texas, with a membership of about five thousand, which forced me to resign the office of Quartermaster General and accept the high honor, which I very much appreciated. Serving in this capacity a year, I decided to decline re-election on account of deficiency in hearing, which almost disqualified me from presiding over this body at its annual meeting and soon after, was appointed by General Stephen D. Lee, Assistant Adjutant-General on his staff, with the rank of Brigadier-General and which appointment I have had from every successive commander and I may, perhaps, hold until death. I certainly appreciate these honors conferred on me by my Confederate comrades, more perhaps than anything that has ever fallen to my lot. This closes my connection with the Confederate U. C. V. organization; many of the details of its works I do not care to record herein, as they might appear too much of egotism.

MISCELLANEOUS CORRESPONDENCE ON CONFEDERATE MATTERS

Columbus, Miss., April 21, 1905.

General H. W. Graber.

My Dear Sir: I have yours of April 18, with enclosures. I had seen the pleasant incidents of return of flags by veterans of Texas, and also the return of the Ranger flag at time it occurred. Let us hope your letter to the President did good, for certainly he has changed his views, and if he has not recanted what he once wrote and spoke, he has for some time spoken and acted in the very opposite way, which virtually is the same thing. This is the country of our fathers, of us all now and of our children, and we should accept any advances of reconciliation and obliteration of sectional lines possible and consistent with our self-respect.

Thanking you for your letter and enclosure, I return them,

With kind wishes,

Your comrade and friend,

STEPHEN D. LEE.

New Orleans, La., April 4, 1909.

Brig.-General H. W. Graber,

Dallas, Texas.

Dear General: I have much pleasure in handing you herein a copy of S/O No. 12, naming the staff of the Commander-in-Chief of the U. C. V.

The General Commanding this glorious Federation feels that the responsibility rests on him to use every effort to bring forth the results that will be for its best interests. He knows that if the earnest workers and progressive spirits in the association will render such services in his aid as he has reason to think they will, our order will make more rapid advances in the future, greatly diminished as are our numbers, than in the past.

Trusting, then, on your love for the organization and your eminent fitness for the position, he has selected you as one of his personal staff; and begs that you will honor him by accepting the position of Assistant Adjutant-General, with the rank of Brigadier-General.

In addition to using every occasion to increase the interest and affection of the veterans in our "social, literary, historical and benevolent" society, and constantly working to bring about peace and harmony among the comrades, he particularly desires that you will, if possible, be in attendance at the Memphis Reunion, in full dress uniform, and meet him at the Headquarters Hotel (the Peabody Hotel) to concert measures that will make this a most memorable occasion. He hopes that you will attend the daily sessions of the convention, be present on the stage with him, and on the day of the parade take part with the entire staff in full uniform.

Trusting that you may be able and willing to assist in this great work in the way indicated, with every good wish for your health, prosperity and happiness,

Most sincerely,

WM. E. MICKLE,

Adjutant-General and Chief of Staff.

War Department,

Vicksburg National Military Park Commission,

Vicksburg, Miss.

January 14, 1909.

General H. W. Graber,

Dallas, Texas.

My Dear Sir: I highly appreciated and greatly enjoyed reading your good letter of the 12th instant, and its inclosures, one of which is herewith returned. Needless for me to say to you that I am in heartiest sympathy with the generous, patriotic and American sentiments so well expressed in the "Concurrent Resolution" of the two Houses of the Indiana Legislature, Session of 1899. Ten years earlier, in 1889, in an address to the veterans of my regiment (24th Iowa Infantry) in reunion assembled, I said, in part:

"In forming the characters and shaping the lives of the future citizens of this great Republic, we fondly hope that the unselfish devotion to duty and the unshaken valor of the volunteer soldier will be a potent influence for good; that his heroism will live in song and story and through all the years to come, be a challenge to patriotism, above the din of party strife ringing loud and clear as bugles that blow for battle. Nor do we forget that our late foes were brave men and gallant soldiers. Their valor, like the valor of the men of the North, illustrates and adorns the character of the American citizen soldier. This character, tempered and proved in the crucible of battle, is the pledge and sure prophecy of the greatness of our common country. Looking into the future, may we not say of the coming American citizen, 'His shall be larger manhood' because of the heroic example of the men who conquered with Grant and Sherman and the no less heroic example of the men who surrendered with Lee and Johnston. Of this coming American, may we not predict that, where need is, he will know that 'not suffering but faint heart is worst of woes.' In the nobler destiny of our country, in the larger and stronger character of its people, will be found the final compensation for all the suffering and all the losses of the war."

Please keep me closely informed in regard to the prospects for the greatly desired Texas appropriation for the Vicksburg Park. Command and direct me whenever I can help in any way.

Very cordially yours,

WM. T. RIGBY, Chairman.

CHAPTER XXXVII

THE TERRY RANGERS' FLAG.

One most remarkable incident I must not fail to add: As stated heretofore, the Terry Rangers of which I was a member, lost a beautiful flag sent us by a couple of young ladies of Nashville, made of their dresses, which after the first engagement wherein it was displayed, near Rome, Georgia, we lost in a stampede and it was found by a scout of the enemy the next day. This flag had worked in beautiful silk letters, the name of Terry's Texas Rangers, beside some Latin, which I do not remember. After the war, on a number of public occasions, such as the several National Expositions in Chicago and Philadelphia, the Grand Army, who had charge of such matters, exhibited this flag, with a tag in bold letters, "Captured from Terry's Texas Rangers in an engagement near Rome, Georgia, by the Seventeenth Indiana Mounted Infantry."

Such a public exhibition of our misfortune was galling to the members of the regiment and when Governor Hendricks, the first Democratic Governor of Indiana, was installed, we made a request through our Governor Hubbard for the return of the flag. Governor Hendricks very properly referred the request to the State Librarian of Indiana, who happened to be a vindictive, howling Republican and in answer wrote Governor Hubbard a very insulting letter, refusing to return the flag. The matter then was dropped.

About thirty-four years after the close of the war, a business friend, Mr. William Burr of Dallas, who was an ex-Federal soldier, came to my office one day, and asked me if I ever drank any cider? I told him I did when I could get good cider. He told me he had a friend in an old shack near the Windsor Hotel, who was making cider, and invited me to go around and have a glass of cider with him. To this I consented. He there introduced me to a Major Weiler, and in conversation with him, I found that he belonged to Wilder's Brigade, who were with Sherman's army in Georgia. While we were sipping cider Burr remarked, "Well, this is pretty good; two Yanks and one Johnny sipping cider together." Major Weiler then asked what command I belonged to? I told him I belonged to the Eighth Texas Cavalry. He said, "Terry's Texas Rangers?" I told him, "Yes," when he said, "I am mighty glad to meet you; I have been trying to find somebody belonging to your command ever since I've been in Dallas. I am the man that found your flag." Of course, I was much gratified at meeting him and told him about our efforts to have the flag returned and the result at the hands of the State Librarian. "Now, Major, this flag is yours; you found it and as you state you want to return it, you make a demand on Governor Mount of Indiana, claiming the flag as yours and return it to our regiment." He said that it had been the ambition of his life to do this and in accordance therewith indited a letter to Governor Mount, requesting the return of the flag to him, for the purpose, he stated, to return it to the Rangers.

He furthermore stated that he was well acquainted with Governor Mount, as the Governor was a private in his command, of which he was a major. Verily, strange are the vicissitudes of life! Governor Mount's major was now making cider at five cents a glass.

In due time Major Weiler received an answer to his request from the Governor's Private Secretary, stating that the Governor had no authority to return the flag, which could only be done through a joint resolution of the Legislature of Indiana. We then both concluded that we might as well give it up; we hardly thought that a unanimous vote could be had on such a proposition by a lot of politicians.

I then requested the major to furnish me a written statement, setting forth the circumstances under which he came into possession of the flag and especially that the flag was not captured in battle, but was picked up in the road the next day after our engagement, encased in a rubber pocket, and he did not examine it until he returned from a scout and rejoined his main command, being much surprised that the package found contained the Terry Texas Rangers' flag, which was forwarded to the State authorities at Indianapolis, Indiana.

In about a month the Terry Rangers had their annual reunion at Austin, Texas, where I had read the statement of Major Weiler, which, of course, was a matter of surprise and deep interest. A resolution by a comrade was offered to appoint a committee, with myself as chairman, to memorialize the Indiana Legislature, requesting the return of the flag, I being the only member of the committee present, the balance not being in attendance at the reunion. On my return home I wrote to each member of the committee, requesting them to draw up a memorial and forward to me, to which I received no response. I then drew up the memorial myself and attached a letter I received from a Colonel Wylie in Dallas, who was a gallant soldier and commanded an Iowa regiment during the war.

I next forwarded this memorial to the Richmond City Mill Works of Richmond, Indiana, a concern I was doing business with, requesting that they turn it over to their Representative in the Legislature, which they promptly did and in due time I received a letter from Senator Binkley, stating that he would take pleasure in introducing it and that I would hear from him in due time.

To my great surprise, in about thirty days I received a printed copy of a joint resolution of the Legislature of the State of Indiana, carried unanimously, instructing Governor Mount to return the flag to the Terry's Texas Rangers in person and appropriating two hundred and fifty dollars to pay the expense of his trip to Texas. The complete resolution follows:

House Concurrent Resolution No. 6

Senate Concurrent Resolution No. 9

Preamble and Concurrent Resolution in relation to the return to the association of the survivors of Terry's Texas Rangers of their battle flag, captured from them during the late war of rebellion by the 17th Regiment of Indiana Infantry (mounted) Volunteers, appointing a commission to discharge said duty, and ordering an appropriation to pay the expenses thereof.

Whereas, On October 13, 1864, during the War of the Rebellion, the flag of the Texas Rangers at a battle near Coosaville, Alabama, was captured by the 17th Regiment of Indiana Infantry (mounted) Volunteers, in command of Major J. J. Weiler, and then belonging to General J. T. Wilder's Brigade, which brigade at the time was in command of General A. O. Miller, and subsequently, by the proper authorities, was deposited in the archives of the State of Indiana, and now reposes in the custody of the State Geologist, and to which is attached the following inscription:

> "Battle flag of the Texas Rangers, captured from the 8th Texas Cavalry near Galesville, Alabama, October 13, 1864, by two companies of the 17th Indiana Infantry, commanded by Major J. J. Weiler, of Company E, Wilder's Brigade."

And, Whereas, H. W. Graber, George W. Littlefield, S. P. Christian, W. D. Cleveland and R. Y. King, all of the State of Texas, as a committee duly appointed by and representing the Association of Survivors of Terry's Texas Rangers, by their petition hereunto attached, have asked the Legislature of the State of Indiana to kindly return to that association said battle flag, that it may be kept and treasured by them, and in said memorial the said Major J. J. Weiler, now a Past Commander of the Grand Army of the Republic for the district of Texas, has united, and which memorial is as follows:

"To the Honorable President of the Senate and Speaker of the House of Representatives of the Legislature of the State of Indiana:

"The undersigned, your memorialists, most respectfully show that they were selected by the Association of Survivors of Terry's Texas Rangers, a committee to memorialize your honorable bodies for the return to said association of the colors of that command, lost during the Civil War near Coosaville, Alabama.

"Your memorialists would show that in a cavalry engagement on the 13th day of October, 1864, the flag of the Texas Rangers was lost near the field and found by one of your memorialists, Mr. J. J. Weiler, then the Major of the 17th Indiana Infantry, and was subsequently deposited in the archives of your State.

"In view of the fact that the American people have forever put behind them the animosities and heartburnings which were incident to our unfortunate Civil War, and are one united, patriotic people, marching shoulder to shoulder under the folds of the Star Spangled Banner, and keeping the step to 'Hail Columbia' in the onward sweep to that high destiny, which, through the providence of God, awaits our grand Republic.

"Your memorialists would most respectfully request that such action be taken by your honorable bodies as will result in the return of the flag to the Association of the Survivors of Terry's Rangers.

"As beautifully and appropriately expressed by Col. W. D. Wylie, in his letter hereto attached, 'We now drink out of the same canteen, sheltered and protected by one common flag,' a sentiment so universal that it is without hesitation we appeal to our countrymen, the brave and gallant and patriotic citizens of Indiana, in even a matter of sentiment so delicate as that involved in our request. And as gracious as the favor will be accounted by the association, we are sure that the still greater pleasure will be with the people of Indiana in bestowing it.

"Most respectfully submitted,

"H. H. GRABER, "W. D. CLEVELAND,

"G. W. LITTLEFIELD, "R. Y. KING,

"S. P. CHRISTIAN, "J. J. WEILER."

And, Whereas, There is attached to said memorial a letter from W. D. Wylie, also a Past Commander, G. A. R., of the Department of Texas, as follows:

"Dallas, Texas, September 30, 1898.

"Col. H. W. Graber, Quartermaster-General Trans-Mississippi Department, U. C. V.:

"My Dear Sir: Referring to the conversation we had in reference to the colors of your old command, which had been lost during the late Civil War, on October 13, 1864, in a battle near Coosaville, Ala., by my comrade and our mutual friend, Maj. J. J. Weiler, of the 17th Indiana, who had, under instructions, turned the flag over to the State of Indiana, where it now reposes in the State library at Indianapolis, and which you are now endeavoring to have returned to the remnant of your old command—as an old soldier, Colonel, I can readily understand the beautiful sentiment which is so characteristic of the American soldier in the desire of yourself and comrades to secure the colors under which you passed through so many dangers, which are now passed and gone, leaving only the memories of a struggle which has resulted, with all its sufferings and animosities, in bringing us closer together, and we now drink out of the same canteen, sheltered and protected by one common flag, and in this connection, at your request, it is with pleasure I give the episode relating to the return of the flag of the 57th Indiana Infantry by Texas, in 1885. While commanding the Department of Texas, Grand Army of the Republic, in 1885, Parsons' Confederate Brigade held their annual reunion at Cleburne, Texas. Myself and others who wore the blue were the honored guests of the brigade. During the proceedings, Major Heath and Capt. W. G. Veal called my attention to the fact that a brave soldier (a corporal) of the 13th Tennessee, now a resident and citizen of Texas, had in his possession and on the grounds the regimental flag and colors of the 57th Indiana, which he had captured at the Battle of Franklin, Tenn., in December, 1864, and had taken careful care of for twenty years, hoping that he would find some representative of that regiment to whom he could return this priceless and precious relic. I received the valued colors from the brave soldier and immediately conferred with Department Commander of the State of Indiana, and was informed that the 57th would hold their annual reunion during the month of September of the current year, and they earnestly requested that Texas be present in person at that time for the return of their long-lost colors. We arranged that Capt. W. G. Veal and Maj. E. M. Heath, of the Confederate Veterans, and Corporal W. M. Crooks, the brave soldier who had captured the colors, should accompany myself and staff to the reunion at Kokomo, taking with us the flag.

"It is needless to give you the incidents of the trip further than that Indiana threw her doors open to give the old Texans who had met them on the field, a royal reception, and Corporal Crooks was received with open arms by the boys in blue, whom he had last met at the point of the bayonet on the field of battle; and the return of that precious relic that had spread its silken folds over the brave Hoosier boys in many a hard-fought battle, wiped out the animosities engendered by the war, especially between Indiana and Texas, and Corporal Crooks occupies an enviable niche in the war history of the Hoosier State, and the boys in blue and the boys in gray are now marching elbow to elbow, side by side, for the honor and integrity of our common country, and I can assure you, Colonel, that when you make the application for the return of your colors it will be as much of a heartfelt pleasure for Indiana to return the flag as for Texas to receive it.

"Sincerely yours,

"W. D. WYLIE,

"Past Commander Dept. of Texas, G. A. R."

And, Whereas, As shown by the correspondence of Governor Mount with Gen. J. T. Wilder and Gen. A. O. Miller, that they severally approve such return, which correspondence is as follows:

"Lebanon, Indiana, January 30, 1899.

"Gov. J. A. Mount:

"Dear Governor: In answer to your letter of the 28th inst., some twelve years ago a representation of Terry's Texas Rangers asked the Legislature to return the flag referred to in your letter, which was not done. I was willing then they might have the flag and know of no reason why it should not be given to the representation of the regiment now.

"The brigade captured two pieces of artillery at the same time. As the guns were captured from our forces at Murfreesboro, Tenn., in 1862, and have long since been made into G. A. R. badges, they are disposed of, and the returning the flag will settle that matter to good advantage.

"Your friend and comrade,

"A. O. MILLER."

"Knoxville, Tenn., February 1, 1899.

"Hon. Jas. A. Mount, Indianapolis, Ind.:

"Dear Governor: I have your favor of the 28th of January, relating to the return of the battle flag of Terry's Texas Rangers, which was captured by the 17th Indiana, near Coosaville, Ga., in October, 1864. In so far as I am concerned, I quite agree with you as to the propriety of returning this flag, but I think that Gen. A. O. Miller is the proper man to consult, as he was in command of the brigade at the time the flag was captured. I would suggest that if the flag is returned to Texas, that you take a clear receipt for it, to be preserved in the State archives. * * * Believe me,

"Your comrade and faithful friend,

"J. T. WILDER."

"Dear Senator: After your call at my office, I immediately wrote to my old brigade commanders, Generals Wilder and Miller. I was in the engagement when the battle flag of the Texas Rangers was captured. I am sure there is but one sentiment at this time, and that is, return the battle flag. Texans and Indianians rally under the one flag now. Generous acts will tend to obliterate the asperities of war.

"I herewith enclose letters of Generals Wilder and Miller.

Yours truly,

"JAS. A. MOUNT.

"February 2, 1899."

Therefore be it Resolved by the House of Representatives of the State of Indiana, the Senate Concurring, That the said battle flag be returned by said State of Indiana to said Association of the Survivors of Terry's Texas Rangers; that the duty of the return thereof be delegated to the Governor of the State and the present Commander of the Grand Army of the Republic for the Department of Indiana, with such other Union soldiers whom the Governor may appoint, and that the Geologist of the State of Indiana, now in charge of said battle flag, do deliver the same to said commission, taking their receipt therefor, to be deposited in place of said battle flag; and that said commission, at such time as may be most convenient, in person return said battle flag to said association; that the actual expense of said commission, not to exceed the sum of two hundred and fifty (250) dollars, be paid by said State of Indiana, and that the same be placed, by the proper committees, in the general appropriation bill to be enacted at this session of the Legislature.

Mr. Speaker: Your Committee on Military Affairs, to which was referred House Concurrent Resolution No. 6, which resolution provides for the return of certain flags to the Association of the Survivors of Terry's Texas Rangers, has had the same under consideration, and begs leave to report the same back to the House with the recommendation that said resolution be amended by inserting the words "the Governor of the State and" between the words "to" and "the," in line 4, page 7. (2) Substitute the word "such" for the word "two," in line 5, page 7. (3) Strike out the words "when the' between the words "soldiers" and "may," in line 5, page 7, and insert therefor the words "as the Governor." And that, as so amended, the said resolution be adopted.

SOMERS,

Chairman.

As soon as it became known to the Grand Army organization of Indiana, a certain post, numbering about four hundred members, passed a resolution denouncing the action of the Indiana Legislature and demanding of Governor Mount not to return the flag. The reporter of a paper, who attended this meeting, on his way home met General Ryan, the Commander of the Grand Army organization of the State and submitted to him the resolution passed by this post, when he unqualifiedly endorsed it and stated that he was going to write to Governor Mount not to return the flag.

Governor Mount then wrote to General Wilder, who commanded the brigade to which Major Weiler belonged, and asked his opinion and received General Weiler's answer, saying the flag ought to be returned. Governor Mount also wrote to General Henry, who commanded the division and had his answer, saying the flag ought to be returned, which Governor Mount determined to do at any cost.

Immediately on my receipt of the resolutions I forwarded it to Senator Wooten in Austin and suggested to him that this was no longer an affair of our regiment, but it was the action of the State of Indiana extending the olive branch to the State of Texas and should have suitable acknowledgment. I requested Senator Wooten to introduce a resolution inviting the whole Legislature of the State of Indiana to come to Texas as the guests of our Legislature and appropriating ten thousand dollars to defray the expense thereof. (This appropriation was unconstitutional and could not have carried, but as it turned out, it was not needed, as the Indiana Legislature, on receipt of same, had already adjourned.)

THE TERRY'S RANGERS' FLAG

CONCURRENT RESOLUTION PASSED INVITING GOV. MOUNT AND PARTY TO VISIT AUSTIN.

INDIANIANS TO BE GUESTS OF STATE.

Resolutions Transmitted by Wire to Governor of Indiana and Mailed to Legislative Officers.

Austin, Tex., March 4.—(Special.)—The correspondence and concurrent resolution relating to the return of a battle flag to the Texas Rangers are of interest. Senator Brinkley, one of the members of the Senate of Indiana, wrote to Mr. H. W. Graber of Dallas. The letter from Hon. C. C. Brinkley and the resolutions adopted by the Indiana Legislature were printed in The News of Thursday, March 2, while the memorial and other letters referred to in the following have previously appeared in The News:

Mr. Graber of Dallas has written to Mr. Wooten as follows:

> Dallas, Tex., Feb. 27.—Hon. Dudley G. Wooten, Austin, Tex.: Dear Sir—Inclosed find copies of memorial, letter and resolution of the Legislature of the State of Indiana, in reference to the return of the battle flag to the Association of Survivors of Terry's Texas Rangers.
>
> You will observe that the resolution contemplates the return of the flag by his excellency, the Governor of Indiana, in person, and an appropriation is made to defray the expenses of the Governor and party.
>
> It occurs to me that this liberal, generous and patriotic action upon the part of the Legislature and Governor of Indiana should be met by appropriate official recognition by the Legislature of the State of Texas.
>
> It has been suggested, and it seems to me rightful, that the Governor of Indiana and his party, while in the State, should be

the guests of the State of Texas, and that a small appropriation should be made and placed at the disposal of Gov. Sayers, to enable him in the name and on behalf of the people of the State, to extend to Gov. Mount and party a royal welcome to Texas. Such amenities are invaluable, and would tend to wipe out the lingering bitterness of the past, more closely connect the American people in common brotherhood, and place Texas in the true light before the world as among the most patriotic and liberal States in the Union.

I would suggest that you confer with Governor Sayers and Major Littlefield (who resides at Austin, one of the officers of the Association of Terry's Texas Rangers) as to the action to be taken.

I assume that the time will be designated for a meeting of the association to be held at Austin for the purpose of meeting Gov. Mount and party. I am sure it is not necessary to say that Texas should not permit Indiana to outstrip her in the good work of joyous reconciliation.

Please return to me the copies inclosed when you have no further need for them, as I wish to present them with my report to the Association.

Yours truly,

H. W. GRABER.

The following is the concurrent resolution introduced by Judge Kittrell and passed:

Concurrent Resolution:

Whereas, the Legislature of Texas has just heard with emotions of sincerest pleasure that the Legislature of the State of Indiana has adopted a resolution providing for the return of the battle flag of Terry's Texas Rangers, which was captured by an Indiana regiment during the late war between the States, and has appointed a committee, including Gov. Mount and his staff to visit Texas and return said flag to the Association of the Survivors of Terry's Texas Rangers. Therefore, be it

Resolved, by the House of Representatives, the Senate concurring, That the action of the Legislature of Indiana is recognized as most generous, chivalric and patriotic and is hailed as a most gratifying evidence of the restoration of that unselfish and unsectional spirit upon the existence and continuance of which so largely depends the prosperity and happiness of our common country, and that the thanks of the Legislature of Texas be and are hereby tendered the Legislature of our sister State of Indiana for its patriotic action. And be it further

> Resolved, That the committee appointed by the Legislature of Indiana to return said flag be and it is hereby invited to visit the city of Austin at the earliest possible day to the end that appropriate ceremonies may mark the occasion of the return of said flag, for which ceremonies the use of the hall of the House of Representatives is hereby tendered. Be it further
>
> Resolved, That an invitation to attend said ceremonies be and is hereby extended to the Governor and other State officers and the Legislature of Indiana and to the Governor and other State officers of Texas, to the Association of the Survivors of Terry's Texas Rangers, John B. Hood Camp, Austin Camp of the Grand Army of the Republic and the inmates of the Confederate Home. Be it further
>
> Resolved, That these resolutions be at once transmitted by wire to the Governor of Indiana with the request that he lay them at once before the Senate and House of Representatives of that State and a duly engrossed copy thereof, signed by the Speaker of the House and the President of the Senate and duly attested by the Clerk of the House and Secretary of the Senate be likewise transmitted by mail to both the Speaker of the House of Representatives and President of the Senate of the State of Indiana.

Governor Mount was taken sick very soon after and was unable to come to Texas immediately, but in a further correspondence with him, asked to have the time of his visit deferred until fall, which suited our purpose exactly. Colonel Wylie, in the meantime, received a newspaper clipping, containing the action of the army post, endorsed by General Ryan, demanding that the flag be not returned, when we both agreed we would keep the matter secret, which we did. There is no doubt it would have marred the pleasure of the Governor's visit had any mention been made to him of the matter.

After my comrades of the committee learned I had been successful in having the flag returned, Mr. W. D. Cleveland of Houston insisted that the meeting on the return of the flag should be had in his city. Mr. Littlefield claimed it ought to be at Austin and so on, but I finally decided that it ought to be at Dallas during our State Fair, when we had low railroad rates and greater crowds than they could gather at any point in Texas. I then submitted the matter to Governor Mount and had his letter, expressing himself highly pleased, as he would thus be enabled to see more of Texas than he would at any other time, having heard a great deal about the extent of our State Fair. He furthermore stated in this letter that when he came to Texas he would come in state, as the representative of the State of Indiana.

During the first week of the fair we had the pleasure of the arrival of the Governor and his magnificent staff, which latter were in brilliant uniform and proved to be one of the most magnificent bodies of men we ever had to visit Dallas. They also brought their horse equipment, such as saddles, bridles, etc., and were accompanied by quite a number of ladies; if I remember correctly, there were fifty-two in the party, on a special train, and with the party was our friend, General Ryan, to whom the Governor had turned over the two hundred and fifty dollars appropriated for him to pay his expenses.

I regret to have to record that I was unable to secure the attendance of a large part of our Ranger organization, who seemed to have taken offense because we had the meeting at Dallas, really prompted by petty jealousies of the cities where they resided and, as a consequence, we had only twenty-four Rangers present.

The meeting of the Governors and the ceremonies attending the occasion, was had in the Machinery Hall at the Fair Grounds, which had a seating capacity, outside of the stage, of only about one thousand to twelve hundred. At the hour of the opening of the ceremonies the Indiana Governor, with his staff and ladies, were seated on one side of the stage with twenty-four vacant chairs in two rows, in front, on the opposite side of the stage and the rear portion of the stage, occupied by the city officials and prominent citizens of the town, the two Governors sitting together in the front part of the aisle.

When everything was ready I marched in the twenty-four Rangers present in column, by twos, headed by myself with Miss Ruth Phelps, carrying a Texas flag. Miss Ruth Phelps was the daughter of one of our Rangers and the only member of the Phelps family living and was lost in the Galveston storm the next year.

After forming the Rangers in two lines in front of their chairs, I introduced Governor Mount to everyone and he, in turn, introduced General Ryan and when General Ryan had reached and shaken hands with the last member on the second row, he came around in front, singing, "There is a land that is fairer than day," in which the whole audience joined, standing, and I believe proved one of the most affecting scenes ever witnessed in this city. We then had several speeches before the Governor spoke, one by General Ryan, which evidenced considerable change in his attitude on the return of the flag and which, of course, was unknown to any one present, except Colonel Wylie and myself.

In the course of Senator Brinkley's remarks he referred to the captured flag, when one of our Rangers jumped up, asking pardon for interrupting him, and saying he wanted the audience to understand that the flag was not captured, but it was found, when another one of our Rangers remarked: "Bill, you know they run us out of it; what's the difference?" which, of course, created considerable merriment. Governor Mount happened to be sitting near me and remarked, "Graber, I thought you Rangers never run," when I said to him, "Governor, if they hadn't run a thousand times, there would not have been one left here to tell the tale. We always knew when to quit and didn't require a bugle call to bring us out."

Governor Mount next made one of the most patriotic speeches, characteristic of the man, ever listened to, which was responded to by Governor Sayers, who also, it is needless to say, did full justice to the occasion, as he, too, had been a gallant Confederate soldier.

After the closing of the speeches Governor Mount had the flag brought forward on the stage and, with a few appropriate remarks, handed it over to Governor Sayers, who also accepted it with appropriate remarks. Thus ended one of the grandest occasions ever had since the Civil War and its salutary effect on sectional feeling cannot be overestimated.

The Governor and staff remained with us three days. We had the best rooms at the Oriental Hotel assigned them and their hotel bills were paid by Camp Sterling Price, the Grand Army Post of Dallas and the Fair Association, and taking their expression on their visit, they left impressed with the grandeur of the Lone Star State and its people. Governor Mount and several members of his staff, among whom was Major Durban, who succeeded Governor Mount in the office of Governor, made me promise if I ever came anywhere near Indianapolis I must be sure to stop, as they wanted an opportunity to entertain me and I regret to have to report that I, on a business trip in that section, made a special visit to Indianapolis to meet them once more, when I found Governor Mount's body prepared for burial. This changed my trip from that of pleasure to one of sadness and regret, and with this feeling, I did not stop, but passed through without making myself known.

CHAPTER XXXVIII

ROOSEVELT'S VISIT TO TEXAS

A few years after this incident Dallas was making great preparations to receive and entertain President Roosevelt, on an invitation extended him by Colonel John N. Simpson of the National Exchange Bank.

Colonel Simpson and Roosevelt were neighbors, on adjoining ranches in the great Northwest and were great friends. When Colonel Roosevelt raised his regiment of Rough Riders at San Antonio, Colonel Simpson's son, Sloan Simpson, quit Harvard College and joined the regiment at San Antonio and was with his regiment in their engagement at San Juan Hill, which furthermore increased their friendship.

In April of that year I received a Congressional pamphlet containing a speech of Congressman Kitchin of North Carolina, scoring President Roosevelt on many of his expressions and acts while in office. This was just preceding his second nomination for the Presidency. We had had some bitter denunciations of the President by Senator Vardaman of Mississippi and Tillman of South Carolina, and after reading the speech of Kitchin, in which he referred to Roosevelt's book on the life of Benton, which had the largest circulation of any he ever published and in which occurs the expression, "Through the Southern character runs a streak of coarse brutality," and another passage, "As long as the word treason is in the English dictionary, so long will Jefferson Davis stand the Archtraitor of this country," and again Kitchin said, "Would I startle this House to call attention to a speech delivered by this man, the President of this great country, in the Capital City of the Nation, denouncing the Confederate soldier as an anarchist!"

In connection with this I would state that President Roosevelt's mother was a Southern woman, born and raised in Georgia, sister of ex-Governor Bullock. How could he reconcile such an expression as his first; certainly it was a strange expression under the circumstances.

Pondering over the situation frequently, I came to the conclusion that this speech of Kitchin's had been sent broadcast over the State and if so, we had a thousand Vardamans in Texas that would be sure to make his visit to Texas unpleasant and might result in his being insulted, which of course, would place Texas in a very unenviable position with the people of the North and East. I finally concluded to write Mr. Roosevelt a letter, calling attention to Kitchin's speech and quoting the above remarks from this speech and suggesting his correction of his position on these matters, before he made his visit to Texas. In my letter I especially referred to the Indiana flag incident, enclosing copies of the affair, which I requested returned.

Dallas, Texas, March 8, 1905.

To the Hon. Theodore Roosevelt,

President of the United States,

Washington, D. C.

My Dear Sir: I have read with deep interest your recent expressions in response to invitations from Southern communities indicating an earnest desire to bring about a better understanding, and forever obliterate the last vestige of sectional feeling resulting from the unfortunate conflict of forty years ago; particularly, your letter accepting an invitation from the Confederate Camp at Paris, Texas, which induces me to offer a few suggestions, and more fully inform you of the position of the Confederate soldier today, who I know is as solicitous of this country's future as you possibly can be, and on which I feel assured, you require no further evidence than he has furnished both in private and public life particularly, in his country's hour of peril incident on foreign war.

Camp Sterling Price of this city—the largest camp in our Confederate organization—immediately on receipt of your patriotic expressions extending the olive branch to the solid South, in which you rose superior to party limitation, originated a resolution inviting you to become the guest of our camp when on your visit to Texas. This resolution was drawn and introduced by a gallant comrade—who has since passed over the River—and supported with one of the most eloquent and patriotic appeals ever delivered in our Camp's meeting, but opposed by me, because of your former expressions on the character of Southern people, and particularly, on the Confederate soldier, which forbid such action until you could correct statements so damaging to our character, so degrading in the estimation of our children and in the eyes of the civilized world, thereby reviving and strengthening the unjust prejudice of a large class of Northern people.

These, your expressions referred to, I find in a speech of the Hon. Claud Kitchen of North Carolina, delivered in Congress on the 23rd of April last, as follows:

> "Mr. Chairman, your party and your section might have expected great things and good treatment at the hands of Mr. Roosevelt, but we of the South could not. We knew that twenty-five years after Lee surrendered this gentleman, in two of his public volumes, had denounced Jefferson Davis as an Arch traitor, and had declared that until out of the dictionary had been stricken the word 'Treason' Jefferson Davis was a traitor. We felt then, and we feel now, that that was a strike across the memory of the idolized dead, at the whole South and the Confederate soldiers. We knew, too, that in one of his volumes—the Life of Benton—perhaps the most widely read work of which he is author, he declared that 'through the Southern character there ran a streak of coarse and brutal barbarism.' We could expect little from him. Would I startle this house to remind it that after the passing of nearly forty years from Appomattox, Mr. Roosevelt, President of the United States and of a united people, stood here in the Capital City of our Nation and proclaimed to the world that the Confederate soldier was an anarchist? So surprising was this utterance, so revolting was it, that the Washington Post, a loyal supporter of Mr. Roosevelt's Administration, was led to observe, editorially: 'It is disagreeable enough to the Southern people to be officially designated as Rebels, and now to add anarchist is an exasperation which we find it impossible to believe the President really intended.' These words from the lips of a President, and at the National capital, while yet the grave at Canton was wet with the tears of Southern grief!"

It is needless to say that these expressions were not known to the members of the Confederate Camp who extended you these invitations, but no doubt will become known before you visit the State, and when so known will prove embarrassing to all concerned. This must, and can be avoided, simply by a correction on your part, a withdrawal of your terrible arraignment of the people of the South, and particularly, the Confederate soldier.

Please understand, the organization I have the honor to represent, as Commander of the Fourth Texas Brigade, United Confederate Veterans, which numbers eighty-nine Camps, the Paris Camp among them, and a membership of about five thousand, is especially charged with the preservation of the truth of history, and the protection of the Confederate character. Northern historians are still branding the Confederate soldier a traitor; what will be the effect on the minds of our children, nay, the entire country, to have Confederates paying homage to one who has even gone a step further, and denounced the Confederate soldier as anarchist? Consider, Mr. President, the lofty character of Robert E. Lee; General Robert E. Lee branded an anarchist by the President of this great Nation! The same sense of duty and sublime patriotism that prompted Lee to take up arms in defense of principle and country, prompted every true Confederate soldier in the ranks.

I do not deem it necessary to enter into a further presentation of the unfortunate attitude you occupy toward the people of the South and the Confederate soldier until a correction is made—which it is in your power now to do, and I am persuaded to believe, as a fearless, brave and honorable man you will not hesitate to do, and by this act of simple justice accomplish more towards a complete conciliation of all sections than anything else done.

To impress on you more fully the importance of such action at this most opportune moment, all Texas is stirred up on your contemplated visit and is anxious to honor you, but the Confederate soldier until this correction is made, is barred by his very manhood from participating in a demonstration that should be one of great unanimity. It should be a true and unreserved Texas welcome, which would have the approval of the entire Southern people.

Please understand, there are more Confederate soldiers and their descendants in Texas today than perhaps in any other four Southern States. To give you a better appreciation of what grand result would follow such a course on your part, I enclose herewith for your careful perusal the history of an incident of but a few years ago, wherein the broad-gauged Governor of Indiana and his patriotic Legislature, extended the Olive Branch to our Lone Star State, which was promptly and properly responded to by our own Executive and Legislature, and permit me to assure you, that the salutary effect of this sublime occasion cannot be overestimated in the accomplishment of its grand purpose. In this instance only two States were participants; what would be the effect to have the President of this great Nation extending the Olive Branch to a remnant band now fast passing away, whose gallant soldier record was never equaled in this world's history?

In conclusion, I will state, although born in a foreign land—in the City of Bremen—I yield to no native born citizen a greater love for, and interest in this country's future. Reared in the Lone Star State from childhood, under the shadow of the Alamo, Goliad and San Jacinto, and through personal acquaintance with participants of the latter engagement, I had instilled within me a kindred patriotism and love of liberty and country that is stronger today than it has ever been, and which must be my excuse for submitting this communication, which I trust will receive your careful and earnest consideration.

Please have returned to me the Indiana papers at your convenience, as they are highly prized by my children.

I am with great respect,

Yours very truly,

H. W. GRABER.

In reply to this letter I received the following:

The White House,

Washington.

March 13, 1905.

Sir: Your letter of the 8th instant has been received, and the enclosures are herewith returned, as requested.

Very truly yours,

WM. LOEB,

Secretary to the President.

Mr. H. W. Graber,

511 Wilson Building,

Dallas, Texas.

When the letter was handed me, with carbon copies, by my stenographer, I happened to have in my office Judges Rainey and Talbot, who were going to take lunch with me. When I handed them the letter, asking their careful perusal of the same, and after their return from lunch, to tell me their opinion about sending it, when Judge Rainey told me to send it, "It's a good letter and may have a good effect."

Some week or ten days after mailing the letter I concluded I would see Colonel Simpson in regard to the matter and handed him a copy of the letter to read, when, after reading it, he became furious, stating that it was an outrage to insult the President, as I had done; first to invite him to our town and after his accepting the invitation, then insult him by asking him to take back what he had said. I called his attention to a clause in the letter, giving my position on a resolution introduced by a member of our Camp, inviting him to be the guest of our Camp while here, which resolution I opposed and succeeded in defeating, however, the matter was passed over with Simpson and I am not advised whether he ever made mention to Roosevelt about this letter. Simpson stated that he believed that he would wire Roosevelt not to come, when I told him he had better do so and not have him come with these expressions hanging over him and lay himself subject to being insulted.

When Mr. Roosevelt started to Texas on his visit, he made a great speech at Louisville, Kentucky, one of the most conciliatory on sectional differences he had ever made and paid a magnificent compliment to the Southern people and especially the Confederate soldiers. This speech was published all over the country, as also here in Dallas, and effectually removed any feeling on the part of the Southern people engendered through his writings and expressions, derogatory to our character.

Then followed the magnificent reception and welcome extended him on his arrival here in Dallas and his subsequent visits to Fort Worth, Austin and San Antonio, where he received grand ovations and also on his subsequent tour of the South, gaining in popularity to the extent of receiving almost the united vote of the South, resulting in his sweeping victory in the November election.

CHAPTER XXXIX

MY FAMILY.

Our married life was blessed with seven children—four girls and three boys—five of whom are living and happily married. Our oldest, Henrietta Louise, married Doctor Frank M. Dannelly at Waxahachie, and they are now living on a large farm about seven miles from Dallas. Dr. Dannelly is a native of Georgia, in which State his father was a prominent physician, and his mother the gifted poetess, Elizabeth O. Dannelly, who published "Cactus" immediately after the close of the war, embracing a number of war poems, notably "The Burning of Columbia," a scathing and true denunciation of this inhuman crime, which gained for it a large circulation, demanding a second edition; a second book entitled "Wayside Flowers," a literary gem, was also very popular. Their union is blessed with three boys. The oldest, Henry G., a graduate of Staunton Military Academy, Virginia, is now in the fire insurance business in Dallas. Henry G. married about three years ago Miss Gwendolyn Dunn of Dallas; they have a sweet baby girl about four months old, which is now our first great-grandchild. The other two boys, Frank C. and Perry, are still at school. Our second daughter, Alice May, married W. D. Hume in Dallas about sixteen years ago and they are now making their home in Muskogee, Oklahoma, where Hume is engaged in the real estate and insurance business; they have no children. Our third child, Augustus Lee, was a fine young man, eighteen years of age, at home with us when, through a mistake of our family physician he was given an overdose of medicine, from the effect of which he never rallied and died in about two hours; this proved the saddest blow of our lives. Our fourth child is Irene, who married B. P. McDonald, Jr., of Fort Scott, Kansas, the son of B. P. McDonald, Sr., one of the builders of the M. K. & T. road into Texas, and for many years treasurer of the road. The old gentleman died here in Dallas a few years ago while still a director in the road and also owner of a short-line road into Cleburne, Texas.

At a meeting of the Board of Directors of this company, held in Parsons, Kansas, April 8th, 1909, the following testimonial to the memory of the deceased director, Mr. B. P. McDonald, was unanimously adopted:

IN MEMORIAM

"Since the last annual meeting of this Board, death has invaded its membership and claimed its oldest member in continuous service. After a brief illness, Benjamin Perry McDonald, of Fort Scott, Kansas, departed this life on February 16th, 1909, at Dallas, Texas, where he and his wife were temporarily sojourning.

"Mr. McDonald was born at Lock Haven, Pennsylvania, October 18th, 1839. He removed to the Territory of Kansas August 1st, 1857, saw the Territory pass to Statehood, and his destiny was ever afterwards identified with his adopted State.

"He was married November 21st, 1860, to Emma A. Johnson, who, with their three sons—William A., Charles B. and Benjamin Perry, Jr., all now arrived at manhood's estate—survive him.

"He was elected mayor of Fort Scott in 1866, and at the expiration of his term re-elected. He early engaged in the mercantile and banking business, and organized the First National Bank of Fort Scott in January, 1871. He was elected a director of our Company at its annual meeting on May 15th, 1872, and continued as such every succeeding year during his life. In 1873 he was elected to the Legislature of Kansas as a representative from Bourbon County. In 1874 he built the line southeast from Fort Scott to the coal fields, a distance of twelve miles, which was afterwards purchased by the Kansas City, Fort Scott & Memphis Railroad Company. In 1881 he built twenty miles of railroad on Long Island, New York, for the Long Island Railroad Company. In 1888-9 he built the Sherman, Denison & Dallas Railway, from Denison to Sherman, Texas, now a part of the Missouri, Kansas & Texas Railway of Texas, and in 1901-2 built the Fort Scott, Iola & Western, from Iola to Moran, Kansas, now owned and operated by the Missouri, Kansas & Texas Railway Company. In 1902 he organized and built the Dallas, Cleburne & Southwestern Railroad, from Cleburne to Egan, Texas, of which company he was the president at the time of his death. This railroad is now operated under a trackage contract by the Missouri, Kansas & Texas Railway Company of Texas. He was a director of the Kansas City, Fort Scott & Memphis Railroad Company and its predecessor companies from their earliest history until they passed to the St. Louis & San Francisco Railroad Company. He lived in Kansas when the Union Pacific Railway Company, Southern Branch, now the Missouri, Kansas & Texas Railway

> Company, was originally incorporated, knew the promoters of the company, and was always a great friend of the enterprise. In those early days his aid and support was of great benefit to the company. He became a director in 1872, while the road was being built through the Indian Territory. As a director he was constant in his attention to the duties of his office, faithful to the interests of the Company, and one of its most active and influential friends. During the receivership of H. C. Cross and George A. Eddy he was appointed by them as their treasurer, and served as such during their whole term, his appointment having been confirmed by the United States Circuit Court for Kansas, and his accounts confirmed by that court and found to be faultless. He was one of the strong men of the West, and ever ready to serve the interests of this Company. His acquaintance extended along the entire line; the people and the employes knew him and loved him. He was of sound judgment and absolute honesty. He had troops of friends. He had a more intimate knowledge of the Company's history from the beginning than any other man. His long career made him seem to be almost a part of the Company's life.
>
> "His health was always robust, his nature cheerful, his sound sense commanding. There was nothing subservient in his nature; it was all open and manly. We were shocked and grieved at his sudden taking off, and unitedly mourn his loss.
>
> "He was buried from his old home at Fort Scott, under Masonic ceremonies and according to the rites of the Episcopal Service, and now sleeps on the banks of the Marmaton which he loved so well.
>
> "We express our deepest sympathy and sincerest condolence to his widow and sons, and direct that this memorial be spread upon the records of the Company and a copy transmitted to them."

B. P. and Irene have their home in Birmingham, Alabama, where he is engaged in the brokerage business; they are blessed with two interesting children, a boy and a girl: B. P. the third, and Emma Louise. Our fifth child, Henry A., is living in Dallas; Henry was connected with the Kansas City Southern Railway for about fifteen years, and finally resigned the general agency of his road in Chicago and returned to Dallas to make this his permanent home. While in Chicago he married Ollie Elizabeth Anderson, who was born and raised in Negaunee, Michigan; their union is blessed with two sweet children, Roy Lee and Alice H. Our sixth child, Roy, died when about five years old at Waxahachie. Our seventh child is Lessis, the baby girl, who married Charles Weems Kidwell, born in Louisiana, but came to Texas with his parents when quite a child; Kidwell is now connected with the house of Sanger Brothers, Dallas, as assistant manager of the retail department, starting in at the wrapping counter about fifteen years ago; his father was a prominent physician in Louisiana and died in Dallas years ago; their union is blessed with two bright boys, Rolla, seven years old, and Graber, five years old. On the 23rd of last April we passed the 49th milestone of our married life and if spared until the next 23rd of April will celebrate our golden wedding, with five loving children and nine grandchildren and one great-grandchild in our family circle. Owing to fast declining health, about four years ago I was compelled to give up business, and take a much-needed rest, the first vacation from business cares in about fifty years; have had two serious spells of sickness, one in Dallas and another in Detroit, Michigan, where we went to spend last summer, but through the loving care of wife and children and the dispensation of a Divine Providence my life was again spared, and I am now enjoying better health than for over fifty years.

CHAPTER XL

IN CONCLUSION.

This is my story, a record of what I think the reader will agree has been an eventful life. I have lived long—I have seen much, both of what was good and of what was bad; and now when my allotted span of years must, in the nature of things, be nearly concluded, I look back and realize that all of what has happened has been for the best.

There is no bitterness in my heart as I indite these closing lines. What has passed is past, and the future, as I see it, holds for the people of the Southland a great promise. It is my most earnest wish that this promise shall have a glorious fulfillment.

My story has not been written for the purpose of adding to the literature concerning the period it covers. Rather, it is a personal record, and makes no claim to literary merit. It is written chiefly for my children, though I hope it may be found to be not without interest to the general public.

I feel that I owe it to myself to state that this book, in its entirety, has been dictated entirely from memory, and from the personal viewpoint I acquired during the years of which it treats. It is quite possible that errors have been made in some matters—that history will not entirely substantiate all of my statements, but, in the main, I believe it will be found that this book is a fairly accurate record of our many movements.

In closing I feel it is but right and just, and I know it to be a great pleasure, that I pay my humble tribute to the great souls with whom I was fortunate enough to be intimately associated during the great Civil Strife. Forrest, Wharton, McLaws, Harrison—they were a gallant company. Dashing, fearless, strong in their conviction of right, they were all but unbeatable, though opposed by overwhelming odds in practically every engagement. I can see them all now plainly and I hope to see them again, more plainly, when the Great Trumpeter shall sound "Taps" for me.

THE END

CPSIA information can be obtained
at www.ICGtesting.com
Printed in the USA
LVHW040728040323
740706LV00028B/729

9 789356 898929